FLIGHT
FROM
FAMINE

The Coming of the Irish to Canada

FLIGHT
FROM
FAMINE

The Coming of the Irish to Canada

Donald MacKay

M&S

Toronto and London

Canadian Cataloguing in Publication Data

MacKay, Donald, 1925–
  Flight from famine

Includes bibliographical references.
ISBN 0-7710-5443-2

1. Irish – Canada – History – 19th century.
2. Ireland – Emigration and immigration – History –
19th century. 3. Canada – Emigration and
immigration – History – 19th century. I. Title.

FC106.I6M33 1990   971'.0049162   C90-093963-X
F1035.I6M33 1990

McClelland & Stewart Inc.
The Canadian Publishers
481 University Avenue
Toronto, Ontario
M5G 2E9

Distributed in the United Kingdom
by Sinclair-Stevenson Ltd.

Printed and bound in Canada

Contents

For Barbara Elizabeth, with love

Acknowledgments

*A*s with most books, many people contributed in one way or another to the progress of this volume since work began two and a half years ago. Doug Gibson of McClelland and Stewart, Professor Carl Berger of the History Department, University of Toronto, and James M. Whalen of the National Archives of Canada, Ottawa, all helped get it started, and in addition Jim Whalen contributed his extensive files on Irish emigration to New Brunswick and read the manuscript, as did Professor Hereward Senior of the History Department, McGill University.

I am grateful to the Canada Council and the writing and research program of the Multiculturalism Directorate of the Secretary of State for grants without which the book could not have been attempted.

I am indebted to the Irish Texts Society and the Mercier Press of Cork for permission to quote from the translations of Humphrey O'Sullivan's diaries; to Marianna O'Gallagher of Ste-Foy, Quebec, whose many years researching the tragic past of Grosse Isle brought its story back to life after half a century of oblivion, for her encouragement, as well as assistance in locating a photo of Dr. George M. Douglas; to Mr. Clare Galvin of Ennismore, Ontario; to Mrs. Mary Gallagher of Cambridge, Ontario, and Olive Doran of Peterborough, Ontario, for photos of their ancestors, who were emigrants in the Peter Robinson migration.

I must also thank the staff of the National Archives of Canada, Ottawa, the National Library of Ireland, Dublin, the Oral History section of University College, Dublin, the Cork County Archives, Cork City Library, the University of Cork, the New Brunswick Museum, Saint John, the Ontario Archives, Toronto, and the Metropolitan Toronto Reference Library.

The seminal genealogical work of Carol Bennett of Renfrew, Ontario, whose work is available in *Peter Robinson's Settlers*, was invaluable in studying the families who arrived with Robinson in the early 1820s and I am grateful for the further advice she provided.

In Ireland, my friends Lee Snodgrasse and Paddy O'Leary of Ballydehob, Mary and Dennis Barrett of Cork City, and Jill Cunningham and Kevin O'Mahony of Durrus were all splendid guides to the secrets of west Cork. In Ottawa my work at the Public Archives was rendered the more pleasant by the hospitality of Penny and Clyde Sanger. I would also like to thank Hilary Chick of Scarborough for keying in the final draft. Having thanked all these kind people, I hasten to add that errors and shortcomings are my own.

I was fortunate, as with four books in the past, in my editor, Robin Brass, without whose painstaking labour the result would have been less than it is. Robin has raised editing to the art of collaboration.

Donald MacKay
Montreal

Introduction

*I*N THE PAST 250 YEARS, more than six million Irish have left their homeland, a figure almost twice the present-day population of Eire, and a million more than that of Eire and Northern Ireland combined. From the 1720s on, Irish emigration gathered momentum through the 18th century, but it was only in 1815, after the Napoleonic Wars, that the major emigration began, culminating in a flood tide during the Great Famine of 1845–50. Thus the major part of Irish emigration to Canada was compressed into four decades.

Given the history of invasion, exploitation and hunger in Ireland, it is remarkable that so many managed to cling to their hearthstones as long as they did. Living fatally close to land-hungry neighbours, the Irish have had to fight many wars of survival since the long ships of the Vikings appeared off their coasts in the 9th century, lured by the riches of Irish monasteries.

The Anglo-Norman invasion late in the 12th century heralded 700 years of English aggression and domination. Though the Normans seized choice regions of the country, their invasion was not as terrible as the English invasions to follow. They provided stability through their feudal laws, a central administration and an Irish parliament, and in the fullness of time the conquered swallowed the conquerors and the Normans became as Irish as the Irish.

It is tempting to romanticize the Celtic culture of ancient days, forgetting that lives were short and primitive, prone to disease and tribal warfare; nevertheless the annals of 16th-century Ireland, before the Tudor invasions, suggest a pastoral society that might well have been the envy of its descendants in the dark years of the 19th century. With hardly a million people to 32,000 square miles, there was enough productive land to feed everyone. Poets sang of the Golden

Vale of Munster, which, if not a land of milk and honey, was at least one of milk and butter, and it is said that every man, woman and child could count on the produce of seven acres of grazing and half an acre of arable, which was much more than most whole families had by the time the English invasions had done their worst. This pastoral world was shattered late in the 16th century by an army sent by a queen intent on anglicizing the Irish once and for all.

Having subdued the provinces of Leinster, Munster and Connaught with fire and sword, the Elizabethan army, 20,000 strong, attacked the last of the great Gaelic chieftains, Hugh O'Neill, Earl of Tyrone, and Hugh O'Donnell, Earl of Tyreconnell, whose strongholds lay in remote Ulster. In their struggle for the integrity of Gaelic Ireland, the earls were defeated at the Battle of Kinsale in County Cork on Christmas Eve, 1601. Their lands were seized and, in the vain hope of pacifying the Ulster countryside, planted with the Scots Presbyterians whose descendants two centuries later were to make up 60 per cent of the Irish emigration to Canada. At a time other small nations – Portugal, Holland and England – were enriching and renewing themselves around the world, Ireland had been forced inward on herself, the first of England's colonies.

When the Irish rebelled in the 1640s, they brought what the Irish call "the curse of Cromwell" on their heads; the invasion of Oliver Cromwell's Roundheads, and the famine and plague that followed, killed a third of the native Irish, leaving a population of 850,000, of whom 150,000 were English and Scots. The Catholics rose again four decades later, fighting William of Orange at the Battle of the Boyne, relived in our own time in the streets of Belfast and Derry and celebrated in Orange parades in Canada on July 12. With the defeat of the Catholic forces, poets wrote despairingly of the "evening and the end of the day."

In a tumultuous century of three major wars, migration was feeble and synonymous with exile. Thousands of vanquished soldiers – the Wild Geese of song and story – fled to France. Some 10,000 convicts were transported to penal colonies in Virginia and Maryland. The figures are vague, but as many as 50,000 indentured servants were sent out as virtual slaves to the Barbados and Jamaica, or to Virginia, Maryland and the Carolinas. Most were Catholics, gathered from regions around the ports that carried on ocean trade.

During the 1700s, remarkably few Catholics left Ireland, though it was the era of the notorious Penal Laws designed to stamp out the threat of Catholic resurgence if not the Catholic religion. The Catholics were deprived of the right to sit in the Irish parliament or to vote for the Protestants who sat there, were banned from public office, the professions and trade, and were deprived of the right to own property. Their religion was repressed, but there was as yet no surge of emigration. Some Catholics did emigrate, and thousands of young men sailed from the port of Waterford each spring for fishing stations in Newfoundland, though most stayed only a season or two. Even so, a sufficient number had put down roots by the 1780s to make St. John's a notably Irish-Catholic community. Some went on from Newfoundland to Nova Scotia, and others arrived in Halifax direct from Ireland.

Most emigrants in the 18th century – perhaps four of every five – were Protestants, mostly disaffected Scots Presbyterians from Ulster. Though never as severely repressed as the Catholics, they were seen as dissenters by their Anglican overlords and were banned from public office and from full religious rights. When oppression was joined by rising land rents, depressions and failure in the linen trade, which was their cottage industry, they heeded the exhortations of their embittered pastors and began to emigrate, first to New England and then to colonies farther south. Some went to Nova Scotia and Upper Canada, once that province was opened to settlement late in the century. Again figures are vague, but there is reason to believe that 300,000 or more left Ireland, three-quarters of them Protestants, in the century that was to end in another rebellion, that of Wolfe Tone's United Irish Movement, supported by the French and inspired by the French Revolution.

Thirty thousand were killed in that brief, ill-fated rebellion of

1798, but as bad as that was it spawned something arguably worse, and that was the Act of Union that dissolved the 500-year-old Irish parliament. Though it had come to be the sole preserve of Protestant Anglo-Irish landowners, the members of the Irish parliament were at least generally pro-Ireland in their deliberations, if nothing else out of self-interest – and there are many who believe that if an Irish parliament had still existed in Dublin in the late 1840s, the starvation and death of the Great Famine would have been greatly lessened.

Fearful that the French would use Ireland as a springboard to invade England, the English hugged Ireland into a tighter embrace. To sweeten their offer of parliamentary union, and make the death of the Irish parliament more acceptable, the English promised that union would be followed by Catholic emancipation so that Catholics as well as Protestants might sit at Westminster. Years earlier Dr. Samuel Johnson had intoned a prophetic warning. "Do not make a union with us," he told the Irish. "We should unite with you only to rob you." The Union became law in 1800, though emancipation, in which Irish Catholics were permitted to sit at Westminster, followed only much later, in 1829, and even then Irish MPs were disproportionately outnumbered on the basis of population.

There was little emigration during the twenty years of Anglo-French warfare; shipping was scarce, the sea lanes were dangerous and Ireland was enjoying a rare spell of prosperity due to England's wartime demand for produce and manpower. The exodus resumed with the peace of 1815, which brought a depression in which hundreds of thousands went hungry and rural terrorist organizations such as the Whiteboys of Munster, now often known as Ribbonmen for the green badges they wore, sprang up to wage a muffled civil war.

At first the new wave of migration was much like that of the late 1700s, with few Catholics and dominated by Ulstermen, though now with a number of Anglican small farmers who could see no future in southern Ireland and left while they still had money to buy passage. Fares being cheaper to British North America than to the United

States, the majority sailed to Quebec City or Saint John, New Brunswick, the two emigrant ports. In 1818, 20,000 crossed the Atlantic, and it was now that Irish Protestants established their predominance in Upper Canada. About 10,000 sailed in 1823, with only a quarter of these going directly to the United States, and in this year the first large contingent of Irish Catholics, subsidized by the British government in a rare instance of generosity, arrived to settle in the Ottawa Valley.

Though Catholics were 80 per cent of Ireland's population, the Irish had long ceased to be homogeneous, Celtic blood having been mingled over the years with that of Anglo-Normans, Anglo-Saxons, Welsh, Scots, Germans and French Huguenots. The Anglo-Irish were 12 per cent of the population and Presbyterians 8 per cent, but English was ousting Irish as the language of the country. There were considerable regional differences between, say, the west of County Cork and County Wexford in the east, and these differences were particularly notable in east-coast Ulster, where the industrial revolution was to gain a foothold as it never did in the rest of 19th-century Ireland.

Between 1825, when the first reasonably complete records were kept, and 1845, at least 450,000 Irish landed in Canada, by far the largest migration from any country. They outnumbered the Irish going directly to the United States in that period, though a third or more of the Irish who came to Canada were to travel on later to the States. Some received government assistance, but most paid their own passage, being small farmers who had saved enough to purchase at easy credit the fifty- or hundred-acre lots the colonial government was selling at five shillings an acre. Poorer emigrants found work as labourers on farms, digging canals, in lumber camps or on the busy timber wharves at Quebec City or the Miramichi ports of New Brunswick. Emigration to Newfoundland, Nova Scotia and Prince Edward Island had declined by the 1830s, but these were the years that the Irish strengthened their positions in New Brunswick, Quebec and Ontario. (While the Great Famine years greatly increased the annual flow, fewer stayed, moving to the States when they had the opportunity.)

Since 1800 the population of Ireland had increased from five to eight million with a large proportion dependent on one food, the potato, whose nourishing qualities were credited in part with the population explosion. Introduced from the Americas in the 16th century, the potato had gradually supplanted a diet of meat, grain and milk, but whatever its nutritional value it was a treacherous friend. Between 1800 and the universal failure of the potato crop in the late 1840s, there had been a dozen serious crop failures in one region or another, regional famine occurring in 1800, 1807, 1817, 1821–22, 1830–34, 1836 and 1839. In hindsight, the Great Famine was inevitable.

Between 800,000 and a million people – no one can be sure – died in those five terrifying years of "famine fever" and starvation. Another million fled across the Atlantic, 300,000 to British North America, where they arrived less like emigrants than refugees from terrible disaster. Of these, up to 20,000 died in the worst year of all, 1847, on the ships, in the quarantine stations of Grosse Isle, Quebec, and Partridge Island, New Brunswick, or out in the towns and roads of Quebec and Ontario.

Black '47 heralded the end of massive Irish migration to Canada, and thereafter the majority of those leaving Ireland in their hundreds of thousands would go directly to the United States, with hardly more than 175,000 landing in Canada between 1850 and 1870. Republican America, free from English rule, had long been the goal of most Irish Catholics, who now made up the majority of emigrants, and now that the fares to America were cheaper than those to the British colonies the door was open.

Between 1825 and 1870, nearly 900,000 Irish arrived, outnumbering English and Scots two to one, changing the nature of British North America, particularly Ontario and New Brunswick, where United Empire Loyalists had once been the majority. After the French, the Irish became the largest ethnic group in the country, and on the eve of Confederation they accounted for a quarter of the population. With the decline of Irish arrivals in Canada and the increase of emigration from England, Scotland and other countries late in the 19th century, the Irish share of the population began to dwindle. In 1961, the last year in which the census differentiated among Irish, English, Scots and Welsh, the proportion was down to 10 per cent. The census reported 1,754,000 Canadians of Irish descent, half of them living in Ontario and the rest spread across the nation.

Considering that they came when the country was new, and have done so much to shape it, accounts of the Irish in Canada, and particularly the Catholic Irish, have been curiously lacking up to fairly recent times, particularly in comparison with all the books about the English, Scots and French. For nearly a century the two major works about the Irish in Canada were those written in the mid-1800s: *The Irish in America* by the Cork City journalist and politician John Francis Maguire, and *The Irishman in Canada* by Nicholas Flood Davin, a journalist and lawyer who emigrated from Limerick, worked in Toronto and moved west, where he sat as a member of parliament for Manitoba and established the *Leader* newspaper in Regina. Whatever else they contributed, these books were not enough to dispel the myths and misconceptions that stemmed from deep English prejudice and from the tendency to confuse the Irish Catholics of Canada with those of the eastern United States. There was a considerable difference. Since the majority who settled in Canada took up farming, there were, for example, few Irish ghettoes and the raw Irish politics of cities such as Boston and New York were foreign to the Canadian experience.

Canadian history books through the first half of this century told of wars, treaties and politics, leaving little space for the likes of humble emigrants. Only in the past two decades, with the new interest in social history, have Canadian writers begun to tell the story of Irish Canadians, though most have dealt with the Protestants who dominated and shaped Ontario society. It is the aim of this book to tell more about the arrival of the Catholic Irish, and the conditions whence they came. Their road was harder and their welcome more uncertain, but their impact on Canada was immense.

Ireland, showing provinces, counties, major towns and other places mentioned in the text.

APPROXIMATE DISTANCES – STATUTE MILES
Cork – St. John's, Nfld. 2,000
Cork – Quebec 3,000
Cork – Saint John, N.B. 2,800
Liverpool – Quebec 3,200
Liverpool – New York 3,400
*Distances to Quebec assume
sailing south of Newfoundland.*

From Ireland to the New World

1

Wild Geese

Wild geese rising on clamorous wing,
to follow the flight of an alien king...
A Song of Defeat
Stephen Gwynn, 19th century

*T*HEY CAME first to Newfoundland, servants of the English fishing companies that brought them out from Ireland each spring to harvest the cod. Indentured labourers, hired on at the port of Waterford, where the ships from Bristol took on provisions, most returned home in the fall with the salted fish. But some stayed on, and as early as 1675, long before Newfoundland was recognized as a British colony, there were Irish living at Ireland's Eye, which gazes eastward over Trinity Bay, and on the Avalon Peninsula, which dangles like a starfish off Newfoundland's southeast flank.

The English merchant adventurers who had laid claim to the fishing rights, in violent competition with fishermen from France, discouraged settlement, the better to guard their monopoly and control the coves and harbours. A law unto themselves, they tried to prohibit settlement within six miles of the shore and demanded that homes be built only with their permission. Only after the Treaty of Utrecht in 1713 had confirmed Newfoundland as a British possession did English civil law – though not justice – come to the lawless frontier.

The growth of the fisheries in the 18th century inevitably fostered settlement, despite the policy of the fish companies to ship their servants home once their indentured time was up. Soldiers of the garrison took their discharges and became farmers, and men who had come out for the companies stayed as artisans or shopkeepers. Catholics from southeast Ireland migrated to Newfoundland in increasing numbers, and though most remained for only a season or two, more and more stayed on. The only other notable migration from Ireland in the 18th century was that of the Presbyterians who went to the thirteen American colonies from Ulster.

By the 1750s the Irish dominated the hamlets of the Avalon, outnumbering English, Scots and French. The enterprising Aylward brothers, John and Paul, Catholics from Waterford, opened a fishing station on Placentia Bay and built an Irish community that was larger than St. John's, where the English fishing firms made their headquarters.

Themselves colonized by the English for centuries, the Irish were now colonizing one of England's first North American colonies. The fishing "plantations" of Newfoundland were a welcome escape from poverty, repression, and the terrible famine of the 1740s that had wiped out a fifth of the population of the province of Munster.

"Newfoundland is a fine plantation," wrote Dunnach Ruadh MacConmara in 1750. "It will be my station until I die." A teacher and poet in his native Waterford, he wrote in Irish, the language of the young men who came each spring to *Talam an Eisc*, the Land of the Fish. Waterford was Ireland's third largest port, after Dublin and Cork, and sent sixty ships each spring with beef, butter, flour, oatmeal, potatoes and West Indies rum. The ships also carried the indentured sons of tenant farmers from the counties of Waterford, Tipperary, Cork and Kerry, few of them older than twenty-five and some in their teens, but whatever their age they were known as "youngsters," as were men at home in Ireland until they married. "The number of people who go passenger in Newfoundland ships is amazing," wrote Arthur Young, an English agronomist who visited Waterford; he estimated the migration in 1770 at 5,000 a year.

As servants of the fish companies of Bristol, Dublin and Waterford, these young Irishmen caught, salted and cured vast quantities of codfish for the Friday dinners of Catholic Europe, particularly Spain and Italy. Most "youngsters" who laboured ashore, carrying barrows, cutting wood, drying fish and the like, tended to serve out their time and go home, but there were always a few who stayed. The expert fishermen who worked offshore were Irish, Englishmen from Dorset, and Channel Islanders. Thomas Saunders, of the Waterford company of Saunders and Sweetman, much preferred the Irish and found the English unsatisfactory. "They run away in winter, they never stick to a place, have any attachment to it, and for hard labour one Irish youngster is worth a dozen of them."

The season opened with a search for herring to use as bait, and a shortage of herring meant a poor year. When bait was collected, from skiffs cruising the bays with big nets, the fishermen put to sea in shallops and jacks, crewed by four or five men, to jig for cod with long lines for most of the summer, a normal catch being 350,000 pounds of cod per boat. Curing began in mid-summer, and men who were kept on for winter work – terms of indenture often required service for "two summers and a winter" – cut and hauled timber for houses, sheds, wharves and new boats.

For the fishermen life was hard and dangerous – in one year alone 263 men lost their lives on the rocky coast or out on the Grand Banks in fog and icebergs. Life was harsh in the raw frontier town of St. John's, and as the Irish population grew, the iron hand of the companies was replaced by official repression which was worse. On September 22, 1755, Governor Richard Dorrill issued an edict designed to impose strict control on all Irish entering the colony:

Whereas a great number of Irish Roman Catholics are annually brought over here, a great part of which have but small wages, so that after paying their passage to this place and the charges of clothing etc. during the fish season, their whole wages are spent and they have not the wherewithal to pay their passage home, or purchase provisions for the winter, by which means they not only become chargeable to this place, but many robberies and felonies are committed by them to the great loss and terror of His Majesty's Liege subjects in this island.

This is therefore to warn and give notice to all masters of ships or vessels which bring passengers to this island that after the fishing season they carry from hence the whole number and same passengers they bring here except such as may have my order to remain in this island, and hereafter they are not to fail, as they will be proceeded against with the great severity the law in such cases will admit.

When this failed to have the desired effect, he later issued another set of regulations, which included the following:

For the better preserving the peace, preventing robberies, tumultuous assemblies, and other disorders of wicked and idle people remaining in the country during the winter ... no Papist servant, man or woman, shall remain at any place where they did not fish or serve during the summer. That no more than two Papist men shall dwell in one house during the winter, except such as have Protestant masters. That no Papist shall keep a public house or sell liquor by retail.

Priests were banned from celebrating mass. When Michael Katen invited a priest to hold service in his fish shed at the outport of Harbour Main, he was fined £50 and his shed was demolished. Michael Landrican, "guilty of the same crime," had his house burned and was expelled from the colony, as were fifteen others. When the magistrate William Keene was found murdered, an Irishman and his wife were hanged and five expelled from the colony.

Dunnach Ruadh MacConmara, who had arrived with such high hopes, went home disillusioned. That so many stayed and put down roots reflected the terrible conditions in Ireland, where Serjeant Fitzgibbon, a member of the Irish parliament, declared that "two thirds of the people are unemployed and consequently condemned to the most deplorable indigence."

To the Irish, a patch of land and a shack on the steep, barren hills around St. John's or the stony Avalon Peninsula was preferable to Ireland. In 1763 there were 8,000 permanent settlers in the colony, with thousands of "youngsters" coming each spring and leaving in the fall. Governor Hugh Palliser, a Protestant from Yorkshire, tried to control the size of the Irish Catholic population with indifferent success. "The simplest method of settling a colony," he complained, "was that practised by the Irish from 1714 onwards. They turned up without funds and stayed on, as their brethren from Ulster did in North Carolina and Nova Scotia, only with this difference, that the latter brought funds with them." Waging what was evidently a losing battle against Irish squatters, Palliser on October 23, 1767, issued the following order to the magistrates of St. John's:

Whereas a great number of hutts are erected, possessed and inhabited by the Irish Roman Catholics in this Harbour who entertain and keep in the country a large quantity of rogues and vagabonds to the great disturbance of the peace and danger of His Majesty's subjects' lives and to the exceeding great prejudice of the fishing trade: You are hereby authorized and directed immediately to pull down such hutts or houses and suffer no more to be erected.

By 1785 the permanent population of the colony had climbed to 10,000, the newcomers including "respectable farmers" such as Thomas Meagher, a Catholic from Ninemilehouse in Tipperary, who became a fish exporter and a founder of the Benevolent Irish Society in 1808. Thomas Foley, who arrived from Dungarvan, County Waterford, as an illiterate young labourer, became a successful merchant, exporting seal oil and skins, lumber, and herring and salmon, as well as the traditional cod. The Irish outnumbered the English two to one, and a small Irish middle class of merchants and master craftsmen was emerging. The punitive anti-Catholic laws had been eased, as they had been in Ireland, and in 1784 Father James O'Donnell, a Franciscan from Tipperary, became the first authorized Catholic Church representative in Newfoundland.

St. John's had become a thriving, if smelly, town of some 300 houses cheek by jowl with fish-drying stages that visitors complained perfumed everything, even the milk. In the town and surrounding districts, 80 per cent of the population of 4,400 were Irish. In 1789 there was a stir in the colony when a ship brought in several dozen Irish convicts, most of them men in their twenties convicted of everything from murder to such minor crimes as picking a lock and stealing a pawnbroker's ticket. In this year, the Governor, Admiral Waldegrave, reported that it was his impression that "nearly nine-tenths of the inhabitants of this island are either natives of Ireland or immediate descendants from them, and that the whole of these are of the Roman Catholic persuasion." However, the harsh conditions and shortage of work were causing many of them to leave.

Many of those who left did not, like Dunnach Ruadh MacConmara, go back to Ireland but went on to Nova Scotia, Prince Edward Island or Boston in search of an easier life.

AT HALIFAX, there had been Sullivans, Hurleys, Haggertys, Callaghans, Malones, Quinns and Lannigans almost from the time the town was founded; in 1760, they numbered a thousand, a third of the population. Most of them lived in Irishtown, south of Citadel Hill, and a magistrate, who had studied law in Dublin, said, "The common dialect spoken in Halifax is wild Irish." As in other English colonies, Catholics in Nova Scotia had been deprived of their priests, barred from professions, and though they could occupy land if granted by the government, they were ignored when settlers were recruited to occupy the choice farms of the 8,000 French Acadians driven from the colony in 1755. The Nova Scotia government desired Protestants, and their advertisement was answered by a flamboyant land speculator named Alexander McNutt from Londonderry in Ulster. He was living in Boston at the time, having first tried his luck among Ulstermen in Virginia.

Whereas few Catholics were emigrating to the American colonies, regarding them as hotbeds of Protestantism, Ulstermen had been arriving there in a steady flow for more than a generation. These were the Scotch-Irish, whose Presbyterian grandfathers had, like McNutt's family, been translated from the Scottish Lowlands by the English Crown to colonize lands that belonged to native Catholic Irish. Despised as dissenters by the Anglican Establishment in Dublin, they were victimized in Ireland by many of the same laws that oppressed the Catholics. They were denied public office, and as their ministers held no status in law, even the most respectable of married Presbyterians were regarded by the state as unwed fornicators. They regarded themselves as Scots, strangers in a strange land. "We are surprised," said one of their ministers, "to hear ourselves termed Irish people, when we so frequently ventured our all for the British Crown against the Irish Papists."

Harassed by prejudice, crop failures and intolerable increases in rent, the Scotch-Irish had been leaving – two or three thousand each year – for New England and the southern colonies, as their cousins in Scotland were doing. Emboldened by ministers "bellowing from the pulpit that God had appointed a country for them to dwell in," the first 750 sailed for Boston in five ships in 1718. Within a decade 15,000 had taken up land, from the Carolinas to New Hampshire.

It was from New Hampshire that Alexander McNutt drew the first fifty Scotch-Irish to settle the vacant French farms in Nova Scotia in 1761, but since they were so few he offered to recruit 8,000 direct from northern Ireland. In the end he brought fewer than 400 before the authorities in Dublin called a halt on grounds the full number would deplete too many Ulster parishes. These people were sent to the townships of Truro, Onslow and Londonderry in Colchester County at the head of the Bay of Fundy. Unlike most pioneers, they had no forests to fell, no roads to build, the French *habitants* having prepared and dyked the rich, red tidelands in the belief the French would be there for a lifetime, and their children and grandchildren after them.

The Provincial Surveyor, visiting the Scotch-Irish settlers in 1764, found the sixty families in Truro township were "a very industrious set of people; have large stocks, and tho' they have settled but two years will this year raise grain sufficient for their support, save for a few families." All but ten of these families had come from New Hampshire with McNutt. The fifteen Ulster families in the township of Londonderry north of Cobequid Bay were also industrious, "doing extremely well, considering they had neither money nor stock." At Onslow, where McNutt's brother William built the region's first Presbyterian church, the Surveyor was disappointed. "Onslow has about fifty families. These are the most indigent as well as the most indolent people in the colony. Several families suffered severely last winter and some were famished. If they are not relieved this winter there will be great danger of their starving or quitting the colony. They have but a small portion of stock, compared with the other inhabitants of the province, and there are very few people of any substance among them."

All told, there were 2,000 Irish in Nova Scotia, which included the territory that later became New Brunswick. They made up a fifth of the colony's population. About 1,000 lived in Halifax, 600 of them Catholics, though it would be twenty years before they got their first priest, Father James Jones from Cork, which was also the home of the Halifax Port Warden, Captain Thomas Beamish. When Irish held positions of power they were invariably Protestant – Governor John Parr from Dublin, Chief Justice Bryan Finucane from County Clare, and Richard John Uniacke, the Solicitor General, whose family came from the Blackwater country in County Cork. Uniacke helped form the Charitable Irish Society in Halifax in 1786, the first of its kind, and started an Irish settlement near Lake Shubenacadie, off the road between Halifax and Truro.

"The first five families that I settled in Irishtown, I am sure had not five shillings amongst them," he recalled. "They subsisted upon potatoes and herrings and things I gave them. They had about six miles to go, into a wilderness from the road; but then the first inhabitants, whom I begged to go and assist them, helped to cut them out a path and they chopped the wood and raised their houses. In the spring they got some potatoes and seed; and those families are now increased to at least twenty-five in the course of about five years; for the people who come out write home to their friends, saying how comfortably they are placed, and those friends raise heaven and earth to come."

THE RANKS of the United Empire Loyalists who fled to Halifax during the American Revolution included Irish, who moved on to the St. John River Valley across the Bay of Fundy and helped found New Brunswick. There were so many Irish in that colony in the late 18th century that there was talk of calling it New Ireland. Writing to his mother in 1788, Lord Edward Fitzgerald, then a young cavalry officer based in Saint John, expressed his surprise at finding so many of his countrymen, most of them Protestants in those early years.

"By what I hear," he wrote, "they are all Irish, at least in this town; the brogue is not in higher perfection in Kilkenny.... I came through a whole tract of land peopled by Irish, who came out not worth a shilling, and now all own farms worth (according to the value of money in this country) from £1,000 to £3,000. The quality of everybody and their manner of life I like very much. There are no gentlemen; everybody is on a footing providing he works and wants nothing; every man is exactly what he can make himself, or had made himself by his industry. The more children a man has the better ... the father has no uneasiness about providing for them, as this is done by their profit of their work.... My dearest mother, if it was not for you, I believe I would never go home." Unfortunately Lord Edward did go home and was martyred in Ireland in the United Ireland uprising for independence in 1798.

Across the Northumberland Strait, where Captain Walter Patterson of Donegal was Governor of St. John's Island (Prince Edward Island), an attempt to name it New Ireland was refused by the British government. The Irish there included demobilized soldiers from County Cork and people who had come from Newfoundland, but they were outnumbered by Scots and English.

Significant Irish settlement up the St. Lawrence River had to await the demise of the French regime, but before the British conquest *l'irlandais* named McCarthy, McNamara and Reille (or Riley) appear on French records. There were said to be 130 Irish families in New France in the early 1700s, two of whom held seigneuries near Montreal. There were several Irish priests, but most of the Irish were soldiers of the Irish Brigade, which served as a foreign legion throughout the French Empire and were called Wild Geese, the nickname given the soldiers of Lord Patrick Sarsfield, who fled to France in 1691 after losing the Battle of Limerick to William of Orange's men. (Wild Geese was also the name for Irish smugglers who plied between Ireland and France to escape English customs.)

Five years after the defeat of the French, the first St. Patrick's Day was celebrated in Quebec City in 1765, but Irish settlement in what is now Quebec and Ontario was slow, apart from those who came among the Empire Loyalists who settled on Lake Ontario and Lake Erie, most of whom, if not all, were Protestants. When Hugh Hovel Farmar, a Cork City merchant, tried to recruit people to start an Irish Catholic colony in the 1790s, after the opening up of the new province of Upper Canada, which began about twenty miles west of Montreal and ran to the west and southwest as far as Lake Huron, his project was ignored. He concluded that "the Irish are not fond of leaving their country," though four years later his neighbour, Robert Baldwin, a Protestant farmer, emigrated to Upper Canada to escape the United Ireland uprising. "The horrors of domestic war conspired to drive us from our native land," wrote Baldwin's son, William, who became a leading citizen of York, the Upper Canada capital, by combining the skills of physician, lawyer and politician. One of William's sons was the statesman Robert Baldwin.

That there were Irish in Upper Canada in 1802 was remarked by a citizen named Ely Playter, who wrote in his diary, "This was St. Patrick's Day, which occasioned a number of drunken Irishmen in town."

ENGLAND'S TWENTY-YEAR WAR with Napoleonic France, and its war with the United States in 1812, reduced Irish emigration to a trickle. England's dependence on Irish produce and manpower created what passed in Ireland for prosperity, which filtered down to the farm people, so that Napoleon Bonaparte, a villain in England, was a folk hero among the Irish for creating a prosperous "Golden Age." Ireland mourned Napoleon's downfall in 1815, for the peace brought economic depression. Grain prices tumbled, and landowners scrambled to convert arable land to pasturage to raise cattle, which were more profitable. They used a new Ejectment Act to evict tenants no longer needed to sow and harvest grain, since one family could now handle farm work previously done by twenty or thirty. Crowds of unemployed tramped the roads searching for work, or simply begging, joined by thousands of demobilized soldiers whose ranks included Irishmen maimed fighting England's war. Their red coats were a symbol of English tyranny, and a cruel ballad questioned their intelligence in going to war for the King.

> Oh were you drunk, or were you blind
> That you left your two fine legs behind
> Or was it walking upon the sea
> Wore your two fine legs from the knees away.

The weak died from "road fever," a combination of dysentery and endemic typhus. The healthy fought back with the only means they had, and that was violence, forming secret agrarian societies: the Hearts of Steel and Hearts of Oak in Ulster, Thrashers in the provinces of Connaught and Leinster, and above all the Whiteboys in the province of Munster, where destitution was at its worst. Men with blackened faces and wrapped in white smocks and sheets stole through the midnight fields like ghosts, burning the crops of unpopular landlords, both Protestant and Catholic, and the thatches of peasants who usurped the homes of the evicted.

In the summers of 1816 and 1817, freakishly cold, wet weather destroyed the crops. "We had seventeen weeks of rain without cessation," wrote Humphrey O'Sullivan, a County Kilkenny teacher. "In 1818, the year of the plague and dire sickness, thousands met their deaths. There were streets in Cork so filled with disease that a wall had to be built at both ends so that healthy people might not go through them."

An anonymous pamphleteer in western Ireland wrote, "Oh what scenes of misery were exhibited in the years 1817, 1818 and 1819. The people were left without cattle, their potatoes and corn were seized and sold, and in some cases their household furniture, even to their blankets." He was talking not of the really destitute, but of "snug farmers" with thirty acres or more, who were turning their thoughts to emigration.

"What could I do?" asked Patrick Condon in County Cork. "I had seen strong and mighty men clothed in rags at work for their masters, often without their fill of shrivelled potatoes to eat. I told myself I would die rather than put up with that."

Newspapers sprouted advertisements soliciting passengers to "America." A handbill circulated in Londonderry, dated March 31, 1817, said:

For Halifax and Prince Edward Island, the beautiful fast-sailing ship *New Brunswick Packet,* burthen 600 tons, copper fastened and coppered to the bends, James Walker, Master, will sail hence for the above ports the first of May.... There is no part of the Continent of America that affords so great encouragement to Mechanicks, Labourers as what British America does; on arrival out, an application being made to the Governor, grants of Land from 200 to 1000 acres will be made out for EVER, according to the number in each respective family.

Claims like this were greeted with derision in Halifax, where a correspondent for the *Acadian Recorder* commented, "Now, Mr. Editor, if any of your readers will take the trouble to go to Belcher's Wharf, they will see this 'beautiful and fast-sailing ship' described as 'copper-fastened, and coppered to the bends and of 600 tons burthen', an old, worm-eaten vessel, with her rotten sides open to be repaired, leaky so as to require a continual working of the pumps, scarcely a dollar's worth of sound copper on her bottom, and in measurement about 350 tons. The falsity of the remainder of the bill, is to the regret of many long resident mechanics, too well known already...."

Since fares to British colonies were cheaper than those to Boston or New York, even those favouring the United States went first to Saint John or Quebec City. A great many of the emigrants landing in British North America – in some years as many as two thirds – went on eventually to the United States. On June 30, 1818, the *Limerick General Advertiser* ran a notice soliciting passengers for a ship bound for St. Andrews, New Brunswick, with the words: "For tradesmen and others, who cannot go to the States, as St. Andrews is within a mile of them." This was the first year that emigrants bound for British North America exceeded those going directly to the United States, and it would be well into the 1840s before the ratio was reversed and the great mass of emigrants went to Boston, New York and other U.S. ports.

Three quarters of the emigrants to British North America were Presbyterians renewing their pre-war exodus, and in 1818, 4,000 farmers and linen weavers left from Belfast. They were joined by Protestants from southern Ireland, privileged members of the Anglican ruling class known as the Protestant Ascendency, who had had little reason to migrate in the past but now were accounting for one in every five emigrants. There were still few Catholic emigrants, for as a Dublin newspaper said, "One of the peculiarities which distinguishes the character of the native [Catholic] Irish is a vehement and, in many cases, an absurd attachment to the soil on which they were born." When the English government mounted a scheme to pay the fares of war veterans and give them land in the British colonies, and extended it to a limited number of farmers, 700 applications were received in one day. The applicants, mostly Protestants, wrote of the "slavery of rents and leases," "stalking starvation in our native land" and "murders and house burnings" perpetrated by their Catholic neighbours. Only recently freed from the Penal Laws, Catholics had little reason to hope for government aid, and few applied.

"Thousands of unfortunate sons and daughters of Ireland were at this time contemplating removal to North America," wrote Edward Talbot, the son of an Anglican applicant, Richard Talbot, who lived in the hills of north Tipperary. "I became an exile, not as a matter of choice, but of necessity, not with a view of realizing a fortune in the transatlantic wilderness, but of escaping penury and its consequent miseries in the land of my nativity."

Richard Talbot, forty-six, a militia officer and squire of Clough-jordan, had enjoyed a comfortable living, as had his ancestors who had come from England 200 years earlier with Cromwell. Now, like many of his kind, he was caught between falling income and rising prices. The end of wartime prosperity convinced him there was no future for his family, or indeed for Ireland, and he sought government aid to emigrate to Upper Canada, where his brother, John, had settled.

It was a measure of the British government's reluctance to spend money on emigration that it took Talbot two years and repeated applications to secure free passage and free land, and then only on the condition that he take a substantial group with him and stand surety for them until they were settled. He chose thirty families and fifteen single men and sent the government the torn halves of £320 in banknotes as an earnest of good faith, the other halves to be sent when the government made good on its offer.

He assured the authorities that his people were all loyal Protestant subjects who would fight for the Crown if need be. They were typical emigrants of the time – young, married with children, some with nest eggs from the sale of their leases. Though they were all described as yeomen, only half were farmers, the rest being shoemakers, smiths, weavers, an army pensioner and two listed only as "gentlemen." The most prosperous, with £300 in his money belt, was thirty-eight-year-old William Geary, an estate agent from County Clare, who had farmed 100 acres of his own. George Foster, thirty, had £30, though the average was £50 per family, equivalent to two years' wages for a skilled worker. William Hodgins, twenty-nine, and his wife Sarah, twenty-one, who had left a farm near Newtown, Tipperary, and Robert Grant, twenty-five, a Limerick City clothier, and his twenty-three-year-old wife, Elizabeth, possessed little money but a great deal of enterprise, which was to make them wealthy in property dealing and lumbering in the Ottawa Valley. Most were leaving for economic reasons, but one man was fleeing because Whiteboys had killed his father for having allowed police to use his barn as a barracks. There was some unpleasantness when a landowner accused some of the emigrants of fleeing debt. They were also accused of being apostate Catholics who had changed their faith to curry favour, since one of their number, Edmond Stoney, was a convert to Methodism.

The government's part in the Talbot emigration was slapdash. Talbot was the only Irishman to secure government assistance – though one Scottish and two northern English groups had successfully done so – so there was no precedent. There were many frustrations, the first at Cork City on May 4 when the ship promised by the Colonial Office failed to arrive from England. The Talbot group waited nearly six weeks, exhausting most of their savings, and departed from the Cove of Cork on June 13, 1818, for Quebec City.

Less than a day into the voyage most were sick, and the weather was bad for ten days, but of all the 4,599 Irish bound for Quebec that year, the Talbot people were probably the best cared for. Their ship, the 540-ton *Brunswick,* was well stocked with food and water, and according to Edward Talbot, the captain "was to all a friend, an attendant and a physician, and constantly solicitous for our health and comfort." Even so, there were twenty-three deaths on board, all of them children, always the first to be stricken. When they came aboard, they had been "cheerful, healthy, and the hope and delight of their parents." Within a few weeks, James Goulding, six-month-old son of a whitesmith, had sickened and died, to be followed by eleven others. Eleven more died on the two-week passage up the St. Lawrence River and were buried on the islands. The voyage took forty-three days, the average for sailing ships in summer.

At Quebec, no one knew what to do with them. Talbot resisted efforts to locate them among the French-Canadian *habitants* and insisted on continuing to Upper Canada, where the language, religion and customs of the people were compatible. They were sent to Montreal by steamer, but from there would have to find their own transportation 350 miles to York on Lake Ontario.

Half the party refused to go farther, blaming Talbot for failure to arrange free transportation and locate the 100-acre lots they had been promised. At nearby Lachine, while Talbot was dickering with French-Canadian boatmen to take them up-river in shallow-draft bateaux, the twenty-fourth death occurred with the passing of John Spearman, a farmer and the oldest member of the party. Travelling by day and sleeping at night on the river bank, nineteen families arrived two weeks later at the village of Prescott, where Talbot chartered a schooner to carry them to York, which they reached on September 3.

At York, as at Quebec, their arrival was unexpected and no one could suggest a suitable location until Richard Talbot chanced to meet one of the oddest figures in pioneer Ontario, Colonel Thomas Talbot. Born to the Anglo-Norman family that inhabited Malahide Castle north of Dublin, Thomas Talbot had served in the army and as secretary to Lieutenant Governor John Graves Simcoe. In 1802 he renounced both his commission and civilization and went off to live in the bush on the north shore of Lake Erie on the western frontier of the province. People said he had done this because of an unrequited love affair, and whether this was true or not, he lived the rest of his life as a bachelor in a rambling wooden structure he called Malahide Castle overlooking the hamlet he named Port Talbot, growing autocratic and eccentric with the years. Having got himself appointed superintendent of colonization for a region that had been known only to Indians and the occasional trapper, he excluded settlers he did not like, including his own countrymen. A few weeks before Richard Talbot arrived, the Colonel had been granted London Township to add to his territory, and, taking a liking to his namesake, he offered the party land.

Within a week, Richard Talbot started the trek to Port Talbot, which, although not much more than 150 miles, took nearly three weeks. The schooner chartered at Fort Erie foundered, Mrs. Benjamin Lewis died of exposure, and they lost their belongings. It was late in October when Richard Talbot's sons took off into the wilderness of London Township to clear some land and build a log cabin. Christmas was a few weeks away when the settlers began to move into their new homes. On December 23, 1818, Esther Thomas, wife of a farmer and weaver from Moneygall, Tipperary, gave birth to the first child born in the township. William Geary's wife, Elizabeth, a clergyman's daughter, remembered a "howling wilderness," with no roads and the nearest mill twelve miles away and provisions carried on the backs of the settlers. Few regretted leaving Tipperary, for a report in 1823 showed they had prospered in London Township; most of them owned 100 acres or more, had cleared about a quarter of their land and owned an impressive number of cattle, oxen and sheep. Richard Talbot himself was not suited to the life of a settler and did not do well, selling off some of his land when he went into debt.

Of the seventeen families of the Talbot group who had refused to proceed beyond Montreal, two settled there and the others accepted government land in the Ottawa Valley near the village of Richmond, which had recently been colonized by veterans of the 99th County of Dublin Regiment and their families. Most were Protestants, though there were some Catholics in the regiment, which had fought in the 1812 war. Richmond was the centre of one of three so-called Military Settlements, the others being Perth and Lanark farther west, which the government wished to populate as a defence against potential American incursion.

Before the War of 1812 there had been few settlers in the vast wilderness triangle whose apex lay at Montreal and whose arms ran west along the St. Lawrence and Ottawa rivers. When the United Empire Loyalists arrived, they settled "The Front," along the north shore of the St. Lawrence and Lake Ontario, and whose supply route had been exposed to American attack. The British planned a safer alternative that would follow the Ottawa River as far as the Rideau, where Ottawa now stands, and from there down to Kingston over what, in time, was to be a canal.

In 1818 when the breakaway group from the Talbot emigration went to Richmond, the only settlement on the Ottawa River was the logging village of Hull, established by the Yankee Philemon Wright at the turn of the century. There were one or two farms on the south bank of the river and the rest was wilderness. When William May travelled from the Ottawa to the Irish settlement called The Derry, a region of hardwood bush and marsh, in Beckwith Township in 1819, he walked more than twenty miles over a blazed trail, carrying luggage and his youngest child on his back, his wife and four other children trudging behind with the pots and pans. Families came in by ones and twos. Andrew Kidd and his family from Coon, County Wexford, suffered hardship on a voyage which took 147 days due to storms and accidents. The wife of his twenty-year-old son, John, died in childbirth and the baby was given to foster parents in Quebec City and only reclaimed two years later when John remarried. Presbyterian Scots and Scotch-Irish predominated in the Military Settlements, particularly in Perth and Lanark.

John Garland, who had been a neighbour of the Kidds in Wexford, settled near them, as did William Kerfoot, a stonemason from Coolcullen, County Kilkenny, whose family of eleven included his widowed father, who died on the journey. They were Protestants, either members of the Church of Ireland or Methodists, and the only Catholic to settle in The Derry at that time was Patrick Madrigan, whose family later moved to the United States, as did so many Irish Catholics. One group of Catholics who stayed was known as the Seven Bachelors, young men from Limerick and Waterford who set up housekeeping in Lanark Township in 1820 and tilled the soil together fourteen miles from Perth until one of them, John Quinn, married Catherine Phelan, whereupon the others married and were Seven

Bachelors no longer. John Boucher came in 1819, at the age of twenty, worked as a labourer, saved some money and cleared a lot in March Township, where his daughter was the first child born of white parents. He was married three times and sired twenty-five children – eleven boys and fourteen girls. At his death he left each of his sons a farm and each of his daughters a portion of money. He worked at farming all his life, except for a stint of the Rideau Canal and twelve years as a hotel keeper, belonged to the Church of England and Ireland, and prided himself on being "a strong conservative."

Farmers who had never contemplated leaving Ireland were migrating, people Ireland could ill afford to lose. "It is a melancholy thing," said the *Dublin Evening Post,* "that the emigration is necessarily restricted to the class immediately above the labouring poor, who cannot raise the money to pay their passage." The emigrants in 1819 numbered 6,000 and included prosperous farmers such as the 254 who left Limerick on the *Camperdown,* "one of the best appointed vessels which has cleared this port in a long time." Most of them were bound for the Military Settlements, whereas poorer emigrants gravitated to Newfoundland. "Nothing can be more deplorable than the situation of those Irishmen who migrate," observed Lieutenant Edward Chapell, RN, who saw them in St. John's. "In order to procure a passage across the Atlantic they enter first an agreement with the master of a trading vessel, whereby they stipulate to pay him a certain sum as passage money immediate subsequent to obtaining employment at St. John's. This makes them for a time a 'double servant.'"

Richard John Uniacke, eager to encourage emigration to Nova Scotia, told a parliamentary committee in London that because the passage to Newfoundland was cheaper, "all our population comes by way of Newfoundland," though this was an exaggeration and some ships were arriving at Halifax direct from Ireland, including the *Hibernia* with 105 farmers and their families from Cork in 1816. Those who came on from Newfoundland were called "second boat men," and in 1817 the Lieutenant Governor of Nova Scotia, Lord

Dalhousie, said: "About 500 fine young men, chiefly Irish, have lately arrived totally destitute of bread or means of sustenance. They are, I am told, the overflow of an increased emigration to Newfoundland last summer. There is no doubt they will prove a valuable acquisition," There were 12,000 Irish in St. John's that year, many of them unemployed after serving their time in outports and with neither wish nor money to go back to Ireland, where conditions since the war had grown steadily worse.

"IN THE FIFTH YEAR OF PEACE," wrote an author in the west of Ireland who described himself as "A Countryman," "the Irish peasant is found without provisions and without money, lodged in a filthy cabin, which is pervious to rain and storm, squalid and meagre in his aspect and ragged in his clothing, reduced to a state worse than the negro slave in the West Indies." In County Monaghan, an aspiring emigrant, Peter Finegan, wrote, "There is nothing in Ireland but failers, bankrupts and business gone to nothing." In Munster most of the banks closed their doors, and rudimentary industries, such as mining and smelting, withered and died. In 1821 the potato crop failed, plunging the provinces of Munster and Connaught into the worst famine since the 1740s. The Irish Census of 1851 describes conditions at the time:

The end of 1820 was distinguished for the great quantity of snow which fell; heavy and extensive inundations followed, which produced remarkable phenomena early in the following year. May and June, 1821, were dry, cold, and frosty, but the autumn was one of unusual moisture; the rain accumulated upon the surface of the ground, the rivers rose, the lakes swelled, and the floods spread far and wide over the face of the land, while the rain continued to pour in torrents during November, December and part of the following January.

It was scarcely possible, and generally unprofitable, to dig out the potato crop – it soured and rotted in the ground; and although a sufficiency was obtained in the dry and upland districts to support human life for some months, it was expended early in the ensuing spring; and then destitution, famine, and pestilence in quick succession followed. Fortunately these effects were not gen-

eral throughout the Kingdom, but occupied a district which might be de
a line drawn from the Bay of Donegal, upon the north side, at the junction
counties of Sligo and Leitrim, to Youghal Harbour, where the counties of L
and Waterford border on the south – thus including the whole western seaboa
of Sligo, Mayo, Galway, Clare, Limerick, Kerry and Cork; all exposed to the ful.
force of the Atlantic, the influence of which though mild is moist.

"It would be impossible to describe the state of the poor among
us," wrote a Sligo journalist. "To know all, you should put your head
into a cabin containing perhaps ten or fifteen squalid inhabitants who
had fasted forty-eight hours; hear the cries of the children, behold the
tears of the mother, and the worn, heavy countenance of the father,
who has neither work to do nor strength to do it. The prospects of
another year are gloomy in consequence of the ground remaining
unplanted for want of seed potatoes."

Though the potato crop had failed in the western counties, there
was a good grain crop elsewhere in Ireland and the government distributed supplies of oats, though communications were so bad people
starved because food did not reach them. Public works projects were
instituted to build roads and provide long-term famine relief. The
plight of the peasantry moved such philanthropic bodies as the London Tavern Committee to raise large sums – more, indeed, than was
contributed during the much more serious famine of the late 1840s.
Lord Carbery of west Cork was known to feed 600 people in a day,
but in many regions local support was disappointing and, as Michael
Sullivan of Bantry said, "Were it not for the aid of the benevolent
British public, the local subscriptions would hardly be sufficient to
purchase the coffins of those who die of mere want."

In Limerick, the Reverend Michael Fitzgerald reported that half
his parish was starving. "There are more than seventy families who are
seldom able to provide more than one meal a day of oatmeal gruel,"
he said, "and it is not always that this miserable meal can be pro-
cured." In County Kerry, where there were many absentee owners,
poor people received so little aid that a Killarney man named Ham-

mond reported people flocking to the seashore to feed on rockweed and limpets. "In some of the wretched hovels may be seen the father and mother lying down in the last stage of fever, surrounded by their starving and half-naked children." Dr. Heise of Borriskane, County Tipperary, said, "The poor people are lying without bed or straw under them, some even without shirts, on the bare floor of a miserable cabin or under cover of a wall or hedge. Their food is half-decayed potatoes and their drink dirty water." On the west coast of County Cork, two thirds of the population was destitute in the parish of Schull, and distress in the nearby market town of Skibbereen was "horrible beyond description."

Landlords were blamed for the crisis, but as one parish priest observed, the system, of which they were only a part, was also to blame. For longer than anyone could remember, farm labourers had been paid not in money but with the use of a small piece of land on which to build a mud cabin and plant a potato patch. Potatoes had become their currency. "This system answers very well as long as the poor man has potatoes enough raised by his own labour," he said. "But whereas in the present case potatoes utterly fail him, his difficulty in procuring food is greater than can be conceived. He may be surrounded by plenty, but in this plenty he cannot share without paying the price, and this price, however, small, he finds impossible to secure." While grain was plentiful, the poor had no money to buy it.

Early in 1822 powerful men in London, headed by the Archbishop of Canterbury and the former Secretary for Ireland, Sir Robert Peel, were shocked into establishing the Committee for Distressed Districts. This was a fund built up by private subscriptions that many thousands and, though never enough, provided much more than that received from the Irish gentry, Protestant or Catholic.

During the worst of the hunger, people had been too rebel. But with the easing of famine in 1822 terrorism reached pitch that the government applied the Insurrection Act, lawed such secret societies as the Whiteboys and made the

a capital offence. Whole communities were fined for refusing to inform on them, but the government failed to stamp out these organizations that fought evictions, high rents and the collection of tithes in
the name of a church the Catholics found alien and heretical, the
Church of England and Ireland.

Attitudes toward emigration changed. Priests had generally opposed emigration because it bled their parishes of the faithful, but now
the Bishop of Limerick promoted emigration as an antidote to violence and hunger. "At present they are in a state of hopeless, despairing recklessness," he said of the people of western Ireland. "Give them
hope, and they will endure, particularly if it is known that good character will be a recommendation." Landowners, who had regarded
emigration as loss of cheap labour, began to view it in a different light.
With the fall of grain prices, pasturage was profitable and fewer hands
were needed, and emigration was one way to rid estates of troublemakers. *The Times* of London no longer railed against emigration as
"treasonous."

Early in 1823, the government devised an experiment – the first
state-aided emigration of a large group selected from the majority of
the population, destitute Catholic farm people. Five hundred were
chosen, not, as might have been expected, from the bogs, mountains
and stony fringes of the Atlantic where people had been reduced to
eating seaweed, but from one of the most fertile regions of Ireland.
They were chosen from the Blackwater River region in the north-east
of County Cork, which the English, who had settled there since Elizabethan times, called the Garden of Ireland.

2

The Garden
of Ireland

*F*EW PLACES have been more blessed by nature than the northeast corner of County Cork. Unlike the barren, windswept country to the west beyond the mountains, it is sheltered land watered by the River Blackwater, which rises in the heather on the Kerry border and flows east for eighty miles to the town of Youghal on the sea.

Cattle grazed in the water meadows among drifts of wild yellow irises, and beyond the flowering hedges, fields of wheat and oats sloped away to the hills. A stranger gazing down from the Galtry Mountains might wonder that people should emigrate from such a place. "With honey and with milk flow Ireland's lovely plains," wrote a medieval poet in the golden age of Celtic culture. He might well have been writing of the Blackwater, before war and famine turned it into a microcosm of the Irish tragedy.

The Blackwater had been part of the MacCarthy Kingdom of Cork before Anglo-Norman invaders pushed the MacCarthy clan into poorer lands to the southwest in the 13th century and divided the Blackwater region – which is fifty miles east to west and thirty north to south – into four baronies, which are territorial divisions next in size to a county. The baronies were Duhallow, Fermoy, Orrery and Kilmore, and Condon and Clangibbon. The Normans – Roches, de Barrys, Condons – built castles and monasteries and imposed their feudal law and systematic agriculture. Land was no longer held in common as patrimony of a whole Celtic clan.

The most powerful were the Fitzgeralds, Earls of Desmond, who married the daughters of Celtic chieftains, learned the Irish language and became, as the saying goes, more Irish than the Irish. While English kings occupied themselves with wars in Europe, the Fitzgeralds ran the country in their own way until England tried to impose its rule. The Fitzgeralds rebelled and the war that followed in the 16th century brought misery not only on themselves but on the Celts who farmed their land. On the theory that a "barbarous country" must be broken by war before being capable of good government, the Elizabethan army reduced the Blackwater and most of the province of Munster to a waste of charred homes, wild grass, and the stumps of the old watchtowers that can still be seen. The Desmond rebellion was crushed and half a million acres of Desmond land in the counties of Cork, Kerry and Waterford were awarded to Queen Elizabeth's officers. The poet and civil servant Edmund Spenser from London received 3,000 acres on the Awbeg River, a Blackwater tributary, where he lived in Kilcolman Castle and recounted the horrors of war, famine and plague in a countryside "once full of corn and cattle."

"Out of every corner of the woods and glens they came," Spenser wrote of the survivors, "creeping forth upon their hands, for their legs would not bear them. They looked like anatomies of death, and they spoke like ghosts crying out of their graves, and they did eat the dead carrion. In a short space there were none left, and a most populous and plentiful country suddenly left void of man and beast." The survivors became serfs for 4,000 English yeomen brought in to farm the plantations, and with the yeomen came opportunists thrown up by war. Richard Boyle, a lawyer with a few pounds and a little jewellery in his pockets, became a trader, founder of an iron works and finally the Great Earl of Cork. Fane Becher, another of the Anglican New English, so called to distinguish them from the Catholic descendants of the Anglo-Normans, founded one of the powerful families to settle in the Blackwater. Sir John Jephson, an Elizabethan captain, claimed the Anglo-Norman seigniory of Mallow.

While completing *The Faerie Queene*, with its Blackwater scenes and its flattery of Elizabeth and his neighbour and fellow poet, Sir Walter Raleigh, Spenser had occasion to wish himself back in London. The Irish, he complained, showed "much hatred" for the English and the Protestant religion. Spenser and his fellow "undertakers," as those who had undertaken to run the plantations were called, were often harassed, and in the late 1590s 2,000 Irish clansmen and Catholic Old English, led by a new Earl of Desmond, invaded the Blackwater and destroyed the plantations. Spenser's castle was burned and his son killed, and he fled to England. Those English who remained adopted the language and customs, which explains why the Greens, Crawleys and Thornhills who emigrated to Canada two centuries later were Irish-speaking Catholics.

On Christmas Eve, 1601, the English had their revenge at the Battle of Kinsale, defeating the Earls of Tyrone and Tyreconnell, the last of the great Celtic chieftains. After the "flight of the Earls" their lands in Ulster were seized, and English occupied such choice regions as the Blackwater in County Cork. Sir William St. Leger, Lord President of Munster, purchased the Spenser estate from the poet's heir and built Doneraile Court. Sir Richard Aldworth, nephew of an Elizabethan planter, founded the town of Newmarket. Sir William Fenton, son of the Secretary of State for Ireland, married the daughter of Sir Edmond Fitzgerald, known as the White Knight because of his pale armour, and inherited Mitchelstown Castle, where he lived for forty years before it was burned in the war the Irish call the "curse of Cromwell." An English general passing through northern Cork in Cromwell's wake in the autumn of 1650 said that not a house was left standing and no people were to be seen. The poet Pierce Ferriter, hanged at Killarney with fifty-three rebels, called Cromwell's invasion "the vengeance of God on a sinful Irish nation."

In the depth of winter, Cromwell banished 2,000 Catholic land-owners to the barren hills of Connaught beyond the Shannon River. Their only crimes were refusal to recognize the Reformation and own-ing lands the English coveted. Cromwell gave their land to his ill-paid soldiers or to the Society of Adventurers, the syndicate of London shopkeepers, retired army officers and English county smallholders who had financed Cromwell's army by way of investment. The poet O'Bruadair called them "roughs formed from the dregs of each base trade, who range themselves snugly in the houses of the noblest chiefs, as proud and genteel as if the sons of gentlemen."

The MacCarthys, O'Mahonys and O'Driscolls in County Cork were stripped of their estates, until all but 5 per cent of the land of Ireland was controlled by a few thousand members of the Protestant Ascendency, which also controlled commerce and the civil service. The Catholics hoped that James II would restore their fortunes, and when James landed with troops at Cork in the winter of 1689, he was welcomed by Blackwater peasants with garlands of cabbages, there being no other greenery at that time of year. A few months later they saw him off to France with curses, following his defeat by William of Orange at the Battle of the Boyne, the third defeat suffered by the Irish in the course of the century. Soon after came the Penal Laws that poisoned Ireland for a hundred years.

Unlike the Penal Laws in England which suppressed a minority, those in Ireland were aimed at a whole nation. Though a Protestant himself, the Irish-born politician Edmund Burke called the Penal Laws an "elaborate contrivance for the oppression, impoverishment and degradation of a people and the debasement in them of human nature itself." The laws decreed that no Catholic could own land, or lease it for longer than thirty-one years, stand for parliament, vote, hold public office, practise law, serve as an officer in the military or own a horse worth more than five pounds. Parish priests were allowed to conduct services, provided they registered with the government, but since church property was confiscated this meant they held mass in a cattle shed or the corner of a field. The monastic orders were banned, as were the bishops, to "prevent the further growth of popery." Catholic schools were closed; learning was kept alive by "hedge school" masters who gathered children around them by the roadside.

Jonathan Swift, the Protestant Dean of St. Patrick's in Dublin, declared, "Whoever travels through the country will hardly think himself in a land where either law, religion or common humanity was professed." Passing through County Cork in 1723, he found landlords "screwing and racking" rents until tenants were worse off than the "peasants of France or the vassals of Poland." The terrible famine of the 1740s prompted his savage "Modest Proposal," the satire in which he suggested the solution was cannibalism, the flesh of babies being a "most delicious, nourishing and wholesome food."

An acre of potatoes was expected to feed a large family for most of the year, but that acre was vital and the struggle for land grew into the greatest peasant revolt in European history. Conquest, confiscation, persecution and humiliation, said Burke, had split Ireland into two nations. "One was to be possessed of all the franchises, all the property, all the education. The other was to be composed of drawers of water and cutters of turf for them."

THE BLACKWATER, with its privileged Protestant gentry, poor Catholic tenants and penniless farm hands, epitomized the divided nation. A dozen titled families and scores of lesser gentry aped the styles and manners of distant cousins in England, built castled mansions and isolated themselves in walled gardens from the rural slums around them. Unlike absentee landlords in less-favoured regions, most lived the year round in the Blackwater. St. Legers, Jephsons, Bechers, Wrixons, Hydes, Bowens, they had been there now for generations, breeding among themselves, neither English nor Irish. They attended the Church of Ireland, sent members to the puppet parliament in Dublin, joined the Cork Militia, and at banquets of the Loyal Protestant Society in Mallow wore orange cockades.

In one of the thickest concentrations of gentry, sixty Anglo-Irish families lived within seven miles of the spa town of Mallow, a replica of Bath in England. The fashionable drove there from Cork City, whose exports of wheat, meat and produce made it one of the busiest ports in Europe. By the ruins of Desmond Castle, beside an artificial canal under the riverside poplars, they took the waters, listened to band music, danced, played cards and bet on horse races. Henry Wrixon of Ballygiblin established Ireland's first hunt club there in 1740, and six years later the first steeplechase was run on a four-mile course between the steeple of St. Mary's at Doneraile and that of St. John's in Buttevant.

In Mallow the Anglo-Irish could be among their own kind and forget for a time the bitterness and poverty of those who worked their lands. The exploits of the feckless sons of the gentry, and the garrison officers who thronged the streets, have been preserved in the words of one of Ireland's liveliest jigs:

Beauing, belling, dancing, drinking
Breaking windows, damning, sinking,
Ever raking, never thinking,
Live the Rakes of Mallow.

A few miles to the north by the River Awbeg, the St. Legers, Viscounts of Doneraile, dwelt amid the wooded walks, lily ponds and the ghosts of Spenser's *Faerie Queene*. Buttevant, an "old nest of abbots, priests and friars," had become a backwater, the friary and abbey in ruins. Charleville, founded by the Great Earl of Cork's son, the Earl of Orrery, was a poor town, though it stood on the border not far from the Golden Vale of Limerick, one of the lushest pasture lands in the world. Twenty miles to the east, past the villages of Farahy and Kildorrery, lay Mitchelstown in the parish of Brigown, home of the King family, better known as the Earls of Kingston. The founder of this Irish dynasty was John King, who had come from Yorkshire with the Elizabethan army and married the daughter of the highest English official in Ireland. His grandson was raised to the peerage and succeeded to the White Knight's estates at Mitchelstown by marriage.

By the time the handsome, twenty-one-year-old Robert King inherited the title, second Earl of Kingston, in 1775, his land stretched from Kildorrery and Ballygiblin in the west to Ballyporeen in County Tipperary, and from the Galtee Mountains to the Kilworth Hills, north of Cork City. He rebuilt the crumbling castle of the White Knight, decorated it with French and Italian murals, and surrounded 1,300 acres of parkland overlooking the village with a ten-foot wall, six and a half miles long. He built stables for forty horses and planted a five-acre rose garden from the hot houses that are all that remain of his work.

On the site of the village, he created a model town for 3,000 people, and though a Protestant he built a church for Catholics as well as one for the town's 140 Anglicans. Showing an unsuspected aptitude for business, he built a mill to process wool from his 200 sheep, and a brewery and a flour mill to process his grain. His wife, Lady Caroline, who hired a doctor to attend the poor, provided free medicine and a store where people could buy clothes, sugar, tea, oatmeal and salt at wholesale prices, and founded a school for orphan girls, "to enlighten the minds of rising generations." The Kingstons were that rarity in 18th-century Ireland – progressive landlords – though as Arthur Young observed when he arrived in 1776 to manage Lord Kingston's 100,000 acres, the prosperity of the town did not extend to the countryside.

"The cottages, which are called cabins, are the most miserable-looking hovels that can be conceived," said Young. Looking into one of them, he found "a pot for boiling their potatoes, a bit of a table, and one or two broken stools; beds are not found universally, the family lying on straw." The house, he said, contained a man, a woman, eight children and a pig. Such were the homes of the cottiers and farm labourers at the bottom of a ladder that descended steeply from landowner down through "snug farmer" or "strong farmer" (a tenant with a good spread of land), and down again to subtenants who rented the six acres officially considered the minimum to support a family. Cottiers, on the bottom rung, were lucky if they had an acre.

"Their acre of garden feeds them the year through," wrote Young, "nine months on potatoes and the other three on oaten bread from their own oats. Except on occasional feast days, at Christmas or Easter, they rarely tasted meat, though in good times most managed to keep a pig or two – which they sold to provide cash for hearth tax, tithes, a few necessities, or to make up shortfalls when rent was increased at short notice and labour alone did not suffice to cover it."

Two of every three men had no steady work. Each Thursday, market day in Mitchelstown, the roads were full of people, some trudging a round trip of twenty miles in hope of selling a pitiful fleece of wool, a yard of homespun linen or perhaps a pig. They lived at the whim of middlemen who rented land from the Kingstons and leased it again in small parcels at inflated rates, so that cottiers were supporting not only themselves but a pyramid of subtenants, tenants, middlemen and landowners. One of Young's first acts was to convince Lord Kingston to get rid of the middlemen, reducing the rent burden on the people, but in no way decreasing Kingston's annual income of £50,000.

His son, the third Earl Kingston, known as Big George, was a tall, strong man, fond of acting the role of medieval lord for which he was born centuries too late. By turns enlightened and bigoted, mean and generous, obtuse and brilliant, but always autocratic, Big George was an Orangeman who described himself as a "pro-Catholic Tory." He was one of the few Irish peers to vote against the Act of Union which swallowed the Dublin parliament into Westminster in 1800. Big George was fifty when he inherited the title and the Mitchelstown lands in 1822 and believed himself "the principal man of County Cork." The golden age of his father had vanished with the end of the war, and rural rebellion had spread south from Limerick and Tipperary.

IN THE FAMINE WINTER of 1822, thousands of hungry, desperate men took to the hills armed with stolen muskets, sticks and spades. Maxwell Blacker, a magistrate administering the Insurrection Act, reported uneasily that there were "lights upon the hills at night in every direction." Conspiracy, said one of Lord George Kingston's friends, Sir William Wrixon Becher, MP, had become open revolt and spread to the gates of Cork City. Whiteboys at the town of Bandon raided thirty-seven homes, stealing twenty-five muskets, eight pistols and some rusty swords. Whereas once they had waited for darkness, they fought pitched daylight battles with soldiers and police, and early in January 300 men attacked a posse of fifty-five gentry, servants and soldiers, led by Lord Bantry, some distance from his home on Bantry Bay. "The insurgents, it appears, were not mere rabble," said a government report, "but they were restrained by some sort of discipline, for they had a regular bugle, which sounded the advance and retreat, and pressed on in a resolute manner."

Three days later, on January 24, 1822, a "large body of persons" attacked the Royal Mail coach at Millstreet, in the Blackwater region, killing the horses, driver and guard and wounding a passenger, before soldiers captured fifteen of the attackers. There was fighting over much of north Cork, at Newmarket, Kanturk, and at Charleville, where rebels stormed the jail and released prisoners. On a lonely road near Mitchelstown they held up a train of Rifle Brigade wagons, raping soldiers' wives and daughters and carrying off provisions.

In tacit admission that Cork was in a state of virtual civil war, Dublin sent the Commander-in-Chief, Lord Combermere, to Mallow and Doneraile, where the danger seemed greatest. His only action was to order reinforcements, a questionable remedy in the hills and bogs of Munster, where the troops knew nothing of the country and the Whiteboys knew it well. "Their perseverance and patience in the pursuit of their object, as well as the fatigue and privations they suffer, are astonishing," said an army report. "It is almost useless to harass them by fatiguing marches at night through country almost unknown to the soldiers. The Whiteboys are not easily surprised, they have videttes and scouts extending to a great distance in every direction, who fall back on the main body on the least alarm, with great expedition and silence so that the military cannot get near them. On the alarm, the party separates, crossing the fields and bogs where troops could scarcely follow, even in daylight. Or they lie behind a hedge or ditch within twenty yards of the military, according as the darkness of night favours them. The Whiteboys themselves at present travel generally barefoot, as much to prevent being heard as through want of shoes."

By day they were farm workers, blacksmiths and tenant farmers, indistinguishable from less militant neighbours. English law ruled the countryside in daylight hours, administered by magistrates supported by the "landlord's garrison" of constables, yeomanry and regular army. Once the sun went down, Whiteboy law took over, and neither Protestant nor Catholic was safe from the Whiteboys' rough justice. Their victims were often tithe proctors like Simon Trasse, who awoke one morning in his house across the border in Limerick to find a notice nailed to the door advising him "to quit this place in the course of eight or nine days time, or you will be made an example of to the Country by burning you alive with your horses and family."

The Whiteboys were led by elected commanders with such fanciful names as Captain Midnight, Captain Fear Not and Captain Starlight, who by day might be shoemaker, disbanded soldier, evicted cottier or perhaps a school master. George Kingston insisted that school masters, "among them some very bad characters indeed," were to blame for the troubles. "We transported one the other day who taught the children nothing but sedition." The Whiteboys swore an oath of secrecy and loyalty, and traitors to that oath lived in danger of execution.

"Not every young man that wished could join," recalled a man whose elders had been Whiteboys. "The inner circle of a group of Whiteboys, that is the leaders, decided at a meeting who were to be enrolled. Good conduct, straight dealings, and a decent family seem to have been the deciding factors in asking a man to form one of their body. A man asked to join a Whiteboy unit was always slow to refuse."

They did not regard themselves as criminals – they viewed their activities as a form of alternative law – and they tried to make their communiqués sound legalistic. "If this my first and last notice does not make the satisfactory impression," said one of their warnings, "I shall unavoidably have resource to assassination which I find so highly essential for the stability of the public cause." They could expect transportation to Australia or execution if they were caught. The 1822 diary of Richard O'Donovan of Bawnlahan House, West Cork, said Whiteboys had been caught in pitched battle with police and troops on January 25, and nine had been found guilty under the Insurrection Act and hanged. That outbreak had begun on New Year's Day when a raid by revenue officers on an illegal still making poteen became a running fight with a band of Whiteboys.

The attacks, which had been directed against local abuses and abusers, took on political overtones. "We are oppressed by the tyrannical laws of the English government, which we cannot endure no longer," said one notice found posted by the roadside. "They crowd us up with rents, tithes and taxes, which we daily sustain the burden of, without least abatement of rents. English laws must be curbed in; for we will never be satisfied until we have the truely Irish Parliament and King crowned in Ireland, as there formerly was. The sword is drawn and the hand of God is with us, and tyranny will soon be swept away."

"The part of the county in the greatest irritation," said Sergeant Lloyd, a Cork County magistrate, "was from Mallow to Fermoy. There were also disturbances in the barony of Duhallow, a very wild part of the country." Doneraile was caught up in violence when estates were converted from tillage to pasture, depriving labourers of jobs, and when the leader was caught he turned out to be William Hickey, one of the gardeners at Doneraile Court.

Hickey was described at his trial as a "very intelligent, smart fellow" who had led an attack on the home of a member of the gentry, Dr. John Northcott. The doctor's daughter, Jane, was at home alone and they did not molest her but looted the wine cellar and set the house on fire. Hickey had a blunderbuss and explained to the sheriff, "We always fired five or six shots whenever we set fire to a place, to intimidate people." This time the blunderbuss had exploded, tearing off three of Hickey's fingers, and although he fled, the fingers were found and traced to their owner.

When the sheriff asked him his motive, Hickey said it was the only means of "getting rid of taxes, tithes, and things of that sort." When the sheriff suggested this alienated landlords who could give Irishmen work, he replied, "Yes, but for every kind gentleman, there are ten to the contrary."

The young gardener, who was hanged for burning the house, belonged to terrorists who called themselves, collectively, Captain Rock. A typical Rockite message read, "Here I am, the bold determined man called Captain Rock." They sometimes displayed a sort of grim humour, and when Rocks failed to find any occupants at the home of James Hill, they left this message: "Notice to Mr. Hill, and whoe it May Consarn, that when Captain Rock and his Adicongs visit you next, you will take care to have Plenti of mate, and praties not Forgetting a smol drop of the Creter. Sind. J. Rock." Whole committees of Captain Rocks were discovered, including two respectable tenant farmers, Maurice Barrett and David Sheehan. Seven "Lady Rocks" who were captured turned out to be male arsonists in dresses, bonnets and veils.

Whiteboy attacks increased, and a man who lived on the road between Mallow and Doneraile said, "Our house and another were about the only houses in that district that had not been attacked by Whiteboys and abandoned by their owners." In Cork City, thirty-six Whiteboys were awaiting execution, and the Undersecretary for Ireland, William Gregory, complained to the Chief Secretary, Henry Goulbourn, "I do not know what can be done, with so many peasants under sentence of death. It will not be possible to execute them all." Goulbourn asked London for a convict ship, stating that the jails were so full that 300 Whiteboys must be transported to Australia.

Having failed to pacify the Blackwater by force, the landowners were ready to turn to other means, and in Mallow the most powerful men in the Blackwater called a meeting. Among those present were Lord Kingston, his brother-in-law Lord Mount Cashel of Kilworth, Lord Woodward of Glanworth, Viscount Ennismore, Sir William Wrixon Becher, MP, Charles Denham Orland Jephson of Mallow, Arthur Hyde of Hyde Castle near Fermoy, and Hayes St. Leger, Viscount Doneraile, a governor and former sheriff of the county. Many years earlier, Arthur Young had offered advice to Lord George Kingston's father. "The gentlemen of Ireland," Young said, "never thought of a radical cure, from overlooking the real cause of the disease, which in fact lay in themselves and not in the wretches they doomed to the gallows. If the gentleman of Ireland were to change their behaviour and provide employment, the poor would have no cause to riot."

In the 1770s when Young made that suggestion, such a course might still have been possible. Since then the population had almost doubled, the post-war depression had set in, and surplus labour was no longer the asset it had been, because arable land was being converted to pasture. With the publication of *The Principles of Population* by the Rev. Thomas Malthus – who demonstrated that when population increased more than food supply, the only relief was emigration – the government had been reconsidering its emigration policy. "One of the great misfortunes is over-population," declared Lord Kingston. He assured his fellow landowners that emigration was better than anarchy.

While Parliament debated the eternal "Irish Question," Lord Kingston wrote to his friend Lord Bathurst, Secretary of State for War and the Colonies. "I think you may help us at very small expense to the government," Kingston said, "if you will send out a few families to Canada and provision them for one year on land given them by the government." Well aware of parliament's reluctance to spend money on Ireland, he was careful to present his appeal in modest terms. "I could send you thirty industrious families in a short time – well calculated for settlers, and they would have many followers."

As it happened, Bathurst's deputy, Robert Wilmot Horton, was studying emigration as a means of relieving distressed parishes. He had been thinking of sending large numbers to Newfoundland when he was visited by the young Attorney General for Upper Canada, John Beverley Robinson, with a plan of his own to supply colonists for the Ottawa Valley Military Settlements, which had recently been taken over by the civil administration and renamed the Bathurst District, which later became the counties of Carleton, Renfrew and Lanark.

Horton was an ambitious young member of parliament from the north of England when he was appointed Undersecretary for Colonies. He had never been to Ireland or North America, and his initial idea of sending 985,000 emigrants to British North America in a decade or so was a measure of his inexperience, since such an emigration would have totally swamped the colonies and created more hardship than it cured. Horton was sidetracked by Robinson's plan and Lord Kingston's proposal for the Irish of the Blackwater. Given the Irish peasant's mistrust of the English, however, the matter demanded some care, and the leader of the expedition should probably not be an Englishman.

For John Beverley Robinson, the man for the job was his brother, who had accompanied him to England to see the sights. Peter Robinson was reluctant: he was anxious to get back to York, where he sat as a member of the Legislative Assembly, owned a flour mill and tavern, and was a land developer. An Anglican of United Empire Loyalist stock, he had been born in New Brunswick and raised in Upper Canada and knew next to nothing about Catholics or Ireland. It was only after his brother convinced him that the emigration must fail without him that Robinson reluctantly accepted the cumbersome title Superintendent of Emigration from the South of Ireland to Canada. Since he was poor at figures, he asked for a commissary officer to help him keep account of government funds but he was turned down. Later, when his accounts were delayed and considered excessive, the government doubtless wished it had listened to him. Before Peter Robinson left for Ireland, Horton provided him with a memorandum stating the government's intentions:

"It is thought prudent to attempt nothing more this year than can certainly be carried into effect with due regard to the comfort of the emigrant, and to public economy in the conduct of the measure. Accordingly, it has been ordered that means shall, with as little delay as possible, be provided in the harbour of Cork, for conveying to Quebec such persons not exceeding 500 in number, as are willing to become settlers in the Province of Upper Canada."

Each family would be granted seventy acres, with an option on another thirty, as well as farm implements, a cow and a year's supply of food. Parliament had voted £12,000 once the project was supported by Sir Robert Peel, the Home Secretary, formerly the Secretary for Ireland. No one in parliament knew Ireland better than Peel, for whom emigration was "one of the remedies for Irish misery."

IN 1822 EMIGRATION to North America was meagre. Hardly more than 8,000 left that year, most of them Protestants bound for the British colonies. The few Catholics among them were the most hard-pressed, such as Cornelius Lyons of County Limerick, who had come home to his field one evening to find it empty, his cattle seized by the landlord for arrears in rent. Like many tenant graziers in the Golden Vale north of the Cork County border, Lyons rented not only his land but his cattle from the landlord. Being a man of daring, he took matters into his own hands.

That night he recruited his cousin, filled two sacks with pebbles from the roadside and crept into the landlord's farmyard. The night, it seems, was cloudy and dark with a threat of rain. Methodically Lyons tossed handfuls of pebbles from his sacks on to the high slate roof of the landlord's house, so that the occupants would think it was raining too hard to venture out. At the same time, his helper led Lyons' cows out of the byre and drove them away, their sounds covered by the rain of pebbles on the roof.

Having made his protest against rack-renting, and with no faith in a justice system controlled by the local gentry, Lyons was forced to flee the district, eventually taking passage with his family in one of the ramshackle timber ships bound for Quebec City. From there he went on to the Irish settlement of Frampton, on the Etchemin River in the hill country sixty miles southeast of Quebec City. His story, which illuminates the pressures forcing the Irish into exile in the 1820s, was preserved for history by the parish priest.

3

Peter Robinson

$\mathcal{T}$HE NEWSPAPERS were heavy with reports of violence and outrage in the early months of 1823, and within a week of Peter Robinson's arrival in County Cork, five houses had been burned. In County Limerick, north of the Cork border, twelve people had been killed when a terrorist named William Gorman burned the home of a rack renter, Edward Shea. The Spring Assizes were crowded with petitioners seeking compensation for crops destroyed and cattle mutilated.

A less conscientious or more timid man might have remained in the security of Condon's Hotel in Cork City, but since Robinson was determined to take as many people as he could from the disturbed baronies of the Blackwater, he wanted to see the region for himself. At the age of thirty-seven, and a bachelor, Robinson had a reputation for courage that he had won as an officer in the 1812 war against the

Americans. Since he knew nothing of Ireland, the Colonial Office had instructed him to take the advice of Lord Ennismore, the Whig member of parliament, who suggested Robinson make his headquarters in Fermoy, which during the Napoleonic war had been built up from a muddy crossroads into a market town and military centre that rivalled Mallow.

On May 20, two days after his arrival from England, Robinson hired a coach and horses and set out for the hills twenty miles to the north, passing through a landscape of fields, pastures of grazing cattle, and rising larks. No season is lovelier than spring in southwest Ireland, and for an outdoors man who had been cooped for months in the smoke of London, it was a pleasant journey. On the steep hill half way to Fermoy, Robinson saw the Bride Valley spread below him, with the Blackwater off in the distance and the mountains behind. It looked very peaceful. It was after noon when he rode down another steep hill, across a stone bridge with thirteen arches, and into Fermoy, a town with whitewashed houses, a bank, brewery, flour mill and barracks, where he installed himself at the inn and purchased a desk.

In the next few days, Robinson introduced himself to the Blackwater landowners. At Moore Park near the village of Kilworth he met the ailing Lord Mount Cashel, who complained of "excess population" impeding progress on his 40,000 acres. He received assurances of cooperation at Glanworth, Lord Woodward's estate, before riding north to meet the "principal person of Cork," Lord Kingston, at Mitchelstown.

Since the Colonial Office had failed to advise Lord Kingston of Robinson's arrival, Robinson approached Mitchelstown with some trepidation, for it was said that Big George had been annoyed. In the event, Lord Kingston received Robinson civilly, invited him to breakfast and assured him that government-assisted emigration was being promoted in the Blackwater solely for humanitarian reasons. It had not, it seemed, occurred to Kingston to finance emigration himself. Much of his conversation reflected his preoccupation with rebuilding his home – which his father had rebuilt fifty years earlier – into a Gothic structure resembling Windsor Castle in England. He had hired a Mr. Claridge, who later founded the famous hotel in London, in the hope of making his kitchen the finest in Ireland, in order to please his boyhood friend, King George IV, who was coming to visit. It was one of Lord Kingston's many disappointments in life that the King was delayed in Dublin and never came, but Kingston consoled himself by building an expensive hunting lodge in the Galtee Mountains.

While Lord Kingston was pouring money into these projects, and going bankrupt, people on his estates were going hungry. Thomas Reid, a prison inspector travelling from Tipperary to Mitchelstown, said, "The general appearance of the poor is truly pitiful." On market day at Ballyporeen, a village owned by Lord Kingston, Reid saw "groups of half naked people of all descriptions of age and sex. Throughout the summer, work could not be obtained at any wage, and in order to eke out life, the poor were obliged to pawn and sell their rags and clothes. Heaven only knows what will become of them in winter. They are the poor, ragged and hungry, who can obtain no employment. What are they to do?"

Robinson rode west through the poor villages of Kildorrery and Farahy, past the grey walls of Bowen's Court and other Anglo-Irish estates, into a land of silent fields, Norman churches, lonely stone bridges and unrelieved stretches of rural poverty. "Crossing the Ballyhourie Mountains toward Doneraile," wrote a traveller, "the huts of the peasant had so cheerless and deplorable an aspect as to awaken a dozen painful memories." Doneraile, once a prosperous centre of the weaving trade, was one of the most disturbed communities in the Blackwater, and the same traveller believed that Viscount Doneraile, for all his position as a governor of the county, "gives little encouragement to anything calculated to improve the place, and evinces but a very moderate sympathy with the condition of the people." As Robinson talked with people at the roadside, or stepped into the cabins for a cup of water, he encountered a depth of hopeless poverty and a dis-trust of landlords that he had never heard of in Canada.

Buttevant, once a market town so rich it sent two members of parliament to Dublin, was now a backwater. Charleville was a "poor town on the borders of the County of Limerick, and contains many wretched cabins." Assisted by Captain Roberts, the local squire, he met with three Protestant families who wanted to emigrate, descen-dants of German settlers who had fled from the Rhineland a century earlier to escape persecution and settled in County Limerick. At Mallow he enlisted the aid of Colonel Charles Orlando Jephson, and found that three quarters of the population of the spa town had no work.

Robinson had little time. Within a month he had to choose 500 emigrants, process them and get them aboard ships bound for Quebec by the end of June so they could be settled and housed in the Cana-dian wilderness before winter set in. He advertised in the newspapers and sent circulars throughout the Blackwater and neighbouring coun-ties soliciting Catholic farmers, forty-five years of age or younger, with no money of their own and no more than three children under four-teen years of age. The response was disappointing. When those who came forward learned that their names would be submitted to scrutiny of the local magistrates, they quickly withdrew. In a countryside un-der the Insurrection Act, a magistrate was a man to be avoided. One farmer believed Robinson was party to a sneaky new method of "trans-porting" people, as Whiteboys were transported to Australia. "The government found they could not get rid of them fast enough by the Insurrection Act and were trying another plan," the man said.

Though he had been told in London to put his faith in the land-lords, Robinson's own encounters with poor Irish caused him to take a more independent path. "The temper and disposition of the lower order of people should not be judged solely by what you hear," he cautioned Horton in a letter to London. "It is not as it is in other countries. The noblemen and gentlemen have not in the least the confidence of the lower orders." Landowners had told him frankly they were primarily interested in removing "fiery spirits," paupers and other undesirables, so those who remained could be given steady employment and the recurring troubles be stopped.

Lord Ennismore, who apparently felt that the young man from the colonies was slipping out of his grasp, complained that Robinson seemed to be attracting "only the most industrious and well-disposed," and advised the magistrates to urge Robinson to take "only those who, if not actually concerned with the disturbances, are likely to be so from their situation." Sir William Wrixon Becher hoped that Robinson would remove a "number of persons who had been brought up in turbulent and irregular habits."

Robinson may have been inexperienced and naive, but he resisted efforts by landowners to turn his emigration into a dumping ground for undesirables. "I have no wish," he said, "to hold out a bounty to persons of bad character." So long as he stayed within certain limits, Horton had promised him a free hand. In the depths of the Colonial Office in Whitehall, or the drawing rooms of the landowners, the people of the Blackwater had seemed shadowy paupers or fearsome rebels, but as Robinson travelled through the countryside they became flesh and blood. "People of a good sort," he called them, "bred to farming but now completely without work. I found them much more intelligent than I expected. Most of them could read and write, and calculate their allowance of rations to the eightieth part of an ounce."

Travelling in a circle of sixty miles through Mitchelstown, Doneraile, Charleville, Kanturk, Newmarket and back to Fermoy by way of Mallow and Castletownroche, he found unexpected allies. He had been told that priests were opposed to emigration and was pleased that Father Jones in Mallow and Father O'Brien of Newmarket were not only helpful but read his appeal for emigrants from the pulpit. Robinson sat down with people to explain what a voyage was like, and methods of clearing and planting virgin land. Peter Fane, for one, was worried about Canadian winters, his children "being not in array to bear any frigids." At the village of Ferahy some suspicious Catholics withdrew from the scheme when they heard that Robinson had rejected the application of a local Protestant, whereupon he got Horton's permission to take some token Protestants to demonstrate that this was not a scheme to transport Catholics into North American slavery.

"All so many questions," he recalled. "Was I an American? Did I live there? Would I go back again? Was I quite sure there was no catch? Were there any pigs, potatoes, priests, wild men, beasts? I was able to set before them the length of the journey, the obstacles on the way, and the means of removing them. I dispatched their apprehension concerning wild beasts, and the danger of being lost in the woods."

He was pleased there had been no disturbances since his arrival, and refrained from asking questions about them. When he got back to Fermoy he found 200 people waiting, such had been the change in attitudes, and by mid-June he was able to assure Horton that his mission would be a success. "I returned this day from Charleville," he said, "and can now positively state that the proposals for emigration are very well received by the people. I have been going around to the smaller villages that I might be able to judge for myself."

The applicants were surprisingly varied. Some bore English names, such as Green or Hodge, descendants of families brought to Ireland by Cromwell or Queen Elizabeth. There were Anglo-Norman Roches and Fitzgeralds descended from the invaders who came over from Wales in the 12th century, following Richard de Clare, known as Strongbow. There were Welsh, Scottish and Flemish names among the people of Blackwater, but of the ancient Celtic names, O'Sullehains had long been anglicized to O'Sullivan, or even Sullivan, and O'Gealhbain to Galvin.

Robinson became known as a man of good will, and people walked long distances to see him, coming from as far away as the counties of Kerry, Tipperary and Limerick, where Blackwater gentry owned land. "When I first made the terms public upon which the government would send settlers to Canada," said Robinson, "they were met with a good deal of jealousy by the people, who seemed to consider it a plan of the government to get rid of them, rather than to relieve them, and this they expressed to me freely. However, after some time they were ready to come forward, and upon meeting with a few of their friends who had been in Canada – discharged soldiers and those who could explain to them the state of the country, and the certainty there was of their getting employment, and finding the information they got in this way to correspond with what I had already told them – they soon began to think more seriously of my proposals, and to come forward and accept them. This feeling to emigrate spread rapidly, and I found no difficulty in getting many to choose from."

Some were desperate, such as James Walsh of Kilworth, a "poor man really famished for want of work," or John Quinlan of Fermoy, who had "wandered from place to place in search of work and can find none." There were illiterate labourers, like young James Sheil of Newmarket, skilled farmers like the thirty-nine-year-old Michael Corkery of Carigroshan near Cork City, and artisans such as Cornelius Roche, the Doneraile blacksmith, James Buckley, a Churchtown shoemaker, Edmond Barry, a Mallow baker – all of them seeking emigration, they said, to give their children better lives.

There were people with formal education, such as George Hanover of Mallow, who, despite a royal and Protestant name, was a Catholic who had attended university in Dublin, and Robert Armstrong of Kilfinnane, Limerick, a former militia captain whose Anglo-Irish wife had grown up in Suir Castle, Tipperary, a daughter of the Honourable Francis Massey. The wife of Garrett Nagle of Fermoy was descended from Patrick Sarsfield, Earl of Lucan, leader of the Wild Geese who fled Limerick for France in 1691.

To avoid trouble with the gentry, Robinson hid his attempts to choose experienced farmers known for loyalty to the crown. "The emigrants I took," he insisted, "were selected from persons who were commended to me by the principal noblemen and gentlemen of the country as being absolute paupers, and as such it was particularly desirous to get rid of." In the end he struck a compromise, and his selection consisted of respectable farmers he wanted as colonists and a sprinkling of paupers and troublemakers the landowners urged on him.

Robinson arranged for the navy to send two transport ships, the 416-ton *Hebe* and 438-ton *Stakesby*, and late in June they waited in the Cove of Cork, each equipped with a doctor, medicine and provisions of beef, pork, oatmeal, cheese, biscuits, tea, cocoa and butter. The emigrants, summoned by messengers, had gathered at Cork City, carrying a few belongings, the people of north Cork clad in worn blue woollen frieze cloth and those from Limerick in grey. The men, no matter how poor and tattered, were dressed in the fashion of an earlier time in swallowtail, high-collared, cutaway coats with tapered skirts, knee breeches and stove-pipe hats. Those who had brogues and stockings carried them over their arms.

There was dockside confusion when a city magistrate arrested some men suspected of Whiteboy terrorism; since these were precisely the men the landlords wished to get rid of, they were quickly released. As sailing time drew near, officers on the *Hebe* had difficulty knowing who was an emigrant, "the settlers being on shore at all hours, it is impossible to distinguish them from others." Of the 600 people on Robinson's list, 140 failed to appear and Robinson attributed their absence to the "tardiness of country people, and the dread the women have of the sea." He replaced them from the hundreds who had come to the city in the hope that a place might be found for them on the ships. "On the 1st July, 460 only were embarked but I was able next day to select 111 more," Robinson said, "making in all 571, which was as many as could be accommodated." Right up to the last moment there were people clamouring to go. "They came alongside the ships in numbers until the hour we sailed," Robinson said, "and were always much disappointed in not being received."

Three people changed their minds and left the vessels before they sailed. Of the 568 remaining, 182 were men, 143 women, 57 boys aged fourteen to eighteen, and 186 teenaged girls and children. The average age of the "heads of family," which were not only husbands but sometimes the eldest son of a widow, plus the thirty-two bachelors, was thirty-five years. All but a dozen families were Catholic, and though most came from the Blackwater region, there were some from the counties of Limerick, Tipperary and Clare, and one or two from Waterford and Kerry.

Several families had adopted an alias, either to escape detection because they had been involved in Whiteboy terrorism or because they had purchased the embarkation certificate of a family that had decided not to go. Since these were not transferable, the name of the original family was retained and ages were falsified to match the certificates. There were a few stowaways, and John Green, a thirty-two-year-old Protestant from Castletownroche, had smuggled his Catholic sweetheart, Catherine Mulcahey, aboard the *Stakesby*.

The voyage of the *Hebe* and *Stakesby* took eight weeks, two weeks longer than most crossings, and though the ships were well provisioned, the food was so strange to the Irish they refused to eat the plum puddings and cheddar cheese served for Sunday dinners. "Children during sickness called constantly for potatoes," said Robinson, but there were none aboard. John and Bridget Ahern from Castletownroche lost their three-month-old daughter, Jane, to smallpox on July 29, and a week later the twenty-seven-year-old mother died, leaving the husband with a three-year-old son. Eight children died during the voyage, their bodies, wrapped in canvas, lowered into the sea.

THE *HEBE* docked at Quebec City on the last day of August, followed two days later by the *Stakesby,* and the emigrants were taken to Montreal at government expense by the St. Lawrence Steamboat Company. The great river and the vast, forested countryside made Ireland seem very small, they said. Robinson said they were in good health. On September 6 they travelled nine miles from Montreal to Lachine, where they boarded twenty-two flat-bottomed bateaux, each manned by two French-Canadian boatmen, for the journey through the rapids and shallows of the upper St. Lawrence River. Five boats carried half a ton of beef and a ton of bread and biscuits to feed them.

The emigrants were expected to row the heavy, thirty-foot boats, learning as they went, for few had ever seen rowboats before. Morale was high, the weather fine, and they made good time despite inexperience and blistered hands. They slept on shore, half of them without blankets, cooked over campfires, and were helped at the difficult portages by teams of French Canadians hired for the purpose. Young Michael Cronin, whose wife, Mary, was expecting their first child, wrote to his mother at Mitchelstown, "We had as favourable a voyage and as pleasant as ever was performed, and as good usage as any person could expect."

They covered 100 miles to Prescott, a village on the upper St. Lawrence, in five days. After swearing allegiance to the Crown, they were issued with printed location tickets that assigned each family seventy acres, on condition three and a half acres be cleared and fenced and a house at least sixteen feet by twenty be erected within two years. An additional thirty acres would be reserved for ten years, should the family wish to buy it at the cost of ten pounds.

"I have the emigrants here," Robinson reported from Prescott on September 15, "and am engaging teams to take them to Beckwith Township, where I am told there is a large government store capable of containing them. I sent an express today to Captain Marshall acquainting him with my arrival here, and my intention of proceeding with the emigrants to Beckwith on the 17th, and to know what description of stores he held in his possession, and whether he had authority to issue them to me. As I understood there were many of the articles the emigrants would require in store, I only purchased axes in Montreal."

Three days later Robinson set out at the head of his party on a forty-mile trek by oxcart over the rough, hilly trail to the village of Perth, a Protestant community of Scots and Ulstermen. From there

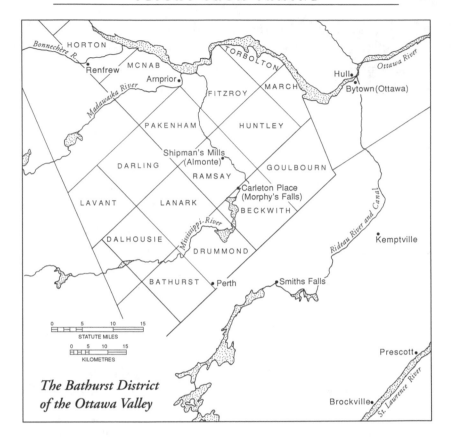

**The Bathurst District
of the Ottawa Valley**

they proceeded twenty miles to the Mississippi River, a tributary of
the Ottawa, and the settlement in Beckwith Township called Shipman's Mills (now Almonte), a community of a dozen families around
Daniel Shipman's mill. "As there were no barracks or government
buildings in the neighbourhood, and the whole party without shelter," said Robinson, "my first care was to provide log houses for them,
and that on their respective lots." In the meantime they camped near
the village. Robinson was disappointed to find that the best land had
already been claimed by earlier settlers in the surrounding townships
of Beckwith and Ramsay. "More than half had been settled by Scotch-
men from the neighbourhood of Glasgow," he reported. "The adja-
cent townships of Huntley, Goulbourn and Pakenham were also par-

tially settled by disbanded soldiers and others. Being anxious to settle the people as near each other as possible, I determined to examine carefully what land remained in these townships at the disposal of the government and fortunately I found a sufficient number of vacant lots for settlement."

Robinson managed to locate land for eighty-two families in Ramsay Township; he placed another five in Beckwith and the rest in the townships of Pakenham, Huntley, Goulbourn, Lanark, Bathurst and Darling. The quality of land varied greatly – hilly, rocky and swampy stretches were interspersed with good loam, particularly in Ramsay and Beckwith. Pakenham, on the fringe of the Canadian Shield, had the least desirable land, western Huntley was rocky but Carp Valley in its north-eastern area was excellent. Poor soil was only discovered when the trees were cleared, and in that sunny autumn of 1823 the Irish had reason to be thankful. On October 6, the resident government agent, Captain William Marshall, having supplied "many articles useful to settlers which remained in the King's stores," wrote that "Mr. Robinson is getting on fast in locating his people." Michael Cronin, writing to his mother, found the prospects pleasing:

The whole crew of settlers which came in both ships were sent out from this place in squads in numbers from six to thirty to look for their lands, with a pilot to show them their respective lots, and it was on Thursday last that I made out my own farm, which was the 23rd of October, and as my own judgment I take it to be as good as any in the country.

Mr. Robinson our Superintendent is uncommonly humane and good to us all. He at first served us our bedding and blankets and all kinds of carpenters tools and farming utensils, and sending people which are in the habit of building log houses with the whole of us, and each man's house is built in the course of two days. And Mr. Robinson promises us a cow to the head of each family next September.

Since we came on shore each man is served out in the day with one pound of bread or flour and one pound of beef or pork, and each woman, boy and girl the same. I do recommend you my Dear Mother to get yourself ready early next Spring to come here. Mr. Robinson tells me he is to go back to Ireland next

Spring to bring a good many more settlers. This is a good and free country, as any in the world, and each man is paid twelve dollars a month … and each woman six dollars each.

Like the other families, the Cronins received a gift of tools and supplies such as they would never have dreamed of owning in their own parishes. Cronin received three blankets, two pairs of shoes, two pairs of moccasins, an iron pot, a spade, saw, adze, plane, hoe, wedge, auger, hammer, two pounds of nails, two files, a gimlet, a pickaxe, a billhook, lengths of flannel and cotton, eight bushels of seed potatoes and eight quarts of corn. The family was promised a cow, and free food until the first crop came in.

A township was usually 10 square miles, divided into 12 concessions and 27 lots; half a lot was allocated to each family. These were marked with a blaze on a tree and were hard to find in the dense bush. "After six days hard labour, travelling through swamps and untrodden paths through the woods, I had to return without selecting land," complained one settler. "I have often heard it said there are few stones in Canada, but Ramsay Settlement abounds in rocks and stones. To give you an idea of the woods in this place is quite beyond my power." But there were few complaints, or if there were they did not find their way into letters home. Robinson reported:

Fortunately the autumn was unusually pleasant and free from rain, and they suffered less from exposure than could have been expected, or than they would have done earlier in the season, and arriving there late there were neither flies nor mosquitoes in the woods to annoy them.

They were first encamped in the immediate neighbourhood of the settlers who arrived three years before, some of these their own countrymen, so they had an opportunity of seeing how far advanced and how comfortable they were after three of four years residence in the country, and this seemed to encourage them very much. They at all times showed the greatest readiness to obey me in everything, and I never met with people more grateful for a little act of kindness.

Robinson helped those not suited for farming to get jobs in Prescott and Perth. Peggy Casey, eighteen, who had travelled out alone, went to work as a servant. Jeremiah Ryan, a Buttevant shoe-maker, got a good wage, twenty-four pounds a year. John O'Mara, a fifty-two-year-old farmer from Rathcormac, wrote on November 20 to his brother James: "Our Superintendent, Mr. Robinson, is behaving as humane and gentlemanly as any man in the world," and called his seventy acres "as good as any land in the country." He asked his brother to send potatoes and a hand loom. There were a few deaths: Patrick Donaghue, a forty-four-year-old farmer from Mallow, died soon after occupying his land, leaving a widow, three daughters and a newborn son.

The fledgling settlement had come to depend heavily on its mentor, and it was a great loss when Peter Robinson left in mid-December to look after his own affairs at York. In a report to London on December 16, 1823, Robinson wrote, "I have great pleasure in acquainting you that the plan of emigration has succeeded uncommonly well. The settlers are much pleased with the country, and I am sure they will be a valuable acquisition." It was not until the spring, when Robinson was back in Ireland to fetch more colonists, that the settlers faced their greatest crisis.

4

The Ballygiblins

*T*HEIR FIRST REAL TEST was the Canadian winter. Coming from a mild climate, the settlers were ill prepared for the iron cold of the Ottawa Valley, and their worn cloaks and swallowtail coats were little protection.

Charles Carrol O'Sullivan of Kilworth, County Cork, who had come out with his wife, Honora, wrote in February 1824 that the cold had been so intense for the past fortnight that people had been unable to work outdoors clearing their land. Even so, said O'Sullivan, Canada was a "fine country," and a temperature of thirty below zero was preferable to having to put up with the "rebuke of a landlord and the frown of a Proctor at home." Informing his uncle James that Robinson would visit the Blackwater again in the spring, O'Sullivan added,

"If you do not come out with Mr. Robinson, you are the fool to stop at home, which I advise you not."

The greatest hardship for these gregarious people, accustomed to constantly visiting relatives and friends in nearby homes, was being snowbound and imprisoned in log cabins scattered over half a dozen townships. Fearful of wolves and bears and of getting lost in the woods and trackless snow, they huddled in drafty dwellings of unseasoned logs, stoked their smoky hearths and prayed for spring. "No one ventured far at night, for wolves prowled around the house in the darkness, uttering the most dismal howls," one settler wrote. When the weather permitted, the men walked to Shipman's Mills to replenish their food from the government depot and carry it home on their backs.

Clearing trees from their lots was slow and dangerous work. Ireland having been denuded of its forests for centuries, the emigrants had no experience at felling large trees. A gust of wind, a moment of carelessness, and a falling tree could kill or maim. Bryan Reilly from Dundrim, Tipperary, a thirty-three-year-old bachelor who had taken up land with his sister, Bridget, managed to clear an acre before he was killed by a falling tree. Katherine O'Brien from Liscarroll, the young mother of four, wrote home from Ramsay Township that her husband, Timothy, had cleared four acres by February 20 "and hopes to have an acre or two again by spring." She invited her brother in County Cork to join them as soon as he could.

"We have every prospect of doing well and having plenty," wrote Katherine O'Brien. "This is the most delightful country. I believe none in the world more healthy. No sickness of any kind affects us, nor any of the settlers here; no want of bread, for all have plenty to spare, and no man living willing to work but may live happy." She had one nagging concern, which was to grow in the coming months. "The rum is very cheap, and a good many of our settlers likes it too well, which may prove their ruin."

In their letters home, they praised the clear air and bright skies, and Thomas Collins, who was twenty-one and came from Kanturk, boasted he was not bothered by the cold. "I would not for £500 be home in Ireland again," he wrote, and added that he and his brothers had cleared seven acres in Goulbourn Township since Christmas. Though Governor Lord Dalhousie at Quebec had disapproved of the scheme from the start and was predicting that once government hand-outs were exhausted the Irish would desert their land and run away to the United States, Wilmot Horton in London found the emigrant letters encouraging. "If accounts of them continue favourable," Horton wrote late in the winter, "North American emigrants will become part of our National Policy. If the contrary event takes place we shall be brought to disgrace, and as far as any individual will suffer, I am sorry to say that I shall be the most prominent one." That the Irish chosen to go with Robinson were well favoured is clear from a report that Horton made to a parliamentary committee on those who emigrated without government support.

In the years 1822 and 1823, 10,300 emigrants upon the average annually arrived at Quebec. By far the larger proportion of these were little better than paupers. Having paid from four to six pounds for their passage and their sustenance on the voyage, they found themselves destitute on arriving at Quebec; they had neither the means of going upon Crown land if granted to them, nor of cultivating it. The greater part, if they had money to pay their passage up the St. Lawrence, or if they could obtain it by a few days labour at Quebec, hastened on to Upper Canada, and of those who did so, perhaps one half went on to the United States. Few remained and became useful and effective settlers in the Lower Province [Quebec]. The proportions of the whole emigration to be assigned to the three nations may be stated at about three-fifths Irish, and the remainder English and Scotch, with a larger proportion of the latter. Of the English and Scotch, perhaps one-fourth at least brought money or other resources with them. Of the Irish, scarcely one-twentieth landed with any but a scanty provision of clothes and bedding. Those who had not the means of settling on land, or who did not, or would not go to Upper Canada or the United States, remained as labourers in the principal towns of the Lower Province; and when the approach of winter at once diminished their sources of employment and increased their wants, they became a burthen on the community.

With the coming of spring, Robinson's settlers sowed their first potatoes, turnips and grain, but unfortunately they had also sown hostility. The trouble had been growing all winter, almost since Robinson's departure, which had left the colony in the charge of an inexperienced young clerk named Thomas Baines, who had neither control over the immigrants nor the respect of the earlier settlers, who were mostly Protestants.

A great deal of the trouble stemmed from religious enmity, compounded with envy. The Presbyterians from the Scottish Lowlands and Ulster who had settled in the townships several years earlier had hacked out trails, cleared the land, planted wheat and built a small export trade in grain and potash from the ashes of their hardwood trees, all with little help from the government. Having no love for Catholics, they did not welcome the newcomers, and their hostility increased when they heard the Irish were being fed for a year at government expense. When the newcomers turned up at the taverns to trade their ample rations for whiskey, hostility grew.

There were occasional reports of drunken quarrels during the winter, and a coterie of young men who called themselves the Ballygiblins, after the crossroads village near Mitchelstown where they had joined the emigration, were especially disliked. They included twenty-two-year-old Bart Murphy, who lived with his sister at Wolves Grove on the road to Perth; Luke McGrath, who like Murphy came from Clogheen, Tipperary; John French and Patrick Sullivan, married men from Bandon, County Cork; and James and William Brown, teenagers from Waterford.

The trouble came to a head on April 23, in what became known as the Ballygiblin Riots, the first major confrontation between Orangemen and Irish Catholics in Canada. It began at Morphy's Falls (now Carleton Place), eight miles up the Mississippi River in Beckwith Township, and the news appeared in the press on May 5. The *Montreal Herald* reported:

The Irish emigrants who arrived in this settlement last season are carrying outrages to such an extent as almost to baffle the efforts of the civil authorities to keep them in check. On the 23rd of April, His Majesty's Birthday, the militia regiment assembled for training at Morphy's Falls. While a party, principally Scots, were drinking His Majesty's health, at the house of Alexander Morris, they were attacked by the Ballygibenets [sic], as the emigrants termed themselves. The windows were stove in and the floor and walls literally washed with blood. A gun was forceably taken from one of the party in Morris' house, and the person who carried it off was wounded by shot fired at him as he was making his retreat with his prize. Since the 23rd, fresh outrages have been committed. A Captain Glendinning of the 4th Carleton Militia has almost been murdered.

This highly coloured report came from a correspondent in Perth, a centre of the Orange Order, which had been introduced from Ulster by Protestant army officers, Perth having one of the first Orange lodges in the country. A government enquiry established the facts more or less as follows: Along with earlier settlers, who included disbanded Protestant Scottish and Ulster soldiers, the Irish Catholics were called out, as the law required, for the first militia drill of the season. With no training in arms, and certainly no love for English officers in red coats, the Irish made a poor impression with Captain Thomas Glendinning, a twenty-eight-year-old Englishman who had fought at Waterloo and had used his pension to build a fieldstone house on Glen Island in the Mississippi River.

At the end of a day drenched with rain, Glendinning stood the Scots to drinks in Alexander Morris's tavern, pointedly ignoring the Irish. When half a dozen Ballygiblins pushed into the tavern and began drinking on their own, words were exchanged and a fracas broke out involving the Irish, Glendinning and twenty Scots. William Loucks, a storekeeper, said he saw Bart Murphy, John Coughlin, John French and William Brown throwing stones through the windows, beating on the door with clubs and attacking three Scotsmen who tried to come out: "They said they would fight any Scotsman in the country." In the confusion, a Scottish settler's rifle went off, John Leahy from Conna, County Cork, was injured, and the Irish beat a retreat across the river to Ramsay Township. Morris, an Ulster Orange-man, was so frightened he locked the tavern and rode through the night to Perth with a lurid tale for the authorities. The next day, Saturday, twenty Ballygiblins came back across the river searching for Glendinning, who was accused of shooting at the Irish as well as insulting them. They found him hiding in Loucks' store, and Loucks said he saw Luke McGrath strike Glendinning on the head with a club.

For the Ballygiblins the affair had become an old-fashioned faction fight, where rival clans battled to decide matters of honour or ownership of land. On Monday, honour still unsatisfied, a hundred Ballygiblins with guns and clubs marched up the road behind an improvised band led by Luke McGrath, who carried an enormous green flag. John Sullivan, a young school teacher, took it into his head to challenge Glendinning to a duel, so they all went to the officer's house but found there only his wife and child, for Glendinning had hidden behind a sliding panel in the living room. Finally, after ransacking Morris's tavern, they decided that honour had been served and they all went home.

For the Ballygiblins, the battle was over, but for the magistrates in Perth, who were Protestants and Orangemen, the "backwoods rebellion" was a matter of concern. Protestants were arriving at Perth with complaints they dare not sleep in their cabins for fear of reprisals. Meeting in emergency session, the magistrates convinced themselves that a "set of lawless banditti were threatening the lives and property of every honest individual in the neighbourhood" and thus set the stage for the second, and more tragic, scene.

The armed posse dispatched from Perth was recruited from Orangemen. The sheriff was ill, and the deputy who replaced him, Alexander Matheson, was a militant Orangeman "of overbearing and insolent conduct," whose father had been murdered by Catholic Whiteboys in Ireland. Matheson arrived with his posse at Shipman's Mills on Sunday morning as the Catholics were gathering for religious service at the smithy of Cornelius Roche of Doneraile, whose building was being used for meetings until a church could be built. Dividing his force, the deputy led one detachment toward a group walking along the riverside, who scattered and ran when one of the posse fired his gun. The second detachment, hearing the shot and taking it as a signal, opened fire on the blacksmith shop, killing one man and wounding two. They accidentally wounded one of their own men and blamed the Catholics. Breaking into the smithy, the posse beat the occupants, tore the roof off and smashed the contents.

The Perth authorities, assuring Lieutenant Governor Sir Peregrine Maitland in York that they had a war on their hands, appealed for an army detachment to fight the "unruly Irish." "They have set all law at defiance, and avow they will submit to no jurisdiction but their own, nor obey any peace officers unless overpowered by force." What had began as a local fracas had become, at least in the eyes of the Perth magistrates, an apprehended insurrection.

The Catholic settlers had powerful supporters in York. Peter Robinson was back in Ireland by now, but his brother, the Attorney General, came to their defence and declared the Perth magistrates were irresponsible in employing a posse of Orangemen who would like to see all Catholics "burned at the stake." Sir Peregrine Maitland not only declined to send troops but appointed a native of southern Ireland to conduct a hearing. The man appointed, Colonel James Fitzgibbon, Assistant Adjutant General, was respected in the Protestant Establishment known as the Family Compact and had the advantage of speaking the Irish language.

After an enquiry, in which witnesses were questioned and sworn statements collected, Fitzgibbon came to the conclusion that his countrymen were more sinned against than sinning. The men in the posse maintained that the Ballygiblins had opened fire from the smithy, but Fitzgibbon believed this was a lie and the wounded Orangeman had been shot by one of his companions when a bullet passed through the house. Fitzgibbon condemned the posse for a "wanton and outrageous attack upon the lives of the new settlers.... For the cruel conduct of the men who attacked Roche's house, in beating and wounding the people they found there, I can find no apology whatsoever." He said the violence "in every instance" had been committed that Sunday by Orangemen.

But despite Fitzgibbon's findings, the justice administered by the magistrates at Perth was one-sided. Glendinning and the Orangemen were found innocent, including the Scot who fired from Morris's inn and those who caused bloodshed at the smithy. Only Irish Catholics were found guilty and convicted of rioting and assault. Bart Murphy, John French, Patrick Sullivan and John Coughlin were sentenced to two months in Perth jail and fined ten pounds each, equivalent to half a year's pay. Such was their bitterness when they were released that all but Sullivan left the settlement.

HEARING OF THIS AFFAIR in Ireland, where he was trying to recruit more emigrants in the summer of 1824, Peter Robinson was afraid it would mean the end of Horton's experiment. Governor Lord Dalhousie at Quebec City urged that Robinson's work "be stopped at once, as a waste of Public monies, and a most serious mischief done to the Canadas." Maitland assured both Robinson and the government in London that all was now "perfectly quiet," there had been no need to call in the army and the "little disturbance among the Irish settlers was quite unrepresentative, though at the time fearfully exaggerated."

Peter Robinson informed his brother he was well received on his second visit to Ireland. "The friends of people I took out last year were very warm in their expressions of gratitude." Lord Ennismore took him stag hunting. Lord Kingston was "civil in the extreme, and I breakfasted and dined daily with him during my stay in his neighbourhood." Kingston made no bones about wanting to get rid of undesirable tenants, and said that unless Robinson accepted the 400 he proposed to send "they will turn out bad subjects" if they remained in

Ireland. What they might do in Canada did not seem to concern him.

Lord Mount Cashel, confined to his bed with a bilious attack, assured Robinson the twenty-three families he wished to send "are just the sort of persons you wish to have in American," while admitting they were "all poor and wretched." Sir William Wrixon offered a more balanced argument. "You are naturally anxious to have steady men with families," he said, "and it is equally natural we should wish to get rid of idle, unmarried individuals who seem likely to keep up the present disturbances, but if once possessed of a little bit of property, would soon change their habits."

Rural violence in northeast Cork had flared again and rarely been more daring. George Bond Low, a magistrate at Doneraile, was the target of three unsuccessful assassination attempts in which his servants were wounded and his brother, an Anglican clergyman, was killed. A government offer of amnesty if stolen arms were surrendered was ignored.

A new law gave landowners still more power to evict, but as Daniel Ryan of County Limerick stated, "There is so much competition for land in this country it may cost a man his life to take it over any other man." Ryan found himself caught between the "tyranny and oppression of the landlords" on the one hand and the "nocturnal enemy," or Whiteboys, on the other. "The existing state of things is truly frightening," declared the Bishop of Limerick, "when tenantry [the under-tenants of under-tenants] are dispossessed. After a season of patient suffering, they go into some other district, perhaps a peaceable one; there they fail not to find friends, clansmen and fellow factionaries, whom they bring back with them by night to avenge their cause; it is avenged in blood; and where occasion offers, the service is repaid in kind. Thus the whole county is set in flames."

A preacher who called himself Pastorini had been forecasting that Christmas 1824 would bring the downfall of the Protestant Ascendency, and the spectre of a full-scale rebellion haunted the English administration in Dublin Castle. Henry Goulbourn, Chief Secretary for Ireland, predicted that 1825 would be "a year of war." The fear at Dublin Castle was that the disparate groups of terrorists, Whiteboys, Rockites and the rest, would unite into one great peasant army, and giving substance to that fear was the emergence of Daniel O'Connell, called "The Liberator." Tall, commanding, with a powerful voice, O'Connell caught the imagination of the people, pledging himself to Catholic Emancipation, a fully enfranchised electorate, an Irish parliament that represented the Catholic majority, protection for tenants, and repeal of the 1800 Act of Union that had done away with the Irish parliament and left Ireland no better than an English colony.

"No more favourable time ever occurred for colonizing Canada," Lord Mount Cashel told Robinson, "for never were people so well disposed to emigrate." Robinson had intended to bring out a large contingent of emigrants in that autumn of 1824, but due to administrative delays and a reluctance in Parliament to vote the money, he sailed to Canada, promising to return in the spring.

Arriving in the Bathurst District, he was pleased that his settlers had cleared an average of four acres and harvested the first of the crops that would make them independent of government help. Their farms were ragged clearings but they had managed to produce potatoes, turnips and wheat, and had learned to make potash, selling it to merchants on "The Front," who shipped it down to Quebec on rafts along with grain and timber for export to Britain. "I found some of them with strong trousers," Robinson noted, "which they purchased from the produce of their ashes."

In a letter to London, Robinson insisted his settlement had been a success, but in preparing for the second migration from Ireland he was wise enough to look beyond the Bathurst District. There was too much ill will in the Ottawa Valley townships, and the best land had been claimed. The Ballygiblin riots had almost wrecked his plans, and he wanted land where settlers might be safe from prejudice. The place he chose, sight unseen, was the Newcastle District north of Rice Lake and 200 miles southwest of the Bathurst settlements. It had been opened to settlement within the last four years, and besides marshes and swamps, the surveyor's report spoke of good soil on the uplands and beaver meadows, and plenty of land for newcomers.

Most of the Newcastle District townships were not yet colonized, with a total population of 500, including a dozen Empire Loyalist families who were still called "the Americans" and a contingent of colonists from the north of England. There was a settlement of Ulster Irish in Monaghan and Cavan townships at the west of Rice Lake, but Robinson felt they were far enough from the townships he had in mind to avoid the trouble experienced at Shipman's Mills and Morphy's Falls in the Ottawa Valley.

The newcomers would not, however, be entirely free of prejudice. Robert Bellingham, a young Protestant Dubliner who had found his way north of Rice Lake that year and gone to work for an Ulster gentleman farmer named Thomas Stewart, wrote in his journal: "A rumour reached us that the British government intended sending 2,000 emigrants. The benevolent intentions were to assist honest, sober, industrious Irishmen living in the counties of Limerick and Cork to emigrate as it was supposed that the landlords would induce the best and most trusted of the tenants to emigrate; but the rumour ran that they selected the vagabonds and scamps in order to get rid of them."

5

"A Perfect Mania for Going to Canada"

*I*N THE SPRING of 1825 the thought of going to Canada spread through the Blackwater like a beneficent contagion. People who had never dreamed of leaving their parish, let alone Ireland, were talking of crossing the ocean and were waiting impatiently for the return of Peter Robinson.

During the winter they had sat by their peat fires and discussed the letters from emigrant relatives and neighbours who had written home of land free for the taking "where all have plenty and to spare." People fated to live off potatoes year in and year out heard of a country where, as one emigrant wrote, the Irish "could eat our fill of bread and meat, butter and milk, any day we like." Some letters had come from the other colonies, but nevertheless in the Blackwater that spring they were all vaguely linked to Upper Canada and Peter Robinson, who had promised to take 1,500 emigrants that year.

People sent in their names, like competitors in a lottery, and when Robinson returned in mid-April he found a "perfect mania for going to Canada." Instead of the four or five thousand applicants he had expected, there were a staggering 50,000, all recommended by magistrates, clergymen and priests. There were, for example, the successful applications of Owen McCarthy of Caheragh and Patrick Twomy of Glouthane, Cork County farmers with large families, recommended by S.W. Hoare, Justice of the Peace. "The excessive population of this little island from many causes induces me to forward the wishes of these people," he wrote, "and indeed, Sir, you have yourself from your kindness to those persons who went from hence in 1823 very much increased the anxiety of the people here to embark under your auspices and for such conduct I am with many others most thankful. The persons I have recommended in this letter are orderly, industrious men, and I think would be useful characters in the establishment of your young colony."

In 1823 Robinson had been at pains to choose the emigrants himself. Now in 1825 with so many tens of thousands wishing to go, this was impossible; moreover, Wilmot Horton was urging him to take as many as he could from the estates of the most powerful landowners, to show them the value of emigration and encourage them to finance future groups themselves rather than leaving it to the government. Robinson had promised to take his draft of 1,500 people only from the estates of Lords Kingston, Doneraile, Mount Cashel and Ennismore, Sir William Wrixon Becher of Ballygiblin House, Colonel Jephson of Mallow, Captain Roberts of Charleville, and Richard Aldworth, Ennismore's son-in-law, who lived at Newmarket. Choosing applicants from towns or other estates was not part of the plan, and he had left the eight major landowners and their agents to make the selections, but when this became known, there were complaints from lesser landlords who wished to send people, and from applicants who felt neglected. On the one hand, the landowners were accused of using the scheme to get rid of troublemakers, and on the other of using it to reward tenants who had remained loyal during the troubles.

The matter was raised in Parliament, and Horton, who wanted no controversy to disrupt his program, urged Robinson to proceed with caution. "Take special and particular care," Horton said, "to have the sanction of the collective magistry as a warrant to the persons taken, coming within the rules prescribed." Robinson reassured him that priority was being given to small farmers calculated to make good settlers and without means of support in Ireland, but in fact Horton's instructions were not always followed closely.

People with relatives already in Canada got special consideration, as in the cases of Eliza Regan of Mallow and Margaret St. Leger of Sixmilebridge, County Clare, who received permission to join their husbands. Johanna Hickey of Mallow, a widow described as an "independent, honest woman," was granted passage because her sons were "good labourers." Margaret Groves, a Wicklow County widow with four sons, a Protestant described as "of the better order of Irish tenantry," emigrated because she feared her Catholic neighbours and there had been terrorism in the area. She was also anxious to be reunited with two daughters, who had emigrated to Ramsay Township in the Ottawa Valley.

Fear was the spur for eight other families, five of them Protestants from County Limerick who came to Robinson because of the "extreme danger to members of the established religion." Thomas Fitzgerald, forty-two, from the grazing country by the River Dee, had received "repeated threats to his family and injuries sustained to his property." The magistrate who supported his successful application was sorry to see him leave the country. "His just sense of Religion, his strict moral example, and very orderly habits gained for him the respect of all classes," said the magistrate, though obviously not the respect of the Whiteboys. Michael Buckley, thirty-one, of Knocknatemple near Cork City, who had a twenty-seven-year-old wife and five children, was also fleeing the Whiteboys. "During the latest disturbances he gave valuable information which placed his life in danger," explained a Cork City official. "He is still obnoxious to his neighbours on that account." And there was David Nagle of Mitchelstown, who had provoked Whiteboy vengeance while serving as a land agent to Lord Kingston.

Francis Young of Newport, in the hill country south of Tipperary town, fled discrimination of another sort. In an era when Catholics were known to embrace the Protestant faith to better their prospects, Young had taken the opposite path and become a Catholic, and was disinherited by his family as a result. His wife, Elizabeth, had also been disinherited by her wealthy Protestant family, and when she died in childbirth, Young resolved to leave forever with his seven sons and two daughters, who ranged in age from eight to twenty-four years. Young was forty-four, and the priest who supported his application called him a "man of most industrious habits and great mechanical ability."

Most were driven by poverty and the belief their lives in Ireland would never improve. Richard Sullivan of Cork assured Robinson that passage to Canada was the "most charitable grant that could be made to individuals perishing for want of means to purchase one meal of potatoes in twenty-four hours." John Lane, a forty-six-year-old shoemaker from the outskirts of Cork City, one of the sixty-nine artisans Robinson selected, said, "Depression and the times, and incredible misfortunes, have left us without house or home or any means."

There were more older men than in most emigrant groups, at least thirty being close to or over the age limit of forty-five – Owen Madigan of Limerick was sixty – and though it was clear that some were chosen because the landlords wanted rid of them, Robinson justified their choice on grounds their knowledge of farming outweighed considerations of age. David Condon, fifty, from Brigown parish near Mitchelstown, and John Condon, forty-five, of Kilworth, were to die during the voyage to Canada. Both had rented land on Lord Kingston's estates, and John Condon had been dispossessed "in consequence of the smallness of his lot, as his Lordship would not allow small lots to be let on his estate in future." Having earlier assured Robinson that he was evicting no tenants, Lord Kingston had evidently succumbed to the temptation to reorganize his farms.

Few of the people who had missed the boat in 1823 got a second chance in 1825, though many applied. Among the fortunate was Henry Maloney of Sixmilebridge, County Clare, who complained that he had sold all his possessions in 1823 to get to Cork City but had been too late. Maloney was accepted in the new draft, but John Burke of Newmarket-on-Fergus in the same county, who had missed the earlier sailing by one day, was turned down for the second group, though he was a good farmer. William Croak of Buttevant begged Robinson to take him, "relying on your Honour's Goodness and humane character," and recalling he had been left behind because the register with his name had been lost at Ballygiblin after he had "disposed of his potatoes and furniture and reduced himself to a state of beggary." There is no record that Robinson gave him a second chance.

Another man left behind in the first emigration because there was no more room fared no better in the second. Richard Fitzgerald, forty-three, from Liscarroll, a few miles west of Buttevant, described by his priest as a "good English scholar," wrote a plaintive letter to Robinson explaining his plight. "My two brothers-in-law," he said, "were next before me on the list, and indeed you desired us to prepare. Depending on God and you I sold my little effects and bought many necessities for the voyage. Alas, others, more prosperous, got the preference. My wife is in a desponding condition from not going with her brothers, being an only sister. I had been a farmer but alas the vicissitudes of fortune have deprived me of it, but earning a little livelihood by teaching school." The unfortunate Richard Fitzgerald was rejected again. Nor did Robert Smithwick of Mitchelstown make the journey. Smithwick, a Protestant, had been the only member of the 1823 migration to return to the Blackwater from Canada. He had stayed at Mitchelstown only a short time, apparently to collect his family, and had been looking forward to returning to Canada in Robinson's second group but he died before the ships sailed. The extent of the depression at Liscarroll was conveyed in the application on behalf of Patrick Callaghan, "who humbly sheweth that he and his family will never recover [from] their present distress if you be not so kind as to take him and family to Kanada."

Whom to choose? This, as Robinson confided in a letter to his brother, was a difficult matter, further complicated by the fact that some of the chosen were selling their tickets. He became aware of this when his friend Father Jones, the priest at Mallow, informed him that Jeremiah Callaghan, teenaged son of a stonemason, had bought a ticket for a pound "from some other Callaghan" and was determined "to impersonate his wavering namesake." The youngster's father wanted Jeremiah at home and was so distressed, said Jones, that "you will do this poor man a favour by not granting passage to his undutiful and disobedient son."

Another young man from Mallow, Patrick Nagle, was more successful, and was safely at sea as a stowaway before he was discovered, as was Laurence Doran of Clonmel, Tipperary, who disguised himself as a girl. Doran's family had been recommended as "sober, quiet and strictly honest," but in the meantime the sixteen-year-old Laurence had got into trouble with the law, for poaching. This was a serious offence, and when the constables came looking for him, his family disguised him and took him to Canada as their daughter.

Among those who changed their names and ages to match those on forged or purchased tickets, Thomas Shenick of Churchtown called himself John Regan, the name of the man from whom he had bought his ticket, and since Regan had no teenaged boy, Shenick's son William had to masquerade as a girl named Abigail. John and Catherine Grady of Mallow, who had seven children, sold their ticket to a family with the same name and same number of children – except that the first family had four girls and the second three. Their son was prevailed upon to dress as a girl named Johanna.

As the families came down from the Blackwater hills in the first days of May, it was clear that Robinson would take many more than the 1,500 agreed to by Parliament. The landlords were insisting on sending more than their quotas, and he was under pressure from the mayor of Cork and others to take more people. In the end, Robinson was able to stretch his supplies and space to take 2,024, partly because 60 per cent were children, who needed less space than adults. On average, each family included six children, more than in most 19th-century emigrant groups. The average age of the adults was thirty-five. They came from the same parishes as the 1823 emigration, and the largest group, 400, came from Lord Kingston's estates. The other seven Blackwater landowners sent slightly smaller contingents, and the remainder, one sixth of the total, were sent by other sponsors, such as the City of Cork.

The Cove of Cork looked like a giant fair, with thousands of people crowded along the shore, and the black ships that were to take the emigrants to Canada already lying out in the stream, and Monks-town shining white in the mist and rain. Nine chartered transports had arrived from the naval base of Deptford, England, and only when the people began to board was Robinson able to "ascertain how far the settlers correspond with the description of persons whom I was in-structed to select." Though several families had some money of their own, Robinson continued to insist he took only the "poor and the deserving," and invited four Cork City officials aboard four of the ships to confirm that the people conformed to his mandate. There was so much coming and going of emigrants, however, it is doubtful the officials knew what was happening. By the time the ships were at sea many families had slipped through Robinson's net. He communicated his frustrations to the Colonial Office:

To choose about 2,000 individuals out of 50,000 applicants was found a very difficult and in many cases an ungrateful task. And although I was assisted in the most friendly and zealous manner by the magistrates and respectable gentlemen of the baronies from which they were taken, the utmost vigilence became necessary to prevent imposition....

The surgeon of each transport had orders to report as soon as he had received his complement of settlers on board, on which I proceeded to the ship and mustered all of them on the main deck. The hatches were then closed, except one, where in the presence of the surgeon and master, I took the original certificates, which had been given over by the head of each family to the surgeon at the time of embarkation, and from these, after comparing them with the duplicates in my possession, I called over the names of each individual belonging to the different families, and when I was satisfied were of the age and description given by the father, and that no imposition had been practised, they were sent below decks.

One of the surgeons, Dr. G.H. Reade, a kindly man who issued blankets and a tot of rum to each emigrant, wrote in his journal:

My charges numbering 228 souls were embarked on the evening of the 5th of May and with few exceptions misery and want appeared to have been their companions. The unfavourable state of the weather added to the misery of their appearance, the rain falling incessantly during their passage in the steamboat from Cork City to Cove and what little covering they brought with them was unfit to make use of, and none brought a second change of clothes. As far as security and embarkation would permit, no apparent contagious disease was among them.

At 7 o'clock the following morning they were served out with provisions for two days – beef, pork, ham, potatoes, tea, sugar and pease and a quantity of oatmeal and bacon. They expressed in very grateful language their satisfaction and they could hardly credit that they were to be dealt with during the passage in a similar manner. Some stated to me that they had not tasted meat for five months, and as to flour they never had any except twice or thrice a year.

As to appearance they were of the very worst character – I mean as to poverty, but it is a pleasing part of my duty to add that I could not speak too highly of their conduct, or say too much in their favour, for their friendly feelings toward each other on board were such as to merit satisfaction.

The *Cork Mercantile Chronicle* of Friday, May 6, reported: "The embarkation on board the first division of the transports, the *Fortitude, Resolution, Albion* and *Brunswick* will be completed this evening and it is expected that those ships will sail, wind permitting, on Sunday." Unlike Dr. Reade, the newspaper reported that some of the families seemed far from destitute, "exempted from the distress which their removal from this country is intended to remedy."

The first four ships sailed on Tuesday, May 10, 1825, followed at intervals by the *Star, Amity, Regulus* and *Elizabeth*. The last to sail was the *John Barry* on May 21. This fleet of nine ships carried the largest single group yet to cross the Atlantic – 385 men, 325 women, 267 boys and 199 girls over the age of 14, and 851 younger children.

"At 12 o'clock we weighed anchor in fine weather and the following morning we lost sight of the land our nativity," recorded Dr. Reade, aboard the *Resolution*. "The wind shifted and blew strongly from the west. The poor people now became seasick and little order or regularity could be preserved. It was in my power to provide arrangements for the young children who did not suffer from sickness...

"May 11. At 9 p.m. a heavy gale began and several times I visited the lower deck during the night and found the children thrown out of their berths and their parents too much exhausted from seasickness to make the least exertion. The gale lasted for two days, and during that period they were unable to prepare nourishment for themselves. I caused gruel and tea to be made ready for all."

When the weather improved, the Irish complained of lack of potatoes but otherwise believed their rations adequate – a pound of salt pork and a pound of ship's biscuits every day for men and boys over fourteen, half that for the women and girls and boys over twelve, and a third for small children. The men got a half pint of rum every day, like the sailors, though Robinson disapproved when he heard of it.

Robinson had not sailed with them, having gone to London to report to Wilmot Horton. Disturbed by the Ballygiblin riots and his brother's comment that those earlier emigrants had seemed uncouth, Robinson assured Horton the second contingent was a "better description of people than those taken out in 1823, although they are wretchedly poor." In fact, they were much like the earlier group.

Along with other duties, the doctors were required to assess each family, with the idea this would be useful once the emigrants reached their destination. Just how useful this was proved questionable, because of the brevity of their reports and because the doctors, being Protestants, showed some bias, and Protestant emigrants tended to get the best marks, followed by those Catholics who went out of their way to be respectful and adopt English ways.

David Hogan of Cork City, for example, made himself popular aboard the *John Barry* because he had served as a soldier in the English army and knew what was expected of him. "He wrought hard and behaved well on the voyage, acting as cook," the doctor on his ship reported. John Kelleher, a fisherman from Dingle, County Kerry, made himself useful by helping the third mate dole out salt meat and ship's biscuits and looking after the two Irish hounds Peter Robinson was shipping to Canada.

John Clancy, a thirty-year-old shoemaker from Rock Mile Creek, County Cork, was a "well behaved man," as was John Daley, thirty, of Buttevant, an "excellent man, worthy of encouragement" who died soon after arrival in Canada. Owen McCarthy of Caheragh, who had been recommended so highly by Justice of the Peace S.W. Hoare, had brought his wife and seven children, a "very well conducted family."

Several families were described as lazy, having failed to make themselves useful during the voyage; as they were not sailors, it is hard to imagine what they could have done. Thomas Murray, thirty-five, of Tipperary, was described as a "well disposed, honest, indolent man," though once settled in Upper Canada he was as hardworking and successful a farmer as could be desired.

At the bottom of the barrel were four hard cases on the *Fortitude*, the sort of men Lord Kingston was glad to be rid of. Michael Elligott, a thirty-three-year-old shoemaker from Mitchelstown, and William O'Halloran of Dungarvan, Country Waterford, were described by the ship's surgeon as "indolent ruffians." James Cotter, forty-five, also of Mitchelstown, and his friend Patrick Leahy, forty, a widower with fourteen-year-old twins, a boy and a girl, were "bad and dangerous characters fit only for any mischief." Just what they were up to on the ship was not mentioned, but it is recorded that they got into a brawl with French Canadians soon after their arrival in Canada.

Three weeks into the voyage the doctors had more serious matters to attend. Smallpox broke out, and a case of typhus was reported. The first death was that of four-year-old Johanna, daughter of Mary and Thomas Stack ("a good and industrious man") from Doneraile, and on May 30 she was buried at sea. A week later, five-year-old Catherine, daughter of Michael and Margaret Sweeney of Kilworth ("a very decent and good family"), fell ill and died. Eleven children and four adults, two men and two women, died at sea, but the ships reached Quebec City with as many people as they had started with – fifteen babies were born during the voyage. All but one ship made the voyage in unusually fast time, thirty-one days. The *John Barry* was late because she ran aground in the St. Lawrence and might have been lost but for the emigrants, who manned the pumps until she was refloated.

The first defections occurred soon after arrival. James Lee, a thirty-year-old shoemaker from Charleville, deserted with his wife and children "taking bag and baggage" and their government-issue bedding. Margaret St. Leger apparently joined her husband, who had come out earlier and settled at Quebec City, where the Irish dominated the work on the timber wharves. At Montreal twelve families went off to the Ottawa Valley to join relatives rather than making the longer trek to the Newcastle District in Upper Canada, where Robinson had intended them to settle.

After more than a month of unfamiliar diet of salt meat and ship's biscuit, and now encountering the humid, almost tropical heat of a St. Lawrence Valley summer with temperatures "at 100 in the shade," the health of the settlers had become a matter of concern. At Lachine, nine miles from Montreal, where boats were to take them up-river, Timothy and Catherine Regan from Donaghmore, County Cork, died, leaving four children aged between six and sixteen. "Timothy

Regan came on board sickly," said the medical officer of the *John Barry*. "Took fever on second of June. Died at Lachine hospital. Wife took sick shortly after and produced a child on the eighth, Monday. Convalesced at Quebec. Hurried off to Lachine. Arrived Saturday evening. Took dangerously sick on Sunday and died at twelve on Tuesday. Child died." Their children, who had lost their belongings in the confusion, were given eight dollars and allowed to continue with other families.

The migration was so large it was split into sections and sent up the river in relays, which went smoothly except for trouble at Île Perrot above Montreal on June 24, when some French Canadians, fearful of this invasion of strange people speaking a strange tongue, refused to let the travellers into their cabin to boil water for tea. James Cotter and Patrick Leahy, who had gained a poor reputation aboard the *Fortitude*, smashed windows and wounded two occupants with stones. A report at the time said they were "dismissed," though they turned up later in Newcastle District.

At Prescott, 120 miles up-river, the settlers camped on the shore while waiting for steamers to take them to Kingston, their next staging place at the head of the St. Lawrence, where they arrived in relays of a few hundred between July 2 and July 30. The doctors who accompanied them said many were "generally in a very weak state," some apparently with typhus and smallpox. In Peter Robinson's absence, Colonel George Burke, an Irishman who had organized settlement in the Ottawa Valley Military Settlements, was in charge of the emigrants at Kingston. The tents pitched for them were on swampy ground near the river; sickness spread rapidly and many contracted ague or "swamp fever," a form of malaria blamed on stagnant water. Dr. Reade, who was ill himself, said there were 190 cases of fever and wrote a letter urging Robinson to come as soon as he could to move the emigrants up-country. Kingston was "unhealthy and fever increasing rapidly," he said, but it would be several weeks before Robinson arrived to get the emigrants moving.

AFTER LEAVING CORK CITY, Peter Robinson had made a long and round-about journey including a fifty-day voyage to New York, and from there via Niagara to York, and the Newcastle District, where he spent a week scouting the land he intended the emigrants to settle in the Otonabee River Valley. For his headquarters, Robinson chose Scott's Plains on the Otonabee above Rice Lake, where the only habitation was a shack and a mill built by Adam Scott, a Yankee who had settled six years earlier. Scott had brought in the millstone by boat in the hope of making a living grinding corn and making lumber for the north-of-England people who had arrived at government expense in 1818 and settled in Smith Township a few miles up-river.

Between Scott's Plains and the English settlers of Smith Township, two emigrants from County Antrim, Thomas Stewart and his brother-in-law, Robert Reid, and their families were trying with indifferent success to farm a few of the 3,000 acres the government had granted them in the newly surveyed township of Douro. Stewart, the son of a Protestant linen manufacturer, had come to Canada in 1821 after losing his inheritance in the post-war depression. He was middle-aged, good-natured and lame, and neither he nor Reid, who had been a businessman, was a competent farmer. Robert Bellingham, the Dublin lad who worked for them, described their layout in his journal:

My first sight of Stewart's residence was not attractive. I saw before me a clearing in the forest of some ten acres; the blackened stumps of the trees were thickly strewn over the ground. I was told that each acre contained 120 trees above six inches in diameter. My future residence was a cottage built of logs of white elm; none of the logs were less than a foot in diameter. The floor had not been secured, the spaces between the logs were open enough to admit daylight.... Our food consisted mainly of pork and pea soup and homemade bread. We never saw fresh meat for months, but as the season advanced we had excellent potatoes, Indian corn and a few vegetables. The work on the farm was of the roughest kind, the hoe being almost the only instrument used, as the undecayed roots precluded the use of a plough. The clearing was surrounded by what was called a snake fence, the rails being obtained by splitting twelve-foot cedar or pine logs, which were built to a height of five feet. The cattle, consisting of two cows, found their forage in the woods, into which the pigs were also turned to get their living.

When Robinson saw him early in August 1825, Stewart had been thinking of abandoning the farm, but decided to stay when he heard that 2,000 Irish were being brought into the district. Stewart's wife, a girlhood friend of the author Maria Edgeworth of Edgeworthtown, County Longford, complained that for a whole year she had seen no other woman except her sister.

South of Scott's Plains, and five miles north of Rice Lake, Lieutenant Charles Rubidge, RN, who had lost a leg fighting under Nelson at Trafalgar, had built a log cabin he called Woodland Cottage. He told Robinson he had been there for five years, but the district was "quite in a languishing state." On the west of Rice Lake were 100 families of Ulstermen who had landed at New York in 1818 and been coaxed by the British consul there, the Irish-born James Buchanan, to move to Upper Canada, where the government was offering land grants to attract settlers. All told, Buchanan sent 3,000 of his countrymen to Upper Canada, reversing the usual pattern of defection of Irish from the Canadas to the United States. There were a few scattered families – seven American and thirty Irish who had come out on their own – in townships north of Scott's Plains, and an iron ore mine run by an Irishman named Charles Large in remote Marmora Township to the northeast, which boasted 400 inhabitants. Otherwise the Newcastle District townships were not yet settled.

When Robinson rejoined his emigrants at Kingston on August 10, three months after he had left them at Cork City, thirty-three had died and 300 were down with fever. Dr. Reade had got hold of a hospital tent and erected it on higher ground, where he cared for those suffering from dysentery, typhus, smallpox and, among the children, whooping cough. "With few exceptions," he said "misery, want and every species of wretchedness appear to have been their guide." An Irish-speaking man named Bastable had appeared to urge the emigrants to desert to the United States, but no one left.

Despite the evidence of his eyes, Robinson's reports ignored the death and misery at Kingston. "Everything has been done for the comfort and health of the settlers that could be," he insisted. "They were quite as well, or indeed better, at Kingston, than they would have been in the woods at that season." Nevertheless by next day Robinson began to move the first relay of 500 people ninety-two miles along Lake Ontario to the village of Cobourg, though it would be another month before all were evacuated from Kingston. So many of his assistants were ill that Robinson was forced to do the work of several men, though suffering with ague himself.

For the next three months Cobourg was a transit camp. "The white tents presented a beautiful and attractive appearance," said the local Methodist minister, Anson Green. "They stretched along the sand beach lying between the lake and a forest of small cedars, which covered the worst part of the swampy ground." The news of their coming was discussed as far away as Halifax, where the *Nova Scotian* inflated their number to 8,000, their tents "whitening the shores of the Lake like the encampments of armies." The newspaper accused them of "abandoning their allotted settlements by companies" and of ingratitude. Rumours reached Colonel Thomas Talbot on Lake Erie that the emigrants were "dying at the rate of thirty a day."

The long weeks of hot, sunny weather had given way to windstorms and rain that reduced the trail from Cobourg to Rice Lake to mud and fallen trees and Robinson's first task was to clear a road. The work took more than a week, spearheaded by twenty hired axemen from the countryside and thirty of the healthiest emigrants. For the first three miles, the party passed through scattered clearings with occasional log cabins before the path plunged into dense forests, where their only companions were flies and mosquitoes, which increased as they approached the swampy margins of Rice Lake.

On the shore of the long lake, one of the men drowned while launching the boats they had hauled on wheels up the twelve-mile trail from Cobourg. During the three-mile crossing to the mouth of the Otonabee, they found clouds of ducks and an encampment of Indians, whose harvest of wild rice had given the lake its name. They had planned to row and pole the three boats twenty-four miles up the Otonabee, a clear river with thickly wooded banks, to Scott's Plains, the head of navigation, but the dry summer of 1825 had lowered the water level and the deep-draft boats were useless. Efforts to deepen the shallows were futile; the workers were suffering from fever and two had died.

There was no road to Scott's Plains, so with no other way to get the people to their land, Robinson set his men to building a sixty-foot scow with shallow draft. They built it in a week and poled it twenty-four miles to their destination, which Robinson called "the prettiest place" he had ever seen. Beyond Scott's ramshackle buildings and the riverside willows stretched a natural park scattered with wild flowers, maples in full colour and oak trees. The berry bushes had attracted bears, and the Indians who used the place on their portages from the Kawartha Lakes to Rice Lake had left the remains of campfires. Several years later Catharine Parr Traill, one of the "writing Stricklands" who made their homes there, called it "superior to any place I have yet seen in the Upper Province.... It is situated on a fine elevated plain, just above the small lake, where the river is divided by two wooded islets.... These plains form a beautiful natural park, finely diversified with hill and dale, covered with a lovely green sward, enhanced with a variety of the most exquisite flowers and planted, as if by Nature's own hand, with groups of feathery pines, oaks, balsam, poplar and silver birch. The views from these plains are delightful; whichever way you turn your eyes, they are gratified by a diversity of hill and dale, wood and water."

To shelter the people until their cabins were ready, out on their lots, Robinson had hundreds of lean-tos built at the depot, using poles, bark and slabs from Scott's mill. He built five log houses, the largest forty by twenty feet, which he grandly called Government House and equipped with a study and a bedroom for himself, sleep-

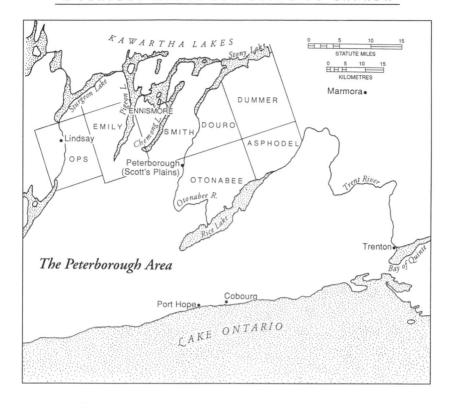

The Peterborough Area

ing space for guests, five gabled windows, a shingled roof, and a fenced garden that ran down to the river. There was a cabin for Dr. Reade, who now served as resident doctor to the settlers, and a smaller structure for Captain John Armstrong, clerk of the commissariat, in charge of issuing rations. John Armstrong, whose brother Robert had settled in Ramsay Township in 1823, was a Protestant from Kilfinnane, Limerick. He was thirty-two years old and, like his brother, had married one of the daughters of the Honourable Francis Massey of Suir Castle, Tipperary.

It took sixty trips to bring all the settlers up from Cobourg, and it was late in October, the days growing chill, before they were assembled on Scott's Plains. William Stewart was fearful when he heard they were Irish Catholics and put locks on his doors, but his wife, Frances, welcomed the colourful bustle. "The arrival of the poor immigrants from Ireland has given us some variety," she wrote. "They are encamped on the Plains, a place about two and a half miles off. Their huts look very odd, being made with poles standing up, boughs and branches of trees interwoven, and mud plastered over them. They live in these until log shanties are ready for the families. The poor creatures suffered a good deal, and many died."

At least twenty died that autumn, among them thirty-year-old William Hagarty from Kerry, who died at Scott's Plains on November 25, leaving a young widow and five children. Mary Flynn, whose family came from Buttevant, died at the depot from exhaustion and fever soon after her arrival. She was twelve years old, and her father, Cornelius, forty-three, died soon after while clearing his land.

Timothy Callaghan of Drishane, County Cork, a farm labourer whose application had stated, "I have four children in distress and a wife for the work," died while building a cabin in Asphodel Township on the banks of the Trent River at the eastern end of Rice Lake. He had left his wife, Nancy, and his children at the depot while he built a home for them, and he died alone. "The poor fellow had built a small log hut and chopped an acre of bush when he was stricken with fever contracted from drinking river water," said the man who found him, "and he was not discovered until aid was to no avail." The ague, which had struck at Kingston, was to claim many lives. Timothy Egan, a twenty-eight-year-old bachelor from Buttevant, became so delirious that he strayed into the forest one evening and was never seen again. Whole families became ill at the same time, shaking so badly, it was said, they could not give each other so much as a drink of water without spilling it.

Robinson was hard pressed to get his people settled on their lots before snow blocked the trails. He hired guides and axemen from the earlier settlements to help them, and to speed the procedure he put the numbers of lots in a hat and had the settlers draw them. Once half a dozen lots had been chosen for a given township, he sent the men out with ten days' rations, a guide and a few local axemen.

To get settlers to the township of Ennismore, seven miles north of the depot, he used the scow to ferry them across Chemong Lake. Sixty-seven families settled there, and the first ashore was twenty-year-old Patrick Galvin, who had come out with his father, Garrett, his mother, and six brothers and sisters. "Behold," he shouted as he jumped ashore, "I am the first settler of Ennismore."

The first task was to make a clearing, and then to build a cabin with log walls and a roof thatched with balsam boughs and wild grass. Cracks between logs were stuffed with mud and moss, the hearth was a circle of stones on the floor, and there was, at first, no chimney, but merely a hole in the roof. Recalling the complaints of the people in the Bathurst District, Robinson said, "It is my wish that no one of the settlers should be placed on a bad lot, or on one that he could not be making a living off. To ensure the latter, I think it requisite that there should be from thirty to forty acres of good land on each lot."

The Scott's Plains depot in 1825 was better organized than Shipman's Mills had been in 1823, and Robinson was determined to remain with his settlers all winter to avoid the incidents that provoked the Ballygiblin riots. "I exact the strictest obedience," he told his brother, "but there are many idle rascals from Ireland frequently inciting our people to mischief and leading them astray." Robinson did not identify these troublemakers, and presumably they were people from other settlements in the district.

Before the snows came, Robinson had settled 1,900 people in six townships spanning an area fifty miles from east to west and thirty north to south, the size of the Blackwater region in Cork that most of them came from. Sixty-seven families settled in Ennismore Township; there were sixty in Douro, thirty-six in Smith, where English colonists had settled some years earlier, 142 in Emily Township, fifty-one in Otonabee, between Rice Lake and Scott's Plains, where Lieutenant Rubidge lived, thirty-six in Asphodel and fifteen in the outlying township of Ops. "The people who come in," wrote Robinson, "seem in good spirits and much pleased with their land."

LORD DALHOUSIE at Quebec City complained the newcomers threw a burden "upon the industrious classes of this young country" and continued to predict they would decamp to the United States once their rations were exhausted. At York the radical journalist and politician William Lyon Mackenzie used them as a pawn in attacks on the ruling clique, the Family Compact. The money that brought the Irish, he said, should have been put to better use, and he printed unfounded rumours in his paper, the *Colonial Advocate*, that "no less than thirty of them decamped lately in one night."

The defence of the Irish was led by Colonel James Fitzgibbon, who had investigated the Ballygiblin affair. "I find the immigrants for the greater part gone to the lands allotted to them," he wrote, "and are making great exertions, some of them to an extent almost incredible.... My countrymen are proving to be all honest men in this province ... better deserving favourable opinion than such slanders as the Editor of the *Colonial Advocate* would have the world believe." Only one family, it seemed, had left Scott's Plains for the United States. An Irish priest, the Reverend James Crowley, who had arrived to look after Catholic emigrants, vowed to devote himself to "establishing order, encouraging industry, suppressing imported prejudices, and reconciling parties of all religious denominations, to arrest the tongue of slander and silence political demagogues." Perhaps the most convincing testimony on the settlers' behalf came from the Ulster Protestant William Stewart, who had worried about putting locks on his doors when he heard that southern Irish would be his neighbours:

I am here in the midst of them. From twenty to thirty of them pass my door every day. I have always found them satisfied and happy. Some of them have told me, with tears in their eyes, that they never knew what happiness was until now. In general they are making great exertions in clearing the land, and their exertions have astonished many of the old settlers. Not one complaint has there been against any of them by any of the old settlers and it is the general opinion that when so large a body of people are brought together none could conduct themselves better.

Poor people, it would delight you to see how happy they are. Of course there are a few black sheep, but though they have been now four months encamped in this neighbourhood, and during that time with nothing to do, yet there has not been one complaint against them. On those plains where they encamped, a few months ago there was only one poor house and a miserable mill. Now we have a flourishing village, containing stores of all kinds of provisions and merchandise, two sawmills, smiths shops, bakehouse, doctor's shops, and dwelling houses. There are shoemakers, masons and carpenters. Every day I go down there is something new to be seen or done. We have laid out lots for the church, school-house, courthouse, jail, etc. on many of which building will begin next spring. We plan to open our new town with a grand dinner. We expect the Governor here this winter.

Lieutenant Governor Maitland came up from York late in February 1826, accompanied by John Beverley Robinson, the Attorney General, and Colonel Thomas Talbot, the latter "clad in a remarkable sheepskin costume, with boots of the same material." They came in five sleighs over the ice of Rice Lake, paid a visit to Lieutenant Rubidge's cottage, where they were welcomed by Peter Robinson, and proceeded up the snowy trail to Scott's Plains, where they were greeted with great excitement.

"On Saturday last," wrote Frances Stewart, "the Governor and his suite arrived. All the immigrants were desired to assemble at the village to welcome His Excellency. They formed a line on each side of the road for a quarter of a mile, and as soon as his sleigh came in sight ten men took off the horses, fastened basswood ropes on, and drew him to Government House. All seem pleased and gratified." Government House was the scene of a banquet in which the growing village received its new name. Someone had taken to calling it Peterborough, and though Robinson had modestly suggested it be named Horton after the Colonial Undersecretary, his guests opted to name it Peterborough in recognition of Robinson's untiring work.

The settlers came from miles around to a gala reception, for which Peter Robinson and Maitland and his retinue donned formal military dress, and Patrick Barragy, an estate gardener from Tipperary, delivered a speech composed of equal parts of thanks, pleas for future consideration and Irish humour. He praised Robinson and the government "for all they have done and we hope will do for us." He assured the Lieutenant Governor that should the colony be attacked the Irish "will follow to a man our brave commanders, and if we have no better weapons in our hands mow them down with our Irish shillelaghs."

All agreed the village of Peterborough, and the townships around, had a promising start. "I cannot perceive that the difference of religions has occasioned or is likely to occasion any disagreeable occurrences among themselves or between other settlers," Maitland reported, recalling the Ballygiblin riots of such ill repute. "On the contrary, though they are in general Roman Catholics they are kindly received by the Irish Protestants settled in the adjoining townships of Cavan and Monaghan."

Even that irascible veteran of Upper Canada colonization, Colonel Thomas Talbot, not known for his love of Irish Catholic emigrants, was pleased. "All of them that I saw had snug log huts," he said, "and chopped down, each, between three and four acres, and I have every reason to think they will realize a comfortable independence in the course of this year and be no more cost to the government; and it was satisfactory to hear them expressing their gratitude for what was done for them."

6

"Independence and happiness"

O<small>N THE EVE</small> of St. Patrick's Day, 1826, Peter Robinson sat in his log mansion at Peterborough to complete his long-overdue accounting of the controversial experiment that brought so many Irish to Canada at government expense. With settlers scattered over hundreds of miles of wilderness in two separate districts, the task had not been easy and, as he had warned Horton at the outset, he was no great hand at keeping books.

Two years had passed since the first contingent had come to the Ottawa Valley, and Horton was naturally impatient to know the result, for he had been greatly criticized by government opponents. Some called his experiment too visionary; others questioned why he was dumping paupers on the colony instead of bringing self-sufficient farmers. In the event, Horton found Robinson's account disappointing.

Critics generally believed the migration could have been achieved at considerably less cost.

Of the 182 families brought to the Ottawa Valley in 1823, a third seemed to have melted away. Of those Robinson could readily account for, some had gone to Perth, Cobourg and Kingston to ply their trades as carpenters, shoemakers and bakers. Nine men had gone to the United States as labourers or millwrights. Eight had died, four by drowning.

The Ballygiblin affair had cast a long shadow. Bart Murphy, John French and John Coughlin, having served time in Perth jail, left for jobs as rivermen at Kingston, and one day in October 1825 Murphy and French drowned in the St. Lawrence River. Coughlin never returned to his family. Cornelius Roche, whose smithy had been destroyed by Orangemen, had picked up his tools and moved to Montreal. The name Ballygiblin had become a word Protestants used in the Ottawa Valley to frighten children.

People brought up as farmers remained on their land, however, and those who had prospered in the old country tended to prosper in the new. Because of their habit of concealing good fortune, it was difficult to determine who had done well, for in Ireland the slightest ostentation had meant higher rents and taxes. Some had acquired the habit of begging during the hard years in Ireland and begged in Canada even when it was no longer necessary. One settler who begged for old clothes around Perth was so affluent he was doing it to get money to buy more cattle, quite happy to wear castoffs. When eighteen Irish settlers petitioned the government for additional aid, it was found they were as well off as Protestant neighbours, who had received little government help. "The man who had the petition wrote," said one of his neighbours, "actually owns three cows and a yoke of steers, has ten acres of land cleared, and received from me eighteen pounds for making hay – I do not think there are eighteen families out of all the settlers who have as much cleared or better prospect of independence than those eighteen families who have stated that they are likely to be in a state of starvation before the next crop comes in."

In the spring of 1826, fifty-eight of Robinson's families were working the land in the townships of Ramsay, Huntley, Goulbourn, Beckwith and Pakenham, having cleared an average of seven acres, which compared favourably with Protestants who had been there considerably longer. They had grown 13,000 bushels of potatoes, 8,000 bushels of turnips and 3,000 bushels of grain and owned 161 cattle and 138 hogs. Half of the families had settled in Ramsay Township, which had the best soil.

"We are doing very well, thank God, and enjoy good health," wrote Michael Corkery, a forty-year-old farmer from Carrigrohan, near Cork City. He and three grown sons had cleared thirty acres in Ramsay Township and owned ten cattle and twenty hogs, but when the inspector came around he was careful to qualify his good fortune. "We had a good crop last year," he admitted, "but my eldest daughter's illness, together with buying clothes and necessities for winter, prevented me from buying a yoke of oxen which are indisputably necessary on a farm. We have a good crop this year also, out of which I expect I can sell about twenty-four barrels of flour and 100 bushels of potatoes; but as I have no market convenient, nor oxen to convey it where there is a market, I don't know how to manage." In fact he managed very well, bought additional land, built a fine house and saw his ailing daughter recover to marry Michael Foley, a graduate of Dublin University who had come to settle on Bart Murphy's abandoned lot at Wolves Grove on the road to Perth.

Half a dozen families prospered exceptionally well in Ramsay Township in the first three years. John Teskey, a Protestant descendant of Rhinelanders who migrated to County Limerick in the 18th century to escape religious conflict, homesteaded on the Mississippi River between Shipman's Mills and Morphy's Falls, where he harnessed the rapids for milling. Now the pretty hamlet of Appleton, it was the site of an Indian encampment when the Teskeys arrived, and the tribesmen came in their blanket coats, red leggings and moccasins, curious and silent, to trade venison or a haunch of young bear for flour and pork.

At Clayton Lake, ten miles west of Shipman's Mills, Martin Ryan from Sixmilebridge in County Clare had "let the sunlight into" twenty-five acres of thick woodland and acquired ten cows and twelve hogs. An illiterate young labourer named James Sheil from New-market declared in a document he signed with his X: "I came to this country with Peter Robinson and have now about twenty acres cleared, a yoke of steers, one cow, three calves, pigs, poultry, etc. I did not receive rations. I am content with my lot, and consider it worth £100."

But even in Ramsay which had the best land, there were those who found themselves on poor or rocky soil and suffered in conse-quence. John Phelan from Kilmore, Tipperary, worked hard to clear sixteen acres but they were so unproductive he gave up in disgust and sold out to a merchant in Perth. "This is a hard case," commented a government agent, "when many of our industrious settlers are strug-gling to make a livelihood on some of the worst lands."

John O'Mara from Rathcormac, County Cork, who had consid-ered his land "as good as any in the country" when he arrived in 1823, cleared twelve acres before he was disillusioned. As acre after acre was laid bare on lot 4 of Ramsay's 4th concession, he saw that his land was poor and rocky, and though he had a wife and eight children to sup-port, he grew only 100 bushels of potatoes and 150 bushels of turnips. He was forced to move to better land. Patrick Lynch on lot 6, conces-sion 3, cleared twelve acres and found a "crop of barren rock." The Killarney man suffered further misfortune when his dog and two of his cows were killed by wolves, which he escaped by climbing a tree.

A notion has come down the years that Protestants were better farmers than their Catholic countrymen, but as the records of the Robinson settlers show this was often not the case. Among Protestants who found the new life difficult was Captain Robert Armstrong from Kilfinane, Limerick, who was forty when he arrived and had no grown sons to help him, a large family of daughters to support and little experience of farming. When a government agent visited him a decade after he arrived in Ramsay Township, he found Captain Armstrong "an aged man with a helpless family of young females," though he was only in his early fifties.

Half the people of the 1823 emigration settled in the townships of Pakenham, to the north of Ramsay, and Huntley and Goulbourn to the east. In Goulbourn, Thomas Collins, who had boasted in 1823 that he would not return to Ireland "for $500" had a thin time of it. He produced only fifty bushels of potatoes and a little grain from the four acres he cleared, though his father, Richard, on an adjoining lot did somewhat better.

The best land in Huntley Township lay in the Carp Valley not far from the Ottawa River, where some of Richard Talbot's emigrants had settled and were doing well. But Michael Cronin, who had written his mother at Mitchelstown with such high hopes in October 1823, had unfavourable ground on lot 18 in the 10th concession, where he was able to clear only two acres and produced no crops at all. He went to work at Brockville, where he became ill, but returned to his land later. Charles Carrol O'Sullivan, who had compared a Canadian winter to a landlord's cold heart, spent his first year working at Shipman's Mills, but cleared four acres in Huntley in his second year and produced 200 bushels of potatoes, some turnips and grain, and acquired two cows and a hog.

The most disappointing land of all lay in western Pakenham on the edge of the Canadian Shield. Nineteen families took lots there, but half gave up and went out to find employment, though they did not give up their property. "Settlers sometimes go to their farms in the woods," noted an observer, "plant a sackful of potatoes, and retreat again with all due precipitation, well stung with insects. Towards winter they will visit the plantation, and dig up a crop, if a wandering sow and her brood shall not have been there previously." Jeremiah Cronin from Buttevant gave up completely and went to Perth to ply his trade as a shoemaker, as did his neighbour, Bustard Green, from Castletownroche. John Green who had smuggled his sweetheart,

Catherine, aboard the *Stakesby* and married her in Perth, he being a Protestant and she a Catholic, struggled with his land for a while before moving to the newly opened township of Fitzroy on the Ottawa River, where he prospered. Seven families of Greens from Castletownroche settled in Pakenham Township and all were related though some were Catholic and some Protestant. The only one to remain in Pakenham was another John Green, twenty-six, who was "still struggling with bad land" a few years later, but he too gave up and opened an inn. George Hanover, the Dublin University graduate, had gone out to work on the Ottawa River but returned to Pakenham, married and found adequate land.

Crime was rare. In Ramsay, Daniel Ryan from Kanturk was banished from the colony for theft and went to live in the United States, and there were a few minor incidents, but there was also the bizarre case of John Dougherty of Churchtown, who had settled in Pakenham with his wife, Judith, and four children. He had not done well, having cleared eight acres but raised only a small crop of turnips. But he did own two cows, a source and a symbol of wealth, and what possessed him to maim one of his neighbour's cattle was never clear, though in his native County Cork it was a common revenge of the Whiteboys. Cattle were scarce and costly, and for slashing the tongue of one of his neighbour's cows he was actually sentenced to death. A short time before his scheduled execution, Judith Dougherty wrote to the Lieutenant Governor:

Your Petitioner is at present one of the most wretched women on earth, with five children in a Strange land, in the poorest of circumstances, and to complete my misery my husband, John Dougherty, is at present confined in Gaol at Perth, under sentence of DEATH.... Your Petitioner prays your Excellency in the most supplicating manner that you will be graciously pleased to permit her husband to return to, and live again in, the world, to be help and support of his unfortunate family. Your Petitioner begs and entreats Your Excellency in the name of Him who wills not the death of a sinner.... With impatient anxiety and trembling hope. Judith Dougherty X Her Mark.

Meantime, Dougherty had escaped from prison, and when he was found, half dead from exposure, his bare feet were so badly frozen he lost some of his toes. Maitland, who found the death penalty excessive for the crime, and believing that Dougherty had suffered enough, pardoned him and sent him back to his family.

When work started on the Rideau Canal in 1826 it provided employment for thousands of Irish for the next six years. Its 135-mile route from the new village of Bytown on the Ottawa River, along the Rideau Valley toward Kingston through the bush, rock and swamp of eastern Ontario, passed south of the region where Robinson's people had settled. Bart Murphy's friends, Luke McGrath and his brother James from Ballygiblin, went to work for the builder, Colonel By, leaving their land in Huntley uncultivated. James O'Mara from Cork City worked on the canal's forty-five locks as a stonemason. Cornelius Ryan made good money hiring out his two oxen. The work attracted Irish veterans of the Erie and Welland canals to the southwest, as well as labourers fresh from Ireland. One of By's engineers, John Mac-Taggert, had no high opinion of them, but he was a Scotsman.

"I would not employ any Irish were it not for mere charity," he declared, and, judging from the book he wrote about his experiences, the Irish he met were young, rootless, hard-drinking men who frequented Mother McGinty's tavern by the canal bank in Corktown, a dismal offshoot of Bytown.

"If they can get a mud cabin they will never think of building one of wood," said MacTaggert. Mud was poor insulation against an Ottawa Valley winter. "At Bytown on the Ottawa they burrow into sand hills. Smoke is seen issuing out of holes which answer the purpose of chimneys. Here families contrive to pig together worse than in Ireland; and when any rows or such-like things are going on, the women are seen to pop their carroty polls out of the doors, so densely, sooty, smoke-dried and ugly that one cannot but be disgusted. You cannot get the low Irish to wash their faces. You cannot get them to dress decently, although you supply them with ready-made clothes. They will smoke, drink, eat murphies, brawl, box and set the house on fire about their ears."

The death rate on the canals was high. Unfamiliar with blasting powder, some of the Irish blew themselves up, or neglected their wounds until it was too late and gangrene had set in. The most serious hazard lay in drinking polluted water, particularly in what MacTaggert called the "infernal place between the Rideau Lake and Lake Ontario, the abode of dreadful ague. Hundreds of labourers and mechanics were laid down with sickness, many of whom never rose again … generally it came on with an attack of bilious fever, dreadful vomiting, pains in back and loins, and general debility and loss of appetite. After eight or ten days, yellow jaundice is likely to ensue, and then fits of trembling. Their very bones ache, teeth chatter, and ribs are sore, continuing in this great agony for about an hour and a half. Those who have had it once most likely have a touch of it every year. A moist, hot summer fosters it very much."

THE WORST OUTBREAK of ague, however, was amid the lakes and swamps of Newcastle District. Weakened by their ordeal at Kingston, ninety-five people had died at the Peterborough depot by the end of 1825 and out in the townships over a thousand were ill. The fever abated during the winter's cold, but returned in the spring. Thirty-two people died that summer, and 172 by the end of the year, or one of every eleven settlers, half of them children. Among them was the forty-seven-year-old widow, Margaret Groves, who had fled Wicklow for fear of her Catholic neighbours, and in the vain hope of joining her daughters in Ramsay Township.

One settler wrote: "Ague is the disease most dreaded by new settlers, and to many persons it has proved a great drawback, especially to such as go into the uncleared lands. They who live in the long settled parts of Canada seldom have ague; it arises from the exhalations of the vegetable soil, when opened out to the action of the sun and air. As long as the soil is unbroken, and the woods uncleared, no such effect is felt. I have heard some of the hardy old trappers say that they never had ague in the woods; but on the newly-cleared land, or by lakes and swamps, where the sun had access, there they would have ague."

Most people recovered, helped by Dr. Reade, who gave them camomile and castor oil in the absence of quinine, and by Indians, who taught them the medicinal values of sarsaparilla, wild peppermint and tansey. The survivors were so weak it is remarkable they achieved what they did that year, clearing and planting an average of three acres per family. They produced 54,000 bushels of potatoes and 23,500 bushels of turnips, and planted their first winter wheat. They learned to tap maple trees and boiled up 900 pounds of sugar, and using whatever money they had brought with them, plus the small profits from the sale of produce, they began to purchase cattle – forty oxen at £7 a head, cows at £4 and 166 hogs at 15 shillings each.

Emily Township, which had received the largest group, covered 110 square miles north of Peterborough, and apart from hills in the north and hills and swamps in the south it had much good land. Over a third of the settlers had been ill, and with so many men down with ague, women worked in the clearings from dawn until well after sundown, burning brush, planting and doing the work of the men. The penalty for delay was recorded in a stark little note beside the name of Edmond Gillman's family from Cork: "Crop failed, put in too late."

All twelve members of the John Harnett family from Churchtown were ill in Emily Township but somehow raised 500 bushels of potatoes and turnips before John Harnett died. Thomas Carew from Faraghy in the Blackwater was ill, but his wife, Esther, and his daughter and son harvested enough potatoes, turnips, Indian corn and maple sugar to see them through the winter.

Despite their illnesses and hardships, the optimistic Robinson found his settlers "in good spirits with the prospect of an abundant crop" that autumn, adding, "They have considerably increased their improvements which look very neat." They hunted rabbits, partridge and deer, and discovered the flesh of the black squirrel was "as good as rabbit." Maurice Clancy of Limerick, the first blacksmith in Douro Township, made fish spears for the Indians, who taught the settlers to spear salmon trout, whitefish, bass and masquinonge. Wayfarers carried torches at night to ward off wolves and kept their homemade lamps, a rag soaked in grease, burning in a window all night as a guide to travellers over the rough trails. Bears were a constant worry, and women working in the fields took their babies with them in case bears tried to break into the cabin. Samuel Strickland, who moved to the Peterborough district a few months after the arrival of the Irish, was told of a bear that forced its way into a kitchen. "The woman and her three children had barely time to get into the potato cellar and shut the trap door."

Prejudice against the Irish Catholics was milder than in the Ottawa Valley, but Strickland's sister, Susanna Moodie, admitted she had a "hard battle" overcoming the traditional English prejudice against Irish peasants. "We shrank from the rude, coarse familiarity of the uneducated people among whom we were thrown," she wrote in *Roughing It in the Bush.* While benefitting from the communal logging, house-raising and harvesting bees, she deplored them as "noisy, riotous, drunken meetings, often terminating in violent quarrels, sometimes even in bloodshed." When she had one at her own house, in which thirty-two men were fed with the usual legs of pork, venison, fish, eels, potatoes, raspberry pie, tea and raw local whiskey, she admitted they were well behaved. "The dinner passed off tolerably well," she said. "Some of the lower order of Irish settlers were pretty far gone; but they committed no outrage against our feelings by either swearing or bad language."

Her sister, Catharine Parr Traill, another of the three "writing Stricklands" who settled near Peterborough, described Irish shanties on "the squatters grounds" as "reeking with smoke and dirt, the common receptical for children, pigs and fowl." Her brother, Samuel

Strickland, assured her that a "disregard for comfort and decency are the general characteristics of the southern Irish." This was the way English travellers had described the homes of the poor in Ireland, but it was rare to find Irish people keeping livestock in their homes in North America. More in keeping with the scene in a drafty Canadian log cabin was Traill's version of a conversation with a young Irish boy she met. "When the weather was stinging cold," the boy told her, "we did not know how to keep ourselves warm; for while we roasted our eyes out before the fire our backs were just as freezing; so first we turned one side and then the other, just as you would roast a goose on a spit. Mother spent half the money father earned on whiskey to keep us warm. But I do think a larger mess of good, hot potatoes would have kept us warmer than whiskey did." Though the Catholics were slower to build themselves the fine, stone houses put up by their Protestant neighbours, most at least had wooden floors and were comfortable.

In Douro Township, where Irish Catholics were the majority, the Ulsterman Robert Reid, William Stewart's brother-in-law, allowed as how they were "doing very well;" out of habit, however, he added that "their former indolent habits" had kept them from doing as well as they might. The belief that Irish Catholics were lazy, rather than ill or starving, had saved the English conscience for centuries, but in Canada it was hard to sustain. A glance into most township cabins after a hard day's work would find the women at their spinning wheels or knitting, the men sharpening tools and carving axe handles or furniture. There were few horses, and people walked great distances. Twenty-year-old Catherine Sheehan, who came with her brother from Cape Clear, County Cork, might be seen every week on the trail from Ennismore Township to Peterborough, ten miles distant, carrying a pail of butter on her head and baskets of eggs in both hands to trade at the depot. She was accompanied by her nieces and nephews, except when they were studying in the school just opened for forty-one children by Patrick Barragy from Tipperary, who taught them reading, writing, arithmetic, grammar and catechism. The children wrote their lessons on birch bark.

"Were it not for the ague, it is a fine country for a poor man if he is industrious," Cornelius Sullivan of Ennismore told a visiting Englishman. "A good country and a rich one, though to be sure it is rather out of the way, and the roads are bad, and the winters very cold. Yet there is always plenty to eat, and sure employment and good pay for them that like to work."

Sullivan was a forty-five-year-old widower who had come from the Dingle Peninsula in County Kerry with his two grown sons and three daughters. The Englishman he was talking to was Captain Basil Hall, a visiting writer and friend of Wilmot Horton. The Robinson emigrants were scattered over such a wide area that Hall was unable to see them all. "I endeavoured by riding from place to place, and calling upon the people without warning, to acquire a general conception of what was going on," Hall said. He found Cornelius Sullivan torn between a longing for his native Kerry and a determination to make good for his family in Canada.

"Would you like, then," Hall asked Sullivan, "to be put down in Ireland again?"

"I would sir."

"Then why don't you go?"

"Because my two sons like this country very well," Sullivan answered. "They have chopped twenty acres of land, and we have got crops of wheat and oats and Indian corn, and potatoes and some turnips all coming up and almost ready, besides five or six more acres chopped and logging, and soon to be in cultivation."

Another Irish settler told Hall, "We have been taken from misery and want, and put into independence and happiness." A third called Canada "a land flowing with milk and honey, or rather, what is better still, potatoes and pork." Hall concluded that the Irish were showing "good sense, moderation and industry, and sufficient strength of mind to bear prosperity with steadiness."

Lieutenant Rubidge, who had helped Robinson get the Irish settled, said the village of Peterborough "grew up as if by magic ... speculators flocked to the neighbouring townships, mills were built, stores opened, and life, bustle and civilization went on with spirit." The government built a bridge across the Otonabee River and property values doubled. There were now twenty houses in Peterborough. William Oakly, a shoemaker in Tipperary, opened the town's first bakery. Michael Elligott, one of the "indolent ruffians" on the brig *Fortitude*, started a shoe repair business, and Moses Begly, who had fled the Whiteboys with his son-in-law, Michael Buckley, opened a smithy. Adam Scott, whose wife had died from an illness brought in by one of the settlers, went into business distilling raw white whiskey and selling it for fifteen cents a gallon, or a pound of pork if the buyer had no cash but had an excess of government-issue rations.

Rubidge grumbled that the government had given the settlers more food than they needed, allowing them to trade it for drink, "thereby injuring their constitutions and morals." With a little more forethought, he said, they could have been settled at fifteen pounds a head, a saving of seven pounds per person, and during a parliamentary hearing in London he said as much. Two separate parliamentary hearings concluded the same thing, and suggested that state-aided emigration continue with a more sensible outlay of money; when Horton and Robinson tried to bring out a third contingent from southwest Ireland, Parliament refused to vote funds. When, shortly after, Horton was posted to Ceylon as governor, the man who replaced him called his experiment little more than a scheme "to shovel out paupers."

Had the scheme been continued, even at a smaller cost, it would have enhanced the course of emigration, providing badly needed regulation in the emigrant trade. But apart from a few timid government programs that involved very few people, emigration to Canada, as to the United States, was left to the emigrants themselves, and any landlords or local authorities prepared to fund them.

Thus the state-aided emigrations devised by Horton and carried out by Robinson were atypical and short-lived. According to A.C. Buchanan, the Ulsterman who was appointed Chief Emigration officer at Quebec City in 1828, the typical emigrant for the next seventeen years, right up to the Great Famine in 1845, was not the destitute but a "small farmer with a large family and an unexpired lease" who could raise money for the voyage with a bit left over to help him get started in Canada. "He disposes of his interest," said Buchanan, "by which he raises a little money, and added to his little stock of other articles, perhaps a web or two of coarse linen, some yarn stockings, and a thread of his own making and provisions of his own raising, off he goes to America."

For most of the emigrants that Robinson brought over, the project was a success. Samuel Strickland, at first critical of them, became favourably impressed by their adaptability and touched by their efforts to send money to relatives in Ireland. "The labouring population of Ireland," he concluded, "do much better abroad than at home – are more peaceable, contented, and industrious, less bigoted; and not so easily duped by political agitators." Rubidge, looking back on the experiment, said, "They are not only independent themselves but their children are independent also, and some even more so than the parents."

Though Robinson had left to take up a post as Commissioner of Crown Lands at York, he kept in touch and did what he could to encourage the settlers, but once their government rations came to an end they were on their own like any other colonists. "The Irish settlers placed in the midst of the woods have already acquired sufficient of the habits of the country," Robinson said, "to enable them to meet all their wants by their own labour, and have before them a fair prospect of comfort and independence."

7

The World of
Humphrey
O'Sullivan

$\mathcal{T}$HE HARM DONE to the Irish by English bigotry, arrogance and ignorance was incalculable. It crippled their lives at home and jeopardized
their chances when they emigrated to British colonies. "The moment
the very name of Ireland is mentioned," wrote the English liberal
churchman Sydney Smith, "the English seem to bid adieu to common
feeling, common prudence and common sense, and to act with the
barbarity of tyrants and the fatuity of idiots."

Queen Elizabeth's soldiers justified their attempts at genocide on
grounds the Irish were wild savages, and Oliver Cromwell defended
the massacre at Drogheda in 1649 as a "righteous judgment of God on
these barbarous wretches." In the 18th century, with Ireland reduced
to a weak, servile colony, fear of the dangerous savage had been replaced by an attitude almost as deadly. The barbarian had become a

contemptible figure of fun, portrayed in *Punch* cartoons, on the stage and in tavern jokes as the witless, loutish, bog-trotting "Paddy."

Arthur Young, the English agronomist, was shocked at the naked oppression he witnessed in 1776. "The landlord of an Irish estate, inhabited by Roman Catholics, is a sort of despot who yields obedience, in whatever concerns the poor, to no law but that of his own will," said Young. "He can scarcely invent an order which a servant labourer or a cottier desires to refuse to execute. Nothing satisfies him but unlimited submission. Disrespect or anything tending toward sauciness he may punish with his cane or his horsewhip with the most perfect security, a poor man would have his bones broken if he offered to lift his hand in his own defence."

Young was one of few English writers who showed some degree of sympathetic understanding of the Irish peasantry, but even he was exasperated by what he described as a tendency to "steal everything they can lay their hands on," ranging from hinges and turnips to whole trees or a field of wheat. "How far it is owing to the oppression of laws aimed solely at the religion of these people, how far the conduct of the gentlemen and farmers, and how far to the mischievous disposition of the people themselves, it is impossible for a passing traveller to ascertain."

A generation later, attitudes were softening, but the ignorance remained, along with a belief that the Irish were genetically feckless and lazy, architects of their own misfortunes. Evidence to the contrary was generally ignored. "It was an injustice to say that they are not industrious," wrote a Belfast man in 1819. "They labour like galley slaves. The wretchedness of their habitations and the want of certain comforts about them often induce careless and superficial observers to pronounce them idle." A parliamentary committee investigating the poor concluded: "So far from being uniformly inactive and idle, the peasantry of Ireland have a considerable anxiety to procure employment." But a widespread view across the Irish Sea was the one put forward by the *Edinburgh Review:* "They scratch, pick, dandle, gape and do everything but strive and wrestle with the task before them. The whole is in the scan of idleness, laziness and poverty strongly indicative of the habits which will long present a powerful impediment to the improvement of Ireland."

There were many books about the Irish countryside, written by prosperous travellers with English middle- or upper-class values, no command of the Irish language, and no understanding of the people they passed on the roadside. To the tourist intent on reaching the famous sights at Killarney lakes, the poverty and begging at every coach stop was an unpleasant distraction. Only a few joined Arthur Young and Henry D. Inglis in comparing the Irish favourably with the farm people of England, particularly in their thirst for education, as evidenced by their homemade hedge schools. And fewer still seemed to realize that behind the poverty life went on, as it had for centuries, with sports, weddings, dances, and even, at times, with gaiety. "To see Ireland happy," suggested the French traveller Gustave de Beaumont, "you must carefully select your point of view." "Their natural condition is turned toward gaiety and happiness," wrote Sir Walter Scott, during his visit in 1825.

No visiting foreigner could capture the life and soul of rural Ireland in the 19th century in the way it was set down in the diary of Humphrey O'Sullivan in the years 1827–35. Schoolmaster, shop keeper, antiquarian, botanist and nationalist, he was born in Killarney, County Kerry, and at the age of nine moved with his father, a hedge school master, to Waterford and then to County Kilkenny. He taught school with his father when the hedge schools were the sole means of education for half a million children throughout Ireland. He married, had four children, and at the time he started his diary was combining his teaching with running his linen draper's shop in the market town of Callan. Though he was perfectly fluent in English, he wrote his diary in Irish, which he rightly feared was a dying tongue.

O'Sullivan's diary touches on the great issues of the time – Daniel O'Connell's struggle for Irish emancipation, the revolt against Protestant tithes, and famine and disease. But mostly he wrote of country matters – fairs and markets, eating and drinking and dancing, music and hurling contests and the characters he met along his way. He wrote of nature and the slow turning seasons: "April, dripping, bleating new," "Victorious, calf-lowing May" and "the Yellow Month of July." Though he offers no physical description of himself, he was clearly a sensual man who loved life, sex, good food, most of his fellow creatures and his country, which he never left, though he took frequent journeys in southern Ireland. As a teacher and merchant he was on good terms with the poor, whom he often helped; his special friend was the priest, Father Seamus Hennebry, who had money of his own and kept a good table.

April 1, 1827…The countryside is beautiful [O'Sullivan wrote]. There are pine trees at Teampall Loisc about four Irish miles from Callan. It is fine country for wheat, oats, barley and potatoes, although they failed last year because of the drought. Livid famine is all over the countryside. Five pence halfpenny for a miserable fourteen pounds of potatoes; eighteen shillings for a barrel of oats, and poor people without any kind of work to buy any kind of food. There are not even alms for the paupers. They are being sent off home to their own parishes. Callan's own paupers, who number 300 families, or 1,500 persons, are reduced to misery. A collection is being made for them by Lord Clifton, the priest, and the minister, the chief magistrate and the Callan merchants but it will not last even half of them for long. God bless them.

Callan contained between four and five thousand people, and Frederick Page, a traveller from Berkshire, England, said it was "distressingly full of poor" because of the evictions from farmland on the fertile plain of the River King. Thomas Cromwell, an Englishman who passed by in the late 1820s, described it as the "very impersonation of Irish poverty and wretchedness." Henry D. Inglis, who counted between 600 and 700 destitute and 200 mendicants incapable of work, blamed absentee landlords, calling Lord Clifton the worst because Clifton visited occasionally and was well aware of conditions. "It is true that his Lordship drives as rapidly through his town as the state of the streets will admit; but it is said that upon one occasion the carriage broke down, and that this patriotic and tender-hearted nobleman was forced to hear the execrations of the crowd of naked and starving wretches who thronged around him."

As a member of the middle class, O'Sullivan ate better than most, his usual diet being oatmeal porridge with milk in the morning, milk and bread at noon, and potatoes with meat or butter at night. "There is joy in the hearts of the poor as they look forward to a bit of meat tomorrow," he wrote on April 14, the day before Easter Sunday. "The dwellers in the country hovels eat meat only three times in the year: Christmas Day, Shrove Tuesday and Easter Sunday." His diary continued:

April 15, Easter Sunday. A beautiful day. Five of us left Callan for Desart, three miles away. The landscape is delightful in this beautiful place. We bent our steps eastwards to Butler's and the green at Ballygell, where we ate white baker's bread, fat pork, delicious mutton, white pudding, and drank a drop of whiskey from a handsome hostess.

April 16. The day of Easter eggs. Every public house full of young people.

April 17. The mob were noisy at 3 a.m., some were still drunk; bogtrotters, dirty mountain people without self-respect or manners....

In mid-May he recorded an attack by a mob of 1,000 people on five boats laden with flour and guarded by police. "A poor hungry crowd tried to take meal from the boats which were sailing from Clonmel to Carrick on Suir, but the peelers fired on them from the boats. Three of the poor Irishmen were killed and six others very badly wounded...."

The hedge schools had helped keep the Irish language alive, and now that the Protestant Ascendency was introducing a National Education system to replace them, he was concerned for survival of the language, although he noted that Protestant missionaries were learning Irish and using it to try to convert people from Catholicism. They were also enticing potential apostates with food, in what most Catholics scorned as "souperism."

May 14. ...Will it be long until this Irish language in which I am writing will disappear? Fine big schools are being built daily to teach this new language, the English of England. But alas! Nobody is taking any interest in the fine, subtle Irish language.

June 29. Feast of St. Peter and Paul, a holiday. Hurling on the Fair Green. It was a good game, the sticks being brandished like swords. ...You could hear the sticks striking the ball from one end of the Green to the other. The well-to-do young men and women were strolling up and down on the Green.

July 12. ...We saw a pretty girl kneading peat. Her foot was slender, her calves and knees as white as bog cotton, her thigh round and beautiful, naked almost to her stout buttocks. She was the daughter of a farmer once rich; but the struggle of life went against him. He became bankrupt, the landlord took his crops, the minister his corn and horses, and the church tithe collector took his table, pot and blankets. Between them they pushed him down in life, along with his wife and handsome children. These are the circumstances that drove him to a small hovel beside the mountain and set his beautiful daughter to kneading peat.

A thousand young girls and boys dancing to music on top of Moin Rua. The brown hillock was shaking under their nimble feet. They are having a fine time – if it does not end in begging.

October 9. ...Rent, taxes, and tithes, county rates and church rates are all too high, and they have to remain so as long as the Royal Debt remains, that is the English Debt, the debt which King William placed on the Kingdom for the purpose of encouraging the foreign religion and destroying the Catholic faith. It was only about a million and a half at first but it is over nine hundred million now. This is a millstone around the neck of the Kingdom, tied by the tyrant's iron chain. The rich collect 30 million pounds a year profit from the people of the country. I don't know how many millions are spent on the upkeep of soldiers and peelers to keep the people quiet but not happy....

On November 25 he admitted he had not been outdoors for a fortnight. The reason, he said, was two black eyes he received in a pub row with a bad-tempered doctor:

We were happy singing and cheering when Doctor Builtear came upon us like a warlike cat would come upon lively mice chewing cheese.

Jan, 4, 1828. Now is the Festive Season. There is not one small farmer who has not pork or mutton or abundant beef, and beggars consequently get a bite.

Jan. 7. Pig Market Day. Windy, boisterous, from seven in the morning to midnight, wet and harsh, unceasing rain and snow. My sister's son, Seamus O'Costigan, was married this evening by Father Seamus Hennebry. We spent the night until three in the morning eating, drinking punch and tea, and singing Irish songs. We came home happily and peacefully, without causing trouble to anyone.

June 20. A meal at Father Hennebry's house. We had two fine, sweet trout, one of which was the size of a small salmon, hardboiled eggs, boiled asparagus dipped in butter melted in hot milk with salt. We had port, hot punch as good as I ever drank.

As Daniel O'Connell's movement for Catholic Emancipation gained strength, O'Sullivan's diary for 1828 reflected the ferment. Except in Ulster, which was more than half Protestant, O'Connell and his Catholic Association had an immense following and every Catholic was expected to contribute a penny a month toward a fighting fund. O'Sullivan was the collector of the "O'Connell tax" in Callan and was urging Protestants to support the campaign to remove the last of the 18th-century Penal Laws against the Catholics which still barred them from sitting in the House of Commons.

July 8. Every window full of lighted candles in honour of Daniel O'Connell, who was elected in County Clare as MP to the parliament in London.

July 10. St. John's Fair Day. Good trade in cattle. The devilish peelers beat a lot of innocent people. They beat up two merchants in their own houses. They can't be tolerated.

July 13. I was one of the jury of twelve that held a coroner's inquest on Michael O'Meagher who was killed by two policemen at St. John's Fair.

Aug. 5. One of the peelers was acquitted by trickery. The other was found guilty of manslaughter. I don't know what the sentence will be.

There was trouble in the district with the shooting death of Patrick Devereux of Cloonygara, who had evicted five families from a forty-acre farm and taken it himself. Two months before this murder, O'Sullivan had met the wife of one of the evicted men – who were the chief suspects – while strolling through the countryside, and described her home as a "mean frail hovel beside the bog" and the woman as tall, thin, ragged, barefoot "and no clothes to her back but dirty soot-coloured rags." She was weeping bitterly.

"Where is the short cut to Callan?" said I.

"I will show it to you myself, and a hundred thousand welcomes," said the poor woman.

"Let us go through this potato patch by this path close to the hedgerow. It is I who set these potatoes but Patrick Devereux will dig them."

After we had gone through a field of wheat, "It is my children," said she, "who sowed the seed, but it is Paddy Devereux who has reaped the harvest, my curse upon him…. It was my husband who built that house. It was I who put soot on the rafters, but Devereux who took the door off the jamb, and the hinges off the hooks. He left the cabin without a door, the window without a pane of glass, the hearth without a fire, the chimney without smoke, the pigsty without sow or boar…. It is far from them all I myself, my poor persecuted husband and my ruined children are being sent…."

The woman's husband and three other men were arrested, tried and sentenced to death.

On August 8, O'Sullivan gives an account of how he conducted his drapery business. "I bought striped and yellow calico from a travelling trader at fourpence a yard." On the 13th he saw reapers who had come east from Tipperary for the wheat harvest, "into our own lovely valley of silver and corn."

September 3. The seed is being blown from the thistle. The thistles are being cut by the paupers for fuel. I see a load of them, as big as a pigsty, being carried on her back by a poor woman. They use cow-dung for fuel as well.

Though Callan was a poor town in a poor district, there is little sense of dispirited destitution in O'Sullivan's daily observations. Young people played games or went swimming, lovers strolled on the green, and on fair days and feast days, at least, people seemed to be able to enjoy themselves with drink and the occasional good meal.

September 14. Sunday. A fine dry, sunny day with few clouds, a fresh lively wind from the north. Four of us had a meal with Father Seamus Hennebry. He had boiled leg of lamb, carrots and turnips, roast goose with green pease and stuffing, a dish of tripe boiled in fresh milk, port and punch and tea. We also had melodious songs in Irish and spent a merry night till eleven o'clock in peace and good cheer.

The autumn of 1828 was a time of great unrest and O'Sullivan complained of a "plague" of soldiers in the town, sent by a government fearful of Daniel O'Connell's influence over the population. Had O'Connell said the word, undoubtedly he could have raised the peasant army so feared by Dublin Castle, but he was seeking a better life for the Irish by peaceful means.

O'Connell was holding vast meetings, attended by many thousands crowding the fields where he spoke. "Whose fault is it," he would thunder, "that so many human beings die annually of hunger? The Saxons! Who has destroyed our manufacture and our industry? The Saxons! Yes, the Saxons, the English! Despotic England is to blame." This was powerful incitement, whatever O'Connell's intent, and late in September 1828 a group of O'Connell's "Liberators" burned a barracks and clashed with police at Clogheen. Lord Kingston, who owned this town, had the leader, Cornelius O'Neil, arrested and jailed at Clonmel in County Kilkenny, not far from Callan.

Efforts were made to reconcile Protestants to the aims of Catholic Emancipation:

September 28, Sunday. Early this morning members of O'Connell's League of Peace gathered with beating drums to go to a meeting of the Tipperary League of Peace. They wore ornate ribbons, green, yellow, red, white … every colour except orange. It is following O'Connell's advice that reconciliation and peace is being sought among the Irish. But the English do not like it, as they think it easier to defeat quarrelling parties than friendly people, and this is true. But I do not like to see women and children, drummers and musicians, with banners with the picture of O'Connell on them, because that will incite King William's followers, that it is the Orangemen, against us.

October 4. I have been very busy this past week trying to persuade O'Connell's followers not to march in green clothes or with O'Connell's image, or with music. The Catholics of Callan have promised not to march any more.

The Protestants pretend they are frightened, but they would be delighted in their hearts to be spilling Catholic blood.... This is the beginning of trouble unless the Catholics stop in time. I hope to Almighty God that they will, and that they won't make their mortal enemies happy, namely the Protestants and the devils.

October 11. A sunny, thin-clouded morning. I went on the priest's mare to Butler Clerke in Newtown to ask him to sign the Protestant Declaration in favour of Catholic Emancipation. He signed, as did Henry Baker, and Arthur Bushe, son of the Chief Justice. I must get the name of every Protestant in the parish on it if I can. Isn't it a sad thing to see the children of the Gael seeking freedom as an alms in their own native land. But they themselves are responsible for being kept in slavery by English foreigners, because of their failure to agree among themselves since the time of Brian Boru up to the recent O'Connell Peace Movement.

October 27. The boreens between the poor hovels on the commons are dirty and muddy. In spite of their wretched condition, Lord Clifton and other landlords are trying to levy a rent on them. May they not succeed.

December 24. Christmas Eve, a fast day. A mild southwest wind. The poor people are buying pork chops, pigs heads, soggy beef, big joints of old sow's loins, and small bits of old rams, as all the good meat has already been bought up by the well-off, well-fed people.

December 25. Before the ring of day the moon was shining from a sky without cloud, welcoming the good Child Jesus. A big drum was beaten at five o'clock, flutes and fifes being played by the youth of the town.

O'Sullivan's diary for 1829 began with another appeal for Catholic Emancipation, and within three months the Emancipation Act was passed and O'Connell led a small band of Irish Catholic MPs into the House of Commons in London. "We achieved emancipation in the most peaceful, loyal and constitutional manner," said O'Connell after a quarter century of effort. "We committed no offence, we were guilty of no crime, we destroyed no property, we injured no man's person," O'Connell was hailed as the "Uncrowned King of Ireland" and his fame spread to Canada. In Quebec City the Irish Emigrant Society passed a resolution praising him, and his framed picture was found on mantles beside the Cross and the Virgin in the homes of French *habitants*.

O'Connell won more fame when he defended twenty-one men from the Blackwater in what was called the Doneraile Conspiracy. They had been charged with attempts to assassinate the magistrate George Bond Low and two other members of the Blackwater squirarchy. Three Whiteboys and an elderly cottier had been found guilty and sentenced to death when O'Connell, whose mother came from the Blackwater, was persuaded to take up their defence. He had the death sentence reduced to transportation to Australia, and for the other seventeen, his skilful defence resulted in a hung jury and they were freed.

The years 1829–30 brought local famine and unusually bad weather. "Uh! it is cold," O'Sullivan wrote on April 2, 1830. "The grey sky is like the face of an old, wizened man in the throes of threatening death." Two weeks later, "two poor spalpeens," itinerant labourers, died of hunger and cold. "They had a miserable wake."

O'Sullivan's diaries contain little reference to emigration, though it had increased, with 11,000 people going to British North America in 1826, due in no small part to poor crops. Kilkenny men were among the 50,000 Irish who settled in Newfoundland between 1800 and 1830, and among them were his sister's son, John Burn, and a brother-in-law, Michael O'Costigan.

April 19, 1830. The weather is very severe for emigrants to the Land of the Fish, as the hard wind is against them. May God help them. The poor Irish must suffer much hardship to earn an honest living in foreign countries since the foreigners came to Ireland.

June 25. The black famine is in Kilkenny and Waterford, etc., in the large towns, but in the small towns like Callan, and in the countryside, alms are to be had more plentifully from the small farmers. It is they who, almost on their own, feed the poor of Ireland. They get little food from the gentry, for it is abroad in distant lands that that devilish crowd spend their time, and the rents which they snatch from tenants, who are crushed in the grip of poverty. Tradesmen and shopkeepers are also generous in giving alms to God's poor.

June 26. There is stark famine in Kerry. It will be well if it is not as bad as the bitter famine of 1740. County Clare is just as bad; nor is Dublin any better off.... The people along the canals are keeping food from getting to Dublin, in case the horrible famine will reach themselves. Things are severe enough here in poor Callan.

July 6. The poor of County Cork are subsisting on nettles and green herbs and weeds, may God shield them from livid famine!

The government had begun to experiment with importing American maize, or corn meal, and O'Sullivan was one of those distributing it to the hungry. "The authorities of the Church and the nobility are going to buy meal to help the poor, until the potatoes are fit to dig. May God reward them for it!" In August he was relieved that the harvest looked promising.

October 28. Myself and another man went around collecting money to bury a poor woman from County Carlow. There is no other way to get a decent wooden coffin for a poor stranger in this land since the foreigners came here. May they not last here long! It is they who destroyed Ireland and the Irish.

The year 1831 saw the escalation of the battle against paying tithes to the Anglican Church of Ireland. Collection of these taxes (one tenth of the produce harvested by the poor) was farmed out to greedy middlemen and tithe proctors. "The proctor has a double objective," wrote Dr. John Elmore of Cork. "First to give a parson as little as he can; second to make as much of a bargain as he can. Therefore he has no feeling at all, but for making money from the transaction." Early in the year O'Sullivan described what came to be called the Tithe Wars, which flared up in his county when a tithe proctor seized the cattle of a priest.

January 6, 1831. A fine, calm, cloudy day. A great crowd in Callan. Hundreds of people seeking exemption from tithes, or a reduction of them, from the Protestant Minister, but there were police and soldiers to keep the tithe collector firm in his demands. This agitation is going on through the county of Kilkenny for the last fortnight, but it is little use going to law with the devil when the court is held in hell. The law is on the side of the ministers, and the Protestant Parliament will make no change until it has no other way out. A similar agitation is going on

St. John's, Newfoundland, in 1831 when 10,000 Irish residents made up the majority of the town's population. Some of the most important years of Irish migration to Newfoundland were 1810 to 1836, after which the influx declined. (National Archives of Canada, C3371)

The English emigrant ship Wellington, *415 tons, in the 1820s. Ships of this tonnage were known to carry as many as 500 passengers, which might mean less than two square feet of space for each person down in the steerage, where passengers were frequently confined because of bad weather. (National Archives of Canada, C1901)*

A silhouette portrait of Peter Robinson (1785–1838), representative of the east riding of York in the Upper Canada Assembly, and later member of the Legislative Council and Commissioner of Crown Lands. As "Superintendent of Emigration from the South of Ireland to Canada" between 1823 and 1825, he played a key role in settling Irish Catholics in the Ottawa Valley and the Peterborough region. (Metropolitan Toronto Library Board, J. Ross Robertson Collection)

Originally known as Shipman's Mills, the community of Almonte beside the Mississippi River became the first stopping place of the 500 Irish emigrants Peter Robinson brought to Canada in 1823. Nearly a century later, when this photo was taken, it had matured into a pleasant Ottawa Valley town. (National Archives of Canada, C59984)

Rice Lake, on the route to Peterborough. When Robinson's 2,000 emigrants crossed it in the fall of 1825, they saw little but an Indian encampment and clouds of duck come to feed on the wild rice that gave the lake its name. (National Archives of Canada, C129703)

Garrett Galvin, who came with his family from County Kerry at the age of twelve with the Peter Robinson emigrants who settled at Ennismore in 1825. The family prospered and the census of 1851 indicates they owned 210 acres, half of it under cultivation. (Courtesy Clare F. Galvin)

Patrick O'Donnell was fourteen when he arrived at Peterborough with the Robinson emigrants in 1825 with his father, Patrick, a stonemason from Mitchelstown, and his mother, Martha. The family settled in Ennismore township, where the father died within two years. (Courtesy Olive Doran)

Coming from a country where trees were scarce, the Irish had to be taught to clear their land, which meant felling enough trees to get their first crop in and planting it among the stumps. Hearing that they could make some cash by burning their fallen trees to make potash, many tried to do so as soon as the trees were felled, learning by trial and error that green wood had to age before it could be burned. (National Archives of Canada, C44633)

Members of the Nagle family which settled
in Ramsay township, Ottawa Valley, in the
Peter Robinson migration of 1823. On the
right is Margaret, first wife of Gerrard
Nagle, who was eighteen when he came out
with his parents, Garett and Honorah, from
County Cork. Below are Garett and
Honorah's four grandsons, the first
generation born in Canada. (Courtesy of
Mary N. Gallagher, Cambridge, Ont.)

Bytown in the early 1830s was one of the roughest communities in the colonies, as Irish migrant labourers, hired to dig the Rideau Canal, found themselves without work when the canal was completed, and fought with the French Canadians for jobs in the new timber industry. (National Archives of Canada, C1200)

Grosse Isle quarantine station in the St. Lawrence River, sketched in September 1832, at the height of the cholera epidemic, with Signal Hill and its tower on the left and cholera hospitals on the right. Thousands of Irish emigrants died that year on the island or in the towns up-river. (National Archives of Canada, C5199)

Established as a quarantine station when Saint John, New Brunswick, was incorporated in 1785, Partridge Island became the graveyard of many emigrants during the cholera epidemics of the early 1830s and the Great Famine, when in one year alone, 1847, 16,000 arrived and 2,000 died. (National Archives of Canada, C30790)

Saint John in the 1840s. Taking advantage of cheap fares on cargo ships sailing out to load timber, emigrants began arriving in the early 1800s, the largest number coming during the Great Famine between 1845 and 1850. By the 1870s the Irish were 55 per cent of the city's population and 35 per cent of that of the province. (National Archives of Canada, C2409)

In the absence of press photography, the Illustrated London News *livened its famine coverage with sketches like this, from February 1847, which shows the watchman's stone shack in Old Chapel Yard, Skibbereen, where six members of a family called Barrett took refuge when they were evicted from their nearby cabin. Elihu Burritt, an American philanthropist, accompanied by a local doctor, found the family huddled, all suffering from fever, in a space seven feet by six, "literally entombed" in the midst of the graveyard. (Metropolitan Toronto Library Board)*

A funeral procession in County Cork during the worst winter of the famine, in 1847. Coffins were fashioned with removable bottoms so they could be reused, such was the scarcity of wood and the number of burials. From the Illustrated London News, *February 13, 1847. (Metropolitan Toronto Library Board)*

With tens of thousands reduced to
starvation, people found whatever
nourishment they could. "I see
hundreds of women and children
going through the stubble fields
striving to get an old stalk of potato,"
wrote a magistrate in County Mayo
in the autumn of 1846. From the
Illustrated London News, *December 22, 1849.*

Some landlords relented during the
Great Famine, ceased evicting their
tenants and helped them survive, but
others continued evictions to clear
their lands for more profitable pasturage. The men on the roof are
breaking the beam to tumble it down
into the cottage, while the tenant
pleads with a bailiff. Nearly 10,000
were evicted in 1848, and 16,000
the following year. From the
Illustrated London News, *December 16, 1848. (Both: Metropolitan
Toronto Library Board)*

A large number of Irish sailed from Liverpool, the busiest emigration port in the United Kingdom. Even allowing for the cost of getting to Liverpool and staying in boarding houses, it was cheaper to travel via Liverpool because of the number of cheap charters available there. Some days twenty or more ships departed, for New York, Quebec City or Saint John. At the heart of the miles of waterfront was Waterloo Dock, whose turmoil was depicted in the Illustrated London News, *July 6, 1850. (Metropolitan Toronto Library Board)*

Not all the emigrant voyages were miserable, and letters home tell of singing and dancing to fiddles when the weather was calm, the captain was kindly and the food was sufficient. From the Illustrated London News, *July 6, 1850. (Metropolitan Toronto Library Board)*

Emigrants left Ireland in their tens of thousands from the sheltered waters of Cork Harbour. In Black '47, that worst of all famine years, 17,519 people embarked on ships in the Cove of Cork, 13,159 bound for British North America. (National Archives of Canada, PA62184)

In normal times Grosse Isle was described by visitors as an attractive island, as suggested by this sketch made in 1850. But it was here, three years earlier, that thousands died of typhus in the terrible summer of 1847. (National Archives of Canada, C120285

Emigrants receiving the blessing of their priest in preparation for the long walk to the ship that would carry them across the Atlantic. Between 1856 and 1860, the period of this sketch, 250,000 people left for the United States and 13,000 for British North America. From the Illustrated London News, *May 10, 1857. (Metropolitan Toronto Library Board)*

In the 1850s, the Great Famine ended and normal emigration resumed. In this scene from the Illustrated London News, *May 10, 1857, the people waiting to embark for Boston, New York, New Orleans and Quebec City are healthier and better clad than the famine refugees of previous years. (Metropolitan Toronto Library Board)*

Alexander Carlisle Buchanan
(1808–1868), who succeeded his uncle,
also Alexander Carlisle Buchanan, as Chief
Emigration Agent in 1838, and served for
the rest of his life. Born in Ireland to a
family of shipowners, Buchanan, like his
father, and his uncle James, who became
British Consul in New York, played a
major role in Irish migration. (National
Archives of Canada, C117427)

Dr. George Mellis Douglas (1809–1864)
medical superintendent at Grosse Isle
during the Great Famine. Though
overwhelmed by successive waves of
thousands of fatally ill emigrants, and
sometimes ill himself, Douglas remained at
his post with amazing energy and courage
throughout the whole of the greatest episode
of human misery in Canadian history.
(Courtesy Marianna O'Gallagher, Ste-Foy,
Quebec, and Dr. Sylvio Leblond)

After the famine, there were thousands of deserted tenants' cabins like this one throughout the west of Ireland. Descriptions of these dwellings in the 1830s said they were usually about sixteen by twelve feet and contained little but a bed, a potato bin in the corner, a few rough stools, a chest and a fireplace. (Courtesy of the National Library of Ireland)

The village of Ballydehob, photographed more than a century ago, after massive emigration had depopulated west Cork. Once a centre of copper mining, Ballydehob suffered severely during the Great Famine. (Courtesy of the National Library of Ireland)

The main street of Skibbereen, County Cork, in the late 19th century, more than a generation after the name of the town had become synonymous with the suffering of the Great Famine. (Courtesy of the National Library of Ireland)

A rebel in his native land, Thomas D'Arcy McGee's zeal for nationhood made him one of the Fathers of Confederation after he migrated to Canada. Fenians had expected him to become one of their leaders, but he opposed their cause in Canada, and his conversion from Irish to Canadian nationalism was to cost him his life. Thousands lined the streets of Montreal (below) for his funeral in 1868. (National Archives of Canada, C44651, C83423)

On Assumption Day, August 15, 1909, 8,000 people gathered on Telegraph Hill, Grosse Isle, for the dedication of a Celtic cross erected by the Ancient Order of Hibernians in memory of the people who died at the quarantine station in the worst year of the Great Famine. Among the throng were some who had arrived on the island as children sixty-two years before. (National Archives of Canada, C136924)

in England. It is dire poverty that is forcing the people of Ireland and England to rise up against the law of the country.

Government efforts to enforce tithe collection with soldiers and police cost more than the tithes were worth. "I am at my wit's end," said Lord Anglesey, the Lord Lieutenant in Dublin. "There exists to the most frightening extent a mutual and violent hatred between the proprietors and the peasantry." A wealthy merchant complained that industrious "strong farmers" were forced to "remove to a distant shore in quest of that peace and security they cannot find at home." They accounted for most of the 240,000 Irish, two thirds of them Protestants, who had arrived in British North America between 1825 (when data become available) and 1831, a year in which emigration reached an unprecedented 41,000.

December 15, 1831. A fine, soft, cloudy day. A number of people were killed in the Walsh Mountains near Carrickshock yesterday. It was said that eighteen of the police accompanying Butler, who was serving summonses because of tithes due, were killed. This is bad for the Children of the Gael, as the English will wreak vengeance on them.

The fighting was northeast of Callan, where forty constables met a mob that would not let them pass. The chief constable, twenty policemen and four civilians were killed and there were many wounded. In similar fighting in County Westmeath seven were killed, and in County Wexford the toll was fourteen. At Schull, in west Cork, the Reverend Robert Traill of the Church of Ireland wrote: "One clergyman within thirty miles of us has been murdered, and another most narrowly escaped with his life by taking refuge in the house of a priest. The ungodly are rising up, and these poor deluded Roman Catholics are caballing to deprive me of my tithes, alas! What wickedness is this?"

There were 203 riots throughout Ireland in this period, 723 attacks on private houses, 568 cases of arson and 280 reports of the maiming of cattle. A secret society known as Whitefeet, formed in the coal mines on the northern Kilkenny border, circulated warnings in Callan that anyone paying tithes would be burned alive. Richard Marum, a landowner who had bought in outside labour after a dispute with local labourers, was killed with a blunderbuss by three terrorists, thought to be Whitefeet, while his tenants looked on and did nothing. A brother of the Catholic Bishop of Kilkenny was murdered for speculating in land. "The Whitefeet are most liberal people," commented a priest, "for they make no distinction between Catholics and Protestants."

May 4, 1832 Callan Fair Day [wrote O'Sullivan]. A grand, delightful, sunny day. There was a good demand for sucking pigs, dry cows, fat cattle, sheep and for shopkeepers' goods. There are soldiers in Callan waiting to levy tithes; though the new tithe bill is not yet law, namely to process a defaulter merely by affixing his name to the door of the Protestant church!

May 5. This week in Kilkenny County fourteen persons caught the 'stingingly painful livid disease,' of whom twelve died in one day. This is great havoc. This deadly plague is in Dublin, in Cork, and in Naas.

Cholera morbus, as it was called, had spread west into Europe from India and in March it had leaped the Irish sea from northern England and appeared in Belfast. A week later people in Dublin stoned the doctors who announced the epidemic had arrived in the capital, and within a month it had spread through Ireland, carried by flies, contaminated food and water. It was at its most deadly in the towns, where tar barrels were burned at street corners and houses painted with lime in an attempt to ward it off. Its victims, identified by their sunken stomachs, contorted limbs and blue lips, were buried in mass graves, wrapped in tarred canvas when the supply of coffins was exhausted.

In Sligo on the northwest coast, a city of 18,000, cholera killed 700 people, including six of the thirteen doctors, and 16,000 people fled into the countryside to find what shelter they could. "It was no uncommon thing in those direful days," said a Sligo writer, "to see persons who had fallen victim to the terrible malady lying dead in the streets. Corpses were wrapped in sheets smeared with pitch to prevent the spread of the disease and were removed by the cholera carts."

Cholera had never been seen before in Ireland, and its rapid spread through the countryside caused mass hysteria. On Saturday, June 9, in the Blackwater area town of Charleville, reports were heard that the Virgin had appeared with a packet of ashes, which were said to be the only cure, and called on each householder to scoop ashes from the family hearth and carry them to four neighbours, each neighbour to do the same until everyone was visited.

"Such was the anxiety to put her orders into execution," wrote Major-General H.G. Barry, "that the whole country was up in a moment, and one of my work people told me that when he was called up at three in the morning he looked out and saw the fields full of people in their shirts running about as if they were mad." All his tenants were visited except for three, who were Protestants, and by 4 a.m. hysteria had spread throughout northeast Cork, one man running thirty miles through the night to carry his "blessed turf" to relatives. When the message reached Callan, O'Sullivan heard it with disgust.

June 11, Monday. A morning of heavy rain. The humbler Irish are superstitious. Some practical joker sent a silly person around the district with a singed stick or other small firebrand that had been extinguished in holy water, which the joker told his dupe to divide into four parts, and give to four persons in four households, telling them that the cholera would carry them off unless each one did the same. In this way, 16 persons, and 64, and 256, etc. etc. got this fire till the whole countryside was a laughing stock for Protestants.

The ashes were carried east to County Carlow and south to County Wexford. People swore they saw a new comet in the sky, others saw angels. Protestants along the way, far from laughing, were convinced the long-feared Catholic uprising had begun. In six days the ashes were spread 400 miles before hysteria died down. "Though this was a bit of barbarous folly," said O'Sullivan, "it shows how easy it is to induce the Children of the Gael towards good or evil, with little urging. People say it was the ministers that set the thing going, in revenge for opposition to the tithes."

September 1. Kilkenny is in a very bad state with the cholera. William M'Cormack the solicitor died suddenly in Kilkenny of it yesterday. He was buried this morning at his family burial ground. It was medical doctors that put the remains into the grave for everybody else was afraid. A hundred and fifteen persons caught this fatal malady in Kilkenny. Only eleven persons recovered. Seventy have died and the remainder are still ill.

Throughout Ireland, 25,000 people died of cholera in the 1832 epidemic.

8

Cholera

*E*ARLY IN 1832 the newspapers of British North America carried fearful accounts of the new disease sweeping through Europe. The opening of the emigration season was awaited with a dread that a well-meaning article in the *Quebec Mercury* did nothing to dispel.

Doctors knew of no cure, said the newspaper, nor did they know what caused the disease. Some blamed the weather and recommended burning barrels of tar and firing off cannon to change atmospheric pressure. Others, somewhat closer to the mark, believed that cholera came from the miasma thrown off by rotting garbage. No one suggested, nor would they for another twenty years, that it was caused by infected food and water and was spread by its victims and by flies and dirt. Cholera, like the Black Plague of the 14th century, thrived on ignorance, but at least the symptoms were known, as the *Quebec Mercury* reported in frightening detail:

Symptoms: giddiness, sick stomach, nervous agitation, intermittent, slow or small pulse, cramps beginning at the tips of the fingers and toes, and rapidly approaching the trunk, giving the first warning. Vomiting or purging come on; the features become sharp and contracted, the eye sinks, the look is expressive of terror and wildness; the lips, face, neck, hands, feet, and soon after, the thighs, arms and whole surface assume a leaden hue, purple or black and deep brown tint, according to the complexion of the individual. The skin is deadly cold, the voice nearly gone. There are spasms in legs, thighs and loins....

The only comfort the Quebec Medical Board could suggest was that the patient be kept warm, with poultices of mustard and linseed on the stomach, and be plied with brandy, sal volatile or peppermint cloves in hot water or, in severe cases, forty drops of laudanum, the alcoholic tincture of opium that the Victorians relied on for a variety of diseases.

In Quebec, a doctor who had served in India and knew of cholera's extreme contagion said the first line of defence must be a *cordon sanitaire* to stop the cholera before it could get in among the population. The authorities at Quebec City, taking his advice, put their faith in quarantine, and time and geography worked in their favour, at least in the beginning. Since the river would be closed by ice until March, there would be time to find and equip a quarantine site far enough away from the city for safety, and close enough for reasonable access. On February 25 the Assembly of Lower Canada created an "Act to establish Boards of Health within the Province to enforce an effectual system of Quarantine." This despite a warning from Lord Aylmer, Governor of Lower Canada, that a quarantine station might do more harm than good by focusing the disease and acting as a breeding ground.

The site chosen was the hilly, wooded Grosse Isle, thirty miles down the St. Lawrence from Quebec City and just off the south-shore village of Montmagny. Despite its name, it was small – a mile long and half a mile wide – and apparently was called Grosse Isle because it was the largest of the islands around, though another theory suggests its name was a corruption of Île de Grace. The clay river bed and the huddle of protective islands provided a natural harbour that stretched for three miles, an anchorage for 150 ships. The government rented Grosse Isle from its owner, a notary who lived on the mainland, without telling the island's sole occupant, a farmer named Pierre Duplain.

Before the first emigrant ships appeared in the St. Lawrence, a company of the 32nd Regiment landed on Grosse Isle, commandeered the home of the indignant farmer and began to put up a few rough buildings to serve as a small hospital, sheds for transients, a bakery and a commissary. On Telegraph Hill, the highest on the island at 120 feet, they erected a mast to semaphore messages to Montmagny and hence by overland relay to the Citadel in Quebec City. To discourage ships seeking to evade quarantine, three cannon were mounted overlooking the anchorage, but in fact they were used only for signalling. No vessel was to pass upstream without a certificate of health, and those with illness aboard were to be quarantined for a month.

Ships started arriving in the first week of May, and by the first days of June the quarantine officers had accounted for 15,000 emigrants on 397 ships without any cholera reported. The most suspicious arrival had been the *Hebron* from Dublin, which reported that thirty-two emigrants had died at sea, but she was cleared at Grosse Isle on grounds there was no sickness aboard when she arrived. Inspections were sketchy because of lack of staff, and some vessels ignored the quarantine station and went right up to Quebec City. There were rumours of cholera at the Marine and Emigrant Hospital at Quebec City, but the city's inspecting physician, Dr. Joseph Morrin, was only prepared to admit there were "symptoms in many particulars resembling cholera" and cases of smallpox.

On June 3 Captain James Hudson brought his brig, *Carricks*, to anchor at Grosse Isle after a harrowing voyage from Dublin in which forty-two of his 133 passengers had died from "some unknown disease." Despite the danger signs, the survivors were given a clean bill of health and allowed to proceed.

On June 7 the survivors of the *Carricks*, released from quarantine, reached Quebec City on the river steamer *Voyageur*, and those who did not go on to Montreal dispersed to their lodgings in the city. Next day a man died in a waterfront boarding house, and two others within twenty-four hours. "Only then," recalled a doctor, "did the truth flash on our minds." The disease the authorities had worked so hard to contain had broken out of quarantine. Given the general ignorance of the disease, this had been inevitable, and the only hopeful aspect was that so many emigrants had already arrived – almost half the Irish emigration for the year – and gone up-river in relatively good health to Upper Canada. On the evening of June 9, the *Quebec Mercury* spread the dreadful news:

CHOLERA

It is our painful duty to appraise the public that this disorder has actually appeared in the city. Since yesterday morning eight cases have occurred which by eleven of the faculty [of Medicine] are declared to have all the symptoms of Spasmodic Cholera. Three deaths have occurred previous to noon this day, and there were two others whose lives were despaired of. The disease first appeared in a boarding house on Champlain Street kept by a person named Roach. The patients are emigrants and are said to be some of those who were landed on Thursday from the Steam Boat *Voyageur*. One Canadian has been seized with the disorder; he had been working on board a ship and a woman is said to have been attacked by it at Cap Blanc.

Three o'clock: We have just heard from undoubted authority that fifteen cases of Cholera have appeared since yesterday and seven have terminated fatally.

Within the next few days the cholera exploded into a major epidemic in the hot, spring weather. The hospital in Quebec City, like the half-built station at Grosse Isle, was overwhelmed, the staff too overworked to keep the wards clean. One doctor was so busy for two weeks in late June he had no time to take off his boots, and napped where and when he could. Medical stations identified by yellow flags were set up to dispense medicine; for those who could find no lodging, tents were erected for 500 people on the Plains of Abraham.

Normal life in the city broke down when farmers refused to come in with food. People fled into the country, spreading infection to the riverside towns of Trois Rivières, Lévis and Sorel, despite guards posted to turn them away. There were sinister rumours, never proven, that victims were dumped into mass graves before they had breathed their last. By the last week of June, 700 cases of cholera had been reported, 420 of them fatal. On some days it seemed the church bells rarely stopped tolling, and Louis-Joseph Papineau, the Quebec nationalist, accused the British of "enticing sick emigrants into the country in order to decimate the ranks of French Canadians." Many believed a great curse had been laid on the province.

Imagine our feelings [wrote young Mary McLean, who came from the village of Leitrim in Ulster] at finding ourselves in a plague-stricken city where men, women and children, smitten by cholera, dropped in the streets to die in agony; where business was paralyzed, and naught prevailed but sorrow mingled with dread and gloom.

The most skilful physicians were baffled by the scourge, and were not unanimous in accounting for even its presence, some asserting it came over in ships, others that the wind carried it, and to prove this latter theory, hoisted a long pole to the end of which was tied a leg of lamb, into the upper air. And certain it is that the side of the leg on which the wind blew turned putrid.

All this was told us by a man whose whole family had been swept out of existence by cholera. While he was speaking, people passed us, each holding between the teeth a piece of stick, or cane, about the length of a hand, as thick as the stem of a clay tobacco pipe on the end of which was stuck a piece of smoking tar. We learned this was used as a preventative.

Mary McLean was sixteen, a "perfectly healthy Irish girl" when she left Leitrim. She became ill during the month-long crossing, and while walking in Quebec City she collapsed in the street and was hurried to the fever hospital on the outskirts of town.

I soon found myself on one of those camp beds which were placed in the wards in such as way as to accommodate as large a number of patients as possible, and off of which many a one rolled while suffering indescribable torments from the deadly cramps of Asiatic Cholera which now had me in its grasp. At the head of each bed was fastened a card on which was written the name of the occupant – provided he or she could tell it. In many cases this was an impossibility, and numbers of victims were never identified.

I was now in a veritable house of torture, where the most appalling shrieks, groans and prayers and curses filled the air continually and, as if in answer to all this, day and night from the shed outside, came the tap, tap, tap of the workmen's hammers, as they drove the nails into rough coffins which could not be put together hastily enough for the many whose shrieks subsided into moans, which gradually died away into that silence not to be broken; and whose poor bodies were then carried to the deadhouse in the hospital yard, coffined, piled on the dead cart – a substitute for hearses – and then hurried off to what was called the cholera burying ground. So great was the mortality at the time, corpses were buried five and six deep with layers of lime between, in one grave.

Mary McLean lay in hospital six weeks, nursed by her mother, who gave her water and lemon juice and thin gruel, and, as she grew stronger, a little milk and porridge and bread and butter. Three of her brothers fell ill and she was the only one to recover. When she left the hospital she saw a pile of clothing "as big as a house," which had been collected from the dead.

By early July there were 1,000 dead in Montreal, which, with a population of 27,000, was the largest city in the Canadas. The waterfront transit sheds of the Emigrant Society were turned into a hospital, forcing healthy inmates on to the streets to make room for the sick. One shed had no floor, and the patients lay on piles of straw, "men, women and children, the convalescent, dying and dead, laid in an irregular line." When the Montreal General Hospital refused to accept cholera patients, a barn-like structure of rough boards with holes for windows was built for them on St. Denis Street.

John Anderson, writing to his parents in Ulster on July 1, said, "It has pleased the Lord to visit Quebec with Cholera of Morbus and it is raging here to a great extent. It has carried off upwards of 3,000 people. It has pleased the Lord to visit our little family by a stroke of death. Little Jane is no more. She took bad on June 13 and died the 17th. She was buried about 4 o'clock in the evening, and she was the 50th corpse entered the graveyard that day, and 28 of them lying unburied."

The Montreal *Gazette,* most of whose printers had failed to show up for work, appealed for calm. "A panic of an almost incredible nature," said the *Canadian Courant,* "seems to have taken hold of the whole body of citizens and deprived them of mind to an extent exceeding nothing of a similar nature which has ever been witnessed in Montreal." "We none of us go into town," wrote a businessman. "Numbers are moving into the country. Yesterday thirty-four *corps* [sic] passed our house. Till this hour, twenty-three. Besides what goes to the old burial ground and the Catholic ground, twelve carts are employed by the Board of Health to carry away the dead who are interred without prayers. All the schools are broke up and it is dreadful to see the immense numbers of carts with yellow flags."

When boatmen began refusing to take emigrants on to Upper Canada, thousands were stranded in Montreal, described by a journalist as an "immense army, much exposed, and ill equipped." Some set out for Upper Canada in wagons and on foot and others spread the disease into New England and New York state.

The first cases in Upper Canada were reported June 17 at Prescott on the St. Lawrence, seven days by boat from Montreal, and threw the town into a "dreadful state of consternation." The next day it was in Kingston, where the *Kingston Chronicle* increased the climate of dread with a poem.

> From south to north hath the cholera come,
> He came like a despot king;
> He hath swept the earth with a conqueror's stoop,
> And the air with a spirit's wing,
> We shut him out with a girdle of ships,
> And a guarded quarantine;
> What ho! now which of your watches slept?

The Cholera's past your line!
There's a curse on the blessed sun and air,
What will he do for breath?
For breath, which was once but a word for life,
Is now but a word for death…
The months pass on, and the circle spreads,
And the time is drawing nigh,
When each street may have a darkened house,
Or a coffin passing by.

On June 20 cholera was reported in York, then a town of 6,000 people, where the *Canadian Freeman* railed against the presence of stagnant pools of water "emitting deadly exhalations" and complained that "yards and cellars sent forth a stench from rotten vegetables, sufficient almost to itself to produce a plague." Magistrates tried in vain to have the streets cleaned, a 10 o'clock curfew was imposed, and families locked themselves in their houses. Sir John Colborne, the Lieutenant Governor, set aside a "day of public fasting, humiliation and prayer, against the dangers threatened by the progress of a very grievous disease which it hath pleased Almighty God in the dispensation of his providence to visit several parts of our Dominion." At Cobourg, the Reverend Anson Green said people were turning to religion: "The excitement created by the cholera induced many careless ones to think of their latter end, and to pray for pardon."

In Hamilton, where cholera appeared early in July, authorities opened the jail and freed the prisoners, except those condemned to death, because "any other course would be downright murder." The dead included two prisoners and a warder, a man who had arrived with Richard Talbot's group in 1818. When the disease appeared in the Niagara Peninsula, all but thirty of the 400 labourers on the Welland Canal threw down their shovels and fled. Cholera devastated the Indian reservation at St. Regis and appeared as far up-country as Peterborough. Thriving on stagnant water and dirt, it spread among the Irish shanties by the Rideau Canal at Bytown, where there were thirty-two deaths in the first week of July. From Bytown it leaped 200 miles up the Ottawa River to a lumber camp at Fort Coulonge, where five deaths occurred.

On July 14 an emigrant newly arrived from Dublin wrote, "The cholera is quite abated at Grosse Isle, but it is taking its course through the towns and now prevails at Montreal and York. The agent, to whom our gentlemen had a letter at Quebec, died of the dreadful epidemic which, from the 4th of June to the 14th of July, carried off 3,500 persons, as I am informed, in that town."

The Chief Emigration Officer in Quebec, A.C. Buchanan, complained that emigrants were passed up-river without the quarantine procedures demanded by law. "Many emigrant ships still continue to arrive in a very dirty state, particularly those from Ireland," he reported. "The *Devoron* from Londonderry, with 250 passengers, arrived on Thursday evening exceedingly filthy; and when visited by this department on the following day at noon, many of the passengers were still in a dirty state."

The epidemic had waxed and waned at Grosse Isle. Late in June it had abated and inspections of incoming ships were abandoned, but were swiftly resumed with the arrival of more cholera ships. Early in August Captain Henry Reid, the military commander at Grosse Isle, reported: "We have upwards of 1,000 emigrants on shore, between the two sheds, and there are about 1,800 more at anchor, ready to take up their quarters as soon as the present occupants be got on board, which we have to effect in the course of tomorrow. The last two days have been very favourable, and you would have been delighted to see how assiduous the poor emigrants are in availing themselves of it, in washing and scrubbing, and we hope to send them to you in a perfect state of cleanliness and purity; but I assure you it requires everybody to be on the alert to preserve anything like regularity among them."

While most emigrants were Irish, there were Scots and English, including the Strickland sisters from Sussex, Catharine Parr Traill and Susanna Moodie. They were on their way with their husbands, retired army officers, to join their brother, Samuel, near Peterborough, and both passed through Grosse Isle quarantine, which they described in their diaries, Mrs. Traill being the first to arrive, on the brig *Laurel*:

August 12: We reached Grosse Isle yesterday evening. It is a beautiful rocky island, covered with groves of beech, birch, ash and fir-trees. There are several vessels lying at anchor close to the shore; one bears the melancholy symbol of disease, the yellow flag.... I amuse myself making little sketches of the fort and the surrounding scenery, or watching the groups of emigrants on shore. We have already seen the landing of the passengers of three emigrant ships. You may imagine yourself looking on a fair or crowded market, clothes waving in the wind or spread out on the earth, chests, bundles, baskets, men, women, and children, asleep or basking in the sun, some in motion busied with their goods, the women employed in washing or cooking in the open air, beside the wood fires on the beach; while parties of children are pursuing each other in wanton glee rejoicing in the newly-acquired liberty. Mixed with these you see the stately form and gay trappings of the sentinels, while the thin blue smoke of the wood fires, rising from above the trees, heightens the picture.

Though not permitted ashore, Mrs. Traill saw enough to condemn quarantine regulations. The emigrant sheds and commissariat buildings were too close to the hospital; the practice of making emigrants, sick and well, go ashore to wash and air their clothes gave the healthy every chance of taking the infection from those afflicted. "Many valuable lives have been wantonly sacrificed," she said, "by placing the healthy in the immediate vicinity of infection, besides subjecting them to many other sufferings, expenses, and inconvenience, which the poor exiles might well be spared."

In Montreal, Mrs. Traill wrote, "cholera had made awful ravages, and its devastating effects were to be seen in the darkened dwellings and the mourning habiliments of all classes." Whole streets seemed depopulated; in one house seventeen had died, the only survivor a child of seven. She found the weather sultry, the oppressive heat unrelieved by the frequent thunder showers. She was about to leave for the healthier region of Peterborough when she contracted cholera herself, and though it turned out to be mild she described it as "mortal agony." "The remedies applies were bleeding, a portion of opium, blue pills, and some sort of broth." The remedies, and the attentions of two maids at Nelson's Hotel, cured her and she continued on her journey to Peterborough.

Susanna Moodie, her sister, arrived at Grosse Isle on August 28 and found twenty-five ships at anchor off what was now called Cholera Bay. From the anchorage on the "broad glittering river" she was struck by the beauty of the scene. To the north lay a range of hills; to the south the fertile fields around Montmagny were dotted with white houses and churches "whose slender spires and bright roofs shone like silver when they caught the last rays of the sun." Grosse Isle, from that distance, was a green, enticing island "with its neat farm houses at the eastern point, and its bluff at the western extremity crowned with the telegraph – the middle space occupied by tents and sheds for the cholera patients, and its wooded shores dotted over with motley groups." On closer examination – unlike her sister she was permitted ashore – she was shocked by the crowding, hardship and "confusion of Babel."

"A crowd of many hundred Irish emigrants had been landed, and all the motley crew – men, women and children – who were not confined by sickness to the sheds (which greatly resembled cattle pens) were employed in washing clothes or spreading them out on rocks and bushes to dry." They crowded around fires cadging pots in which to boil water, "all shouting and yelling in his or her uncouth dialect, and all accompanied their vociferations with violent and extraordinary gestures." The sergeant in charge, hard pressed to maintain order, assured her, "They have no shame – and under no restraint." There were thieves among them, he said, and they celebrated their arrival with "singing, drinking, dancing, shouting and cutting antics that would surprise the leader of a circus."

After a week in quarantine, Mrs. Moodie, her husband and baby proceeded to Montreal where the "cholera was at its height, and the fear of infection, which increased the nearer we approached the shore, cast a gloom over the scene. The sullen toll of the death-bell, the exposure of ready-made coffins in the undertakers' windows, and the oft-recurring notice placarded on the walls, of funerals furnished at such and such a place at cheapest rate and shortest notice, painfully reminded us at every turning of the street that death was everywhere – perhaps lurking in our very path."

"It will be a miracle if you escape," the customs officer told her. "Hundreds of emigrants die daily." He also told her about Dr. Cholera, otherwise Stephen Ayres, who had appeared from the United States and was administering a cure of boiled maple bark. "For some days we all took him for a quack," said the customs man, "and would have no faith in him at all, although he performed some wondrous cures upon poor folks who could not afford to send for a doctor.... The very doctors sent for him to cure them, and it is to be hoped that in a few days he will banish cholera from the city." When Mrs. Moodie saw Dr. Cholera he looked like a gypsy with long black hair and beard. It was impossible to know how many people benefitted from his free ministrations, though Ayres himself later said his "visit to this city is generally acknowledged to have dissipated panic and restored confidence."

Canadians, who in happier times would have helped the 37,000 Irish emigrants who arrived that year, shunned them now as carriers of death. The mood among the French of Lower Canada was reflected in the words of Charles-Seraphin Rodier, a popular politician: "When I see my county in mourning and my land presenting to my eye nothing but one large cemetery, I ask what has been the cause of these disasters. To which my father, my brother and my beloved mother and the voices of thousands of my fellow citizens respond from their tombs – it is immigration."

Sampson Brady, newly arrived from Ulster, wrote from Montreal on September 17: "There are many tradesmen and labourers going about idle and can't get work. The poor emigrants that went up country are dying in hundreds. Those who have money enough are returning to their native homes as soon as possible."

By the end of September most of the emigrants had arrived for the year, though a few ships, such as the *Billy Booth* from Belfast, which had taken three months to make the voyage, continued to limp in. One of the passengers was Dr. William Campbell of Belfast, en route to Peterborough to take up practice:

We left Belfast on Sunday morning, July 1, and the day following the work of Death commenced. The first death was that of an old man of Cholera Morbus. Then came Tuesday when our carpenter lay down, affected in the same manner. My professional skills and ingenuity were called into action. He died in the course of a few hours, affected in the strangest manner I have ever beheld. The fates preserve me from the ague of Upper Canada, but God deliver me from cholera. Then four of the sailors took badly, I think mainly from imagination, and the passengers began to take alarm. Some would have the captain put into harbour. Others wished him to proceed. The storms arose and the winds blew. The captain cursed so that he might have been heard distinctly on the coast of Waterford. All was confusion. I was as busy as a journeyman grave digger, some-times in the cabin, sometimes in the steerage, and often in the forecastle. The sickness prevailed for twelve weeks before we anchored at Quebec. We had not less than twenty-four deaths, mostly cholera. The captain took it himself the very night we anchored at Grosse Isle, where we were in quarantine for a fortnight.

Only with the coming of cold weather in November did the authorities feel safe in declaring the epidemic at an end. An estimated 10,000 people had caught the disease, on ship or ashore, and the death toll figures varied wildly depending on the source. A.C. Buchanan estimated 2,350 had died on the ships or in quarantine. The number buried on Grosse Isle in what was called the Valley of Death, one of the few places where the soil was deep enough for graves, was never established but rumours persisted that 1,000 had been buried there.

Inland, where municipalities had been obliged to deal with the epidemic, records were either neglected or inaccurate in the midst of the crisis, though the available figures from health boards, burial records and the like suggest a total of upwards of 6,000 deaths, or half the people estimated to have contracted the disease. The heaviest casualties were in Montreal, where close to 2,000 died, followed in Quebec City with 1,500. In these cities the cholera struck with greater force than in towns of similar size in Ireland and England. In York the Board of Health put the death toll at 273, and that for all Upper Canada at well over 500.

At Cobourg late that year there was a curious footnote to the cholera epidemic, when the body of an emigrant was found cast up on the shore of Lake Ontario. The *Cobourg Star* of November 14, 1832, published a poem about the incident, which said in part:

> On the sand of the shore, a bloated corpse,
> He lay where the waves had thrown him,
> No wail of the widow lamented his loss,
> No friend stood by to own him.
>
> Yet was he unknown? Ah no! for his ways
> Had been one wild course of error;
> And some there were who remember'd the days
> When his name was a name of terror ...

The dead man was one James Dempsey, who had been a leader of a band of terrorist Whitefeet in County Offaly. While nearing Cobourg on the steamer *William IV,* he had fallen overboard and drowned. His body was found on the shoreline of property owned by James Calcutt, who claimed to have fled Ireland to escape the very terrorists whom the dead man had led.

IN 1833, THE EMIGRATION to British North American totalled only 17,500, much less than half the number of the previous year. As for the past decade and more, virtually all the emigrants to British North America came to the Canadas or New Brunswick, a trend a Colonial Office memorandum explained as follows: "The colonies in North America to which emigrants can with advantage proceed are Lower Canada, Upper Canada and New Brunswick. From the reports received from the other British colonies in North America, namely Prince Edward Island, Newfoundland, Nova Scotia and Cape Breton, it appears they do not contain the means either of affording employment at wages to a considerable numbers of emigrants, or of settling them upon land."

Few cases of cholera were reported in 1833, and those like Thomas Radcliffe of Dublin who had survived the 1832 epidemic were able to get on with their lives. Radcliffe wrote of the grief of having lost a child, as he worked his farm at Adelaide between Lake Huron and Lake Erie: "The despondency we suffered at having our dear little girl taken off in a few hours by that fatal pestilence, and our anxiety for the safety of the other children, caused our difficulties and privations in settling to be doubly felt. We now, thank God, are in perfect health, our spirits beginning to revive, and absolutely enjoying, if not a luxurious, at least a comfortable residence in our own log house. It consists of a cellar, three rooms, and a small store room in the principal storey, and two bedrooms in the roof. My lot is beautifully undulating, a creek or small river winding through its entire length between rich flats."

An emigrant from County Roscommon, writing from the Huron Tract in Upper Canada where the recently-formed Canada Company had acquired land which it was selling off in parcels, wrote: "The cholera raged very much when we arrived, taking numbers off in every quarter, yet we all escaped, thank God, nor have we had any cases of it since last fall. We find ourselves tolerably well settled though so short a time in the country. We have got a great many Irishmen on the Tract, who are good neighbours and settlers."

The spring of 1834 brought a renewal of the heavy migration that had begun in the famine conditions of 1830 and, despite a new flare-up of cholera in Ireland, the weekly reports signed by A.C. Buchanan at Quebec City were encouraging, with no mention of the disease. He was mainly concerned, it seemed, with the large number of ship-wrecks, which totalled seventeen. At the end of May he noted "a better class of emigrants," and on June 21 he reported: "A considerable number of persons of the working classes arrived this week, principally from Ireland; they apparently were all able to pay their way; the greatest demand in Upper Canada for persons of the working class, particularly at public works for labourers and artificers, with the high rate of wages, induced the whole to proceed thither. I have reports this week from the emigrant agents at Toronto, Lachine, Prescott and Bytown, all testifying as to good circumstances of the emigrant population, and the total absence of sickness or distress among them so far this season. This city and Montreal have never been more free from inconvenience from emigrant population, and the interference of the benevolent has been less required this season than for the last five years."

Despite Buchanan's optimistic reports, all was not well at Grosse Isle. Requests for more staff had been refused and there was animosity among the team assembled for what, considering reports of cholera in Ireland, threatened to be a difficult season. Dr. Charles Poole, the medical superintendent, was accused by a staff member of tyranny, whereupon Poole counter-charged that his accuser was a drunk and got his resignation. The supply of fresh water was a problem, and it was discovered that the physician responsible for boarding incoming ships was failing to visit vessels suspected of carrying cholera. He tried to excuse this dereliction of duty on grounds his visits would tend to spread the disease. Once the season began, promising an influx of emigrants almost as great as that of 1832, the staff at Grosse Isle was overwhelmed with work.

One of the first ships, the *Mary* from Cork, had lost seven passengers and fifty of her 300 emigrants were suffering from fever which the Grosse Isle doctors diagnosed as typhus and measles. Little attention was paid to the ship once it was decided there was no cholera aboard, and the captain protested, "There are fifty of my passengers in hospital at present, and the remainder must soon be there if something is not done for them." Throughout May and June ships were permitted to sail on to Quebec City. If there was cholera aboard it was either not diagnosed or not mentioned. The government was suspected of suppressing news of disease for fear of causing panic.

Then on June 29 the Emigrants Hospital in Quebec City admitted a patient from the *Elinore*, from Dublin, said to be suffering from ague. It turned out to be cholera and within a few days there could be no doubt that Canada faced another epidemic. Eighty-seven deaths were reported at Quebec City for the week ending July 14, the first week records were kept that year, and the outbreak had spread to Montreal, where the toll reached forty a day by the end of the month. The Montreal Sanitary Committee complained that, far from being a safeguard, Grosse Isle was propagating the disease.

"The sheds erected there do not in size or structure appear to have been for the protection of human beings," the committee said. "Indeed, the emigrant possessed of self respect often preferred remaining on the bare rock, exposed to the inclemency of the weather, rather than sleep among the congregated hundreds in the sheds, lest he should thereby hasten the approach of a disease, that was hurrying on every side, his fellow passengers to eternity."

On August the 10th the *Mercury* of Quebec City reported that as of the previous day there were 2,300 emigrants on Grosse Isle, and many vessels waiting offshore. Among them were the ship *Ganges* from Liverpool with eight sick and forty-five deaths among her 393 passengers, and the bark *Larch* from Sligo with 150 sick and 108 deaths while at sea, which accounted for half her passenger list. The bark *Naprima* of Dublin carried seventeen sick and seven dead. The newspaper said hospital space on the island was overcrowded and the tents supposed to be for the healthy were filled with dying people "by the dozens," among them two ship masters. More than a thousand had died at Quebec City and 880 in Montreal.

In Upper Canada, where the outbreak ran a course similar to that of 1832, but with fewer deaths, a correspondent for the *Montreal Gazette* with a taste for the biblical, reported, "We have been visited with a noisome pestilence that walketh in darkness and wasteth at noonday." The death toll at York, which had now been renamed Toronto, was close to 200.

There was confusion, as usual, over the total of cholera deaths that year, though it was in general lower than in the previous outbreak, perhaps less than half the total of 1832. At Grosse Isle, where reasonably complete records were kept, 264 people had died, 158 from cholera, and 844 patients had been admitted to hospital. The dead included five soldiers pressed into service as nurses.

Cholera appeared in Nova Scotia and New Brunswick, though when it broke out in Halifax, a city of 14,000, the authorities, fearing panic, had said nothing. Only when people began to talk of seeing bodies transported through the streets before dawn was the epidemic officially confirmed. As the deaths mounted, Dalhousie College, then situated on Grand Parade at the foot of Citadel Hill, was turned into a hospital, trenches were dug in the burial grounds at Fort Massey south of the town, barrels of tar were burned in the streets and large quantities of lime were distributed to disinfect houses. By the time the epidemic ran its course in October, 320 people had died, including sixty soldiers from the garrison.

In Saint John, New Brunswick, which received 2,000 emigrants that year, the cholera came late, detected in the York Point emigrant neighbourhood in September. A cholera hospital was established and an effort made to isolate the houses of the sufferers, but by the end of November, when cold weather came to contain the disease, the toll stood at fifty. Road blocks and the fumigation of travellers and mail kept it from spreading up the St. John River Valley, but there were reports of cholera in the Miramichi ports of Newcastle and Chatham.

9

"Off We Go
to Miramichi"

*I*N THE 19TH CENTURY no province was more Irish than New Brunswick. There had been Irish putting down roots long before the Loyalists arrived in 1783, but it was the collapse of the Irish economy in 1815, coupled with New Brunswick's labour shortage, that brought the colony its Irish flavour. During the next decade an estimated 35,000 arrived.

They settled in Saint John, where they built their first Catholic church, and in Irishtown, where Moncton now stands; and a group of Protestant Irish established in 1817 the community of New Bandon on the Baie des Chaleurs. In Northumberland County, where the Miramichi River ports of Chatham and Newcastle had become the centres of the booming timber trade, Irish competed for work with lumberjacks from Maine, and such were the battles that troops had to be called in from Fredericton, the capital, to keep the peace.

A steady flow of Irish tradesmen and farmers was also arriving in the Miramichi, respectable family men who established a Hibernian Society at Chatham in 1824. The white pine trade was booming and the region was prosperous when, in the autumn of 1825, tragedy struck. The Great Miramichi Fire of October 7 and 8 that year swept down on the towns of Newcastle and Douglastown, destroying at least 200 homes, killing 160 people and blackening hundreds of square miles of timberland. "In the awful light," wrote Robert Cooney, an Irish journalist who worked for a local newspaper, "the terrified people were seen hurrying for their lives and not knowing where to look for safety. Many of them believed the Day of Judgement was at hand." In the damp and relatively treeless Ireland such fires were unknown. That there was no greater death toll was due to the Miramichi River, which halted the fire so that Chatham was spared.

In the wake of the fire, hundreds were forced to seek new homes. Some treked north up the coast to establish Irish communities at Pokemouch and Tabusintac. Others went south to Buctouche on the Northumberland Strait, where Francis McPhelan of Donegal was to become the first Catholic to join the Executive Council of the New Brunswick Assembly. Timothy Lane led a group down the coast, where he established the Catholic settlement of Melrose near Cape Tormentine and the Nova Scotia border. He was joined by such Newfoundland Irish as James Carrol, a wounded veteran of the Wexford rebellion of 1798, and Timothy Harnett, a scholar and poet who arrived by way of Halifax.

Though the older settlers, the Empire Loyalists, controlled the colony's political life, they were rapidly becoming outnumbered by the Irish. In prosperous years, when labour was needed, Irish immigrants were usually welcomed, but in the boom and bust of the lumber trade there were many lean years when they were shunned. "The most miserable and squalid emigrants ever beheld here this season have landed

on our shores," grumbled John Street,. a Chatham merchant-politi-
cian, in 1827. "Many of them are disabled, unable to work, by which
measure the country is inundated with the scum of the population at
home, and half of the paupers shipped off." Though the passenger
laws were never adequate, the government had temporarily abolished
all of them that year.

In what was a particularly miserable year for emigration to New
Brunswick, an emigration official complained that the brokers showed
little concern over "whether the helpless victims of their cupidity perish on the voyage or live to spread disease and death among the people
on whose shores they may be landed." As early as May 29, the season
hardly begun, the Chatham *Mercury* reported, "The number of emigrants who have already arrived at the port is about 1,500." At Saint
John a shipload of needy Irish was sent back to Ireland. The policy of
granting free land had recently lapsed, and the efforts of Sir Howard
Douglas, the Lieutenant Governor, to help settlers with free tools and
seed were thwarted by penny pinchers at the Colonial Office, who
did, however, allow him to make contributions to the various emigrant societies springing up to help the needy.

Another Lieutenant Governor, Sir Archibald Campbell, urged a
few years later that emigrants be limited to Scots and English, burying
his bigotry in rhetoric. "No one more appreciates than I do, or is more
ready to do justice to the many excellent qualities inherent in the Irish
character, and in any other Colony than a frontier one in North
American I should be the first to encourage and invite the Irish to the
Country," he said. "But it cannot be too often or too strongly repeated
that the facility, which this province affords them of indulging a naturally wandering disposition, added to the ties, associations and in-
ducements, which lead them to the States – have hitherto rendered the
great body of Irish emigration to this quarter, not only useless, but
extremely burdensome to the Province, and worse than a dead loss to
the British Empire." For Sir Archibald, turning a blind eye to the Irish
contribution to the lumber industry, no Irish need apply.

But still they came, from Ulster, Tipperary, Clare, Limerick, Kilkenny – and particularly from County Cork, the home of William and Ann Fitzgerald, and when the Fitzgeralds arrived in the summer of 1830, the Irish accounted for at least a quarter of New Brunswick's population. The Fitzgeralds were Catholics, like so many emigrants to the Miramichi, but the notable thing about them was not their religion but where they came from – the coastal region of bare hills, wind-bent hedges and precious gullies of arable land on the western edge of County Cork. Known in ancient times as Ivagha, the Western Land, it had been a separate world, isolated from such rich and coveted lands as the Blackwater, sixty miles to the east over the mountains. In the past it had produced few emigrants, but by 1830 the tide of emigration was washing into remote parishes that few had normally left except by way of the graveyard. Now, as Lord Carbery, the major landowner, noted, people were starting to leave, and among them the Fitzgeralds from the parish of Schull.

The few glimpses of the parish, and village, of Schull – named for ancient Sgoil Mhuire, or Our Lady's School – reveal great poverty for all but the handful of English who had seized the land from the O'Mahonys in the 17th century. Richard Boyle, the English-born Earl of Cork, controlled the market town of Skibbereen in the Ilen Valley, twelve miles south of Schull, and with his crony Sir William Hull established a fishery on the Schull-Mizen Peninsula, the Land's End of Ireland. Hull, who assumed the title Vice Admiral of the province of Munster, though he had no navy, increased his profits by trading with pirates who infested the coves around Leamcon House, which overlooks Roaring Water Bay to this day.

By the 1820s, 15,000 people lived in the parish of Schull: Fitzgeralds, Harrigans, O'Sullivans, Luceys, O'Mahonys, O'Driscolls and the other children of the birthrate explosion that had doubled Ireland's population in two generations. They lived in little farm clusters, or clachans, on the third of the parish – hardly more than 30,000 acres – that provided arable ground. Their farming methods were ancient, depending on the long, narrow spade with which they planted potatoes and dug peat to warm their whitewashed cabins of stone, mud and sod. Through the worst years of the 18th-century Penal Laws they had clung to their Catholic faith. A correspondent for the *Cork Mercantile Chronicle*, writing on December 12, 1825, said: "I saw from the public road at least 2,000 men and women kneeling on the side of a barren mountain, assisting in silence and apparent reverence at the ceremony of the Mass, literally no canopy over them but the broad expanse of the heavens, whilst a heavy winter's shower descended on their uncovered heads."

In the parish's two villages, Schull and Ballydehob, there were hardly more than 1,000 people, several hundred of whom were employed at Lord Audley's copper mines at Cappach and Audley's Cove, and others in the slate quarry at Foilnamuck. Those who found work on the roads earned seven pence a day, and those who could find none tramped east each summer for seasonal work on the harvests.

Outside the villages, most of the people were cottiers, living on an acre of land rented in exchange for labouring on the landowner's fields. Under the system known as conacre, they had tenure from one year to the next, and once the potato crop was harvested their acre reverted to the landlord, who might, if he wished, rent it to someone else entirely.

"All tenants may very properly be called labourers," wrote the local priest, Father James Barry, "as they hold in general but small lots, and till them with their own hands. Such may be said to have constant employment; there are others who have no ground and only occasional employment, in number about 500 or 600." Father Barry was replying to a questionnaire circulated by the government, and when asked what the people ate and what they wore, he replied, "Potatoes and milk in the interior of the parish, potatoes and fish by the seaside, and the great majority of all parts, potatoes only; clothing wretched, perhaps one in every six may have clothing to appear at a house of worship on Sundays." While there had been no actual cases of starvation since he had arrived – he was new to the parish – there had been times when the "ordinary necessities of life would have prolonged the existence of our fellow beings."

Two thirds of the landowners were absent, their estates managed by agents or middlemen, or as Father Barry put it, "the middlemen and their poor tenants who sublet to labourers, who, in turn, work out the rent in seasons of hurry," which is to say the seasons of planting and harvesting. Among those landlords in residence was the aging Richard Hull, Sir William's descendant, at Leamcon House. Widely regarded as an "improving landlord," Hull claimed he had never evicted a tenant and though a Protestant he had given stone, timber and money to build a Catholic chapel when the old one fell down. Skibbereen, owned by the Anglo-Irish family of Bechers, and once a centre for the textile trade, had little industry now except brewing. Henry Inglis called it a "small, ugly town" when he rode through.

Of all the reasons for leaving the parish of Schull, the most pressing were economic. Ingles believed that religious discrimination played no large part any more, since the Catholic Emancipation Act in 1829. "In those districts where people find employment," he said, "Catholic and Protestant are alike comfortable, while in those where people are unemployed, Protestant and Catholic are alike miserable."

It was easier now to leave remote parishes such as Schull because timber ships in recent years had been fetching cargoes from Quebec and New Brunswick to the little west coast ports of Baltimore, Bantry and Crookhaven a few miles away. Ship masters, seeking some profit for their return voyage, were willing to take passengers at a cheap rate, more or less as human ballast. If people were willing to risk life and limb on one of these decrepit timber droghers, known as coffin ships, they could make the voyage for as little as thirty shillings a head, half the fare demanded for departure from Cork City, more than sixty miles away.

Protestant emigrants "in comfortable circumstances" now were being joined by people Father Barry described as "tradesmen, hardy labourers and farmers" such as William and Ann Fitzgerald and Ann's brother, Cornelius Harrigan. Neither William nor Ann was young, William being forty-three and Ann forty-one. They had eight children between the ages of two and twenty-three, some of whom had to be left behind for a year until their parents could find their feet in northeastern New Brunswick.

Like their neighbours, the Fitzgeralds and Harrigans probably could not read or write, and they left no account of their migration. The only reference to their voyage came from the Fitzgerald's daughter Mary Ann, who was seven at the time and recalled in later life that the ship "took a great deal of time" to reach New Brunswick and "there was a great deal of crying among the women." They had either saved money for the trip, or perhaps were helped by Ann's Harrigan relatives, since three Harrigans were listed among the most substantial Catholic farmers in the parish, partners in farms of twenty to thirty acres.

There is a gap in the history of the Fitzgeralds and Harrigans for the next two years. Perhaps they worked, like so many Irish, on the timber wharves or shipyards at Chatham or Newcastle on Miramichi Bay to earn money to buy some land, since the government had ceased granting it free. In 1833, the records show they had settled near Williamstown, seven miles up-river from Newcastle in the parish of North Esk. Known also as Irish Settlement, Williamstown had been colonized by Methodists from County Leitrim and consisted of a dozen log cabins scattered in clearings along the new road between the villages of Redbank and Middleton. The rocky soil was marginal, but it was their own, and ten miles away at Nelson they had their own place of worship, St. Patrick's Church, where Father Michael Egan served Catholics as far away as Chatham, Bartibog and Boisetown. Dennis Harrigan got a job as road supervisor and his twenty-three-year-old daughter, Ann, married an emigrant from Tipperary and lived nearby.

The Fitzgeralds and Harrigans around Williamstown – numbering twenty adults and children – touched off a chain migration of relatives and neighbours in the next few years, including John Kingston, his wife, Catherine, and their three children; Michael O'Brien and his wife, Bridget; and John Regan and Margaret Lucey, who married after their arrival in the province. A school was built despite conflict between Catholics and Methodists over how it should be conducted.

The Miramichi watershed, hundreds of miles of flat land covered by dark forests of pine and spruce, was so different from the breezy open landscapes and seascapes of west Cork that people called it the Black North. The whole population of Northumberland County was less than that of the parish of Schull in Ireland, and animals they had heard of only in tales – bears, wolves and moose – came down to their clearings on the tangled rivers that emptied into the Northwest and Southwest branches of the Miramichi and into Miramichi Bay.

Timber and fish were the main exports from the Miramichi when the Irish arrived, and though the land that slopes back from the river is shallow and stony they scratched a living selling farm produce to the lumber camps and the towns, where they also got winter work. One of the Irish success stories was how potato-planting cottiers learned to be lumbermen though they had never seen forests before or handled a felling axe. Robert Young, a Miramichi farmer, said he knew Irishmen "who had never previously touched an axe become first-rate choppers in three months." Within one or two generations, skilled Irish lumberjacks could be found not only in New Brunswick and the Canadas but out in the woods of Michigan, Wisconsin, Minnesota and farther west, harvesting the giants of the North American forest and running large timber companies.

"Our pleasure," wrote a correspondent for the *Gleaner* of Fredericton on May 14, 1833, "is to see a gang of stout fellows at dawn of an early morning with their axes on their shoulders, marching with a firm step 'to the woods'." There were dangers in the woods as well, and memorials to these perils are embedded in New Brunswick folksongs (most of them based on traditional Irish tunes) with their tales of death by falling trees and drowning on the timber drives when the logs were floated down-river in the spring.

"They were a hardy lot," said the New Brunswick lumberman Isaac Stephenson, "who mastered the variety of trades required by their occupation and were at home alike in forest, on farm and on stream." John McGregor described how, with the coming of autumn and the harvest in, they went about their logging. "Several of these people form what is termed a 'lumbering party' composed of persons who are either hired by a master lumberer who pays the wages and finds them provisions, or of individuals, who enter into an understanding with each other to have a joint interest in the proceeds of their labours. The necessary supplies and provisions, clothing, etc. are generally obtained from the merchants on credit, in consideration of receiving timber."

Farmers and their sons, seduced by the promise of cash and the glamour of a lumberman's life, neglected their land, and the province, unable to grow enough to feed itself, was forced to import most of its food, including potatoes, from other colonies or from Ireland. Almost 80 per cent of the population depended on the lumber industry which, according to Abraham Gesner in his book of advice to emigrants, "has taken away the bone and muscle from husbandry." Saint John, Chatham and Newcastle had been built on the timber, shipbuilding and fishing industries, with farming a poor fourth.

The eight years from 1827 to 1835 brought 65,000 Irish to New Brunswick, and though many used the province as a stepping stone to the American states, a large number stayed. Among them were Ann Fitzgerald's brother, Dennis Harrigan, who was fifty-one, and his wife, the former Catherine Driscoll, and their eight children, and they were only one of the ninety families that left Schull in 1835. There was a song the emigrants used to sing:

Off we go to Miramichi,
Off we go for sugar and tea,
The quicker we get there,
The better for we.

It was common practice for established settlers to arrange passage by mail for relatives and friends through shipping agents in Chatham, Newcastle or Saint John, and by 1839 the 245-ton brig *Dealey* was making regular runs from west Cork to New Brunswick. William Justice Deeley, a Bantry merchant, had her built in Saint John, and she made two or three trips a year, carrying out emigrants and bringing back timber, as did other vessels such as the *Wanderer*, which sailed out of Baltimore, the port for Skibbereen.

Patrick Nelligan came out in 1839 with his bride, Johanna Sullivan, from Dingle in County Kerry, sailing from Cork City in the brig *Ponsila* to Chatham, Johanna's father having emigrated several years earlier. The *Ponsila* took six weeks, colliding with an iceberg in dense fog on the Newfoundland Banks but escaping serious damage, and Johanna's father gave them a forty-acre farm he had hacked out of the wilderness at Escuminac on Miramichi Bay. They had three daughters and two sons, one of whom, John Emmett Nelligan, became a major lumberman in Wisconsin. He recalled in old age the way the Irish had lived in the Miramichi when he was a boy.

The Nelligans had half a dozen cows which the girls milked every morning and evening, a few sheep, a hog or two, and a few chickens. They were never short of milk, butter, beef, mutton, salt pork, or the wool from which they made their clothes. Wheat and potatoes were their crops, along with some vegetables. The Nelligan boys went hunting with an old flintlock rifle and fished for cod and herring in the bay. Tea was their only beverage, they ate a lot of berries, and the children went barefoot all summer, wearing their homemade leather boots only in the winter. They lived in a log cabin and their neighbours were Irish, French Canadians, English and Scots. The school was six miles away and closed in winter because of deep snow. The boys made friends with the Irish crews of the timber ships coming into the bay.

About 8,000 Irish came to New Brunswick in 1840, from the counties of Cork, Sligo and Londonderry, but by 1841 New Brunswick authorities were doing all they could to discourage emigration because the protective tariffs, on which the timber trade had been founded during the Napoleonic Wars, were withdrawn and New Brunswick was plunged into depression. It was not the first time, for timber was ever a boom and bust business, but it was worse than most of the depressions that plagued the province. "I am sorry to inform you that the province is in a bankrupt state," wrote Joseph Hunter, an army veteran from Sligo who had settled at Dalhousie in northern New Brunswick. "There is a Great Depression of trade here. We have now only twelve square rigged vessels in our harbour, whereas in former years at this period there were fifty to sixty. In Saint John there are no less than 5,000 paupers receiving relief from the province." Michael Whelan, whose parents came from County Laois, described that period in his poem "The Woods of Miramichi:"

> Our lumber is taken for half its cost,
> While the merchant profit reaps,
> Our farms are mortgaged away and lost,
> While the farmer works and weeps.

In 1843 the number of Irish arriving in New Brunswick dwindled to 1,000, and these often had to be supported by charity. Coming to Chatham with his wife, six children and a grandchild, Edward Carmony from Limerick sought work for more than a month. With nowhere to live and no prospects, he set off on foot with his family on a two-week journey of a hundred miles to Fredericton. Three of his sons found work on farms along the way, but Carmony himself found nothing and was reduced in Fredericton to begging.

Thousands of Irish who had put down roots were forced to move on. One group went up the St. Lawrence to establish themselves in the Ottawa Valley, where they were known for their song "Off We Go to Miramichi" for years to come. Most went to the United States, following the lumbering. William and Ann Fitzgerald went to Wisconsin, and one of Ann's nephews, William Sauntry, became a timber baron in Minnesota, where he was known as the King of the St. Croix River.

Dennis Harrigan Junior, born in the Miramichi, travelled to Minnesota and then to Washington state, where his daughter gained some fame as the mother of Bing Crosby.

Those that remained – a half to two-thirds of those coming to New Brunswick over the years – made up about a third of the province's population. The greatest concentration was in Saint John and the surrounding countryside, where they were considerably more than half the population and included many Catholics, followed by the Miramichi, where they were somewhat less than half. In Charlotte County, which contains St. Andrews, a way station for people going to the States, half the heads of households were Irish in the 1840s.

There were several reports at this time that the Irish as a whole were settling in as good and useful citizens, despite a flareup in the early 1840s when there were political riots in the Miramichi in which gangs of Irish lumbermen, hired by the timber barons to pack the ballot boxes, staged riots in which one of them, James Ryan of Newcastle, lost his life. In 1844, for example, a correspondent for *Simmonds Colonial Magazine* reported that many thousands who had landed without a penny to their name had "become thrifty farmers in a very short time, having around them such comforts as they never enjoyed, nor ever could have enjoyed, in their own country." There were no particular reports of trouble between Irish Catholics and Protestants at this time, and it was only after the large influx of Catholic Irish during the Great Famine that trouble between the Orange and the Green flared up in the city of Saint John.

10

The Green and
the Orange

$\mathcal{F}$OR THE IRISH in Upper Canada, and particularly in the Ottawa Valley, where good land was scarce, the timber trade was a godsend. "It appears a matter of surprise," said a land surveyor in the Bathurst District, "how many people manage to obtain a livelihood." The answer, as often as not, lay in the lumber camps, with their prodigious appetite for manpower, and for pork, flour and potatoes for the woodsmen, and hay and oats for their horses and oxen. For the settler struggling to make ends meet, the lumber camp provided seasonal work.

In New Brunswick, where conditions were such that a settler could become a logging entrepreneur on his own, the lumber trade was a serious detriment to farming, for many neglected their farm work, but in the Ottawa Valley the Irish generally looked upon the lumber trade as a means of making extra money once their crops were in. The difference was principally due to the great distances involved in getting timber from the Ottawa Valley to market at Quebec City, calling for a great deal more capital than a settler could command. Those Irish who made good in the timber trade in the pioneer years were Protestants like Robert Grant and William Hodgins who came to the Carp Valley in 1818 with the Talbot group and were able to forge commercial ties in a Protestant-dominated province. Even so, Grant and Hodgins were essentially farmers and timber land speculators who avoided the major risks of the trade. Grant, the drapery clerk from Limerick, had apprenticed himself to Philemon Wright of Hull, the Yankee farmer who pioneered the Ottawa Valley timber trade in 1806, and then set up on his own as a supplier to the camps and finally owner of 1,400 acres of timber land.

The outstanding Irish lumberman of his time was John Egan, a Protestant from Galway, who arrived at the age of nineteen, worked as a clerk, went into business on his own as a camp supplier in the 1830s, and progressed to logging the Mississippi Valley and the Bonnechère farther north, where he established the town of Eganville. Known as the King of the Ottawa, Egan controlled 2,000 square miles of timber land, a territory a third the size of the province of Ulster, operated 100 camps and employed 3,500 men to topple the red and white pine, carve it into baulks of square timber and raft it to Quebec City for shipment overseas. The settlers were content to work for timber barons such as Egan, or George Bryson on the Mississippi, in the months when their farms were dormant and to go back to their land in the spring, nor did they venture far from home, leaving the lumbering that was reaching ever farther up the Ottawa River to the French Canadians who came from Quebec.

A similar pattern on a smaller scale developed on the Kawartha Lakes watershed behind Peterborough, where Mossom Boyd, whose roots lay in Ulster, rafted timber down the Trent River to Lake Ontario. One of the few Catholic settlers to try his hand, Dennis Shanahan, a Kerry man who had settled in Ennismore Township with the Peter Robinson people, turned to logging after first hiring out on the canals. Francis Young of the Robinson settlers operated a successful sawmill at Young's Point.

It was only in the early 1830s that Irish Catholics on the Ottawa began to go into the timber trade in a big way as hewers of wood. These were not settlers, but navvies brought in to dig the Rideau Canal, and when that was completed in 1832 they sought logging jobs traditionally held by French Canadians. Since the Irish had little experience in the woods, their method of seeking employment was to try to scare the French Canadians off, and this involved fighting. Bytown, once a canal construction camp and now a glorified timber depot, gained a reputation as the roughest community in the country.

The Irish lived in the east end of the town, in the miserable huddle of cabins called Lowertown or Corktown in the cranberry bog by the Rideau. They included young men like Martin Hennessy, Bobby Boyle and the seven Slavin brothers, brutalized by the hard, dangerous work on the canals. In Bytown the privileged were English or Scots, except for the likes of Nicholas Sparks from Wexford, who owned real estate, or Daniel O'Connor, a magistrate from Wexford.

Farmers in surrounding Nepean Township were Protestants, who outnumbered Catholics more than two to one. Alienated from the society around them, the Irish of Corktown found that even their church failed them, for the priests sent out from Ireland to Bytown in those early years were incompetent or worse. So their one abiding comfort lay in the nine drinking establishments in town where raw, white Canadian whiskey might be purchased at two shillings the gallon. Their favourite spot was Mother McGinty's, run by a woman who inspired verse.

> She kept the reckoning, ruled the roost,
> And swung an arm of potent might
> That few would dare to brave in fight;
> Yet she was a good natured soul
> As ever filled the flowing bowl.

When the lumbermen came in from the woods, Mother McGinty's was filled to overflowing. Some of their capers were light-hearted, as on the occasion burly young lumbermen were seen buying up all the green silk parasols in town and mincing around the streets in a parody of the local ladies of fashion. Just as often, high spirits ended in trouble, and their capacity for violence was demonstrated in 1828 when their St. Patrick's Day parade of 200 men, "drunk, danc-ing and fighting," degenerated into a riot in which one man was killed and several injured. They were called the Shiners, though precisely why has been lost in the mists of Ottawa Valley folklore. Some say the name was bestowed by the French because the Irish had worked for a time cutting oak, or *chêne*, and *chêneurs* was Anglicized to Shiners.

It was only after the Shiners were united under a powerful leader that these unruly men became a threat to Bytown and Nepean Town-ship, though at first glance Peter Aylen seemed an unlikely "King of the Shiners." Unlike his followers, he was a successful timber mer-chant, owned a fine home on Richmond Road and had a wife related to the cream of Bytown society. He had come to the Ottawa Valley twenty years earlier, having run away from the ship on which he was cabin boy, and gone to work for the Wrights at Hull.

Aylen adopted the Irish of Corktown because he had use for them. Timber operators were fighting each other for prime forest land, hir-ing gangs to enforce their dubious claims, and with 200 Shiners under his thumb Aylen had created his own private army. As events un-folded, he also found use for them in his political aspirations, and he appeared to enjoy their rough company, for he invited them to his Richmond Road home for wild parties that scandalized the neigh-bours. In exchange for their loyalty, he helped them get jobs.

With Aylen backing them, the Shiners swaggered around town, frightening citizens, with nothing to restrain them except a few elderly magistrates and timid part-time policemen, the sheriff and his jail being fifty miles away at Perth. What became known as the Shiners War began early in 1835 with the daylight murder of a Shiners' opponent on the streets of Lowertown followed by mounting violence throughout the spring. The Shiners attacked French raftsmen and threw them into the boiling waters of Chaudière Falls, and scattered enemies with a vicious weapon called the "Limerick whip," a willow switch topped by a sharp chisel. Martin Hennessy started one riot all on his own by riding his horse into a French-Canadian tavern. He lost an eye in the fracas, and in retaliation the Shiners drove the French-Canadian owner and his family out of town, after blowing up his house with a keg of powder ignited by a Shiner called "Hairy Barney" who was killed in the explosion. Shiners' control of Lowertown extended to exacting tolls from people trying to use the government bridge across the Ottawa River to Hull.

Having vented their wrath on the French Canadians, the Shiners, most of whom were Catholics, turned on more traditional foes – Irish Protestants. "Of this place I am pretty sick, what between treacherous Papists and truculent Orangemen it is hardly safe to walk the streets even in daylight," said an English visitor. "A greater set of ruffians than the whole population of Bytown it would be hard to find out of Tipperary." That the troublemakers were not all Irish timber workers was made clear, however, by the *Bytown Gazette* of February 23, 1837: "Although these disturbances were in general attributed to lumbermen, under the cognomen of Shiners, there have been instances in which our yeomanry have been the aggressors."

When Aylen assaulted a Protestant lawyer from Perth, the magistrates summoned up courage to arrest him and put him in Perth jail, but he was soon back in Bytown after serving a short sentence. "No person can move by day without insult or at night without risk to life," said the magistrate George Baker. "Thus whole families of unoffending people are obliged to abandon town, and nothing except a military patrol will succeed in arresting the evil and dissipating the general alarm."

The incident that convinced the gentry there was more than random aggression in Aylen's activities was his takeover of the Bathurst

District Agricultural Society, a stepping stone to local political power. When members of the society gathered for their annual election of officers, they found that Aylen had purchased memberships for his Shiners and packed the hall with tough and irreverent lumberjacks who lolled and guffawed in their chairs as if they were sitting in Mother McGinty's tavern. When it came to a vote, there were enough Shiners to make Aylen president of the society.

In 1837, with the timber trade in one of its periodic depressions, the Shiners War reached its climax. Early in the year, Aylen made his bid for political power by packing the meeting to elect the Nepean Township Council, but this time people were ready for him. James Johnston, an Orangeman, merchant and publisher of the *Bytown Independent,* opposed his takeover and the meeting broke up in a fight. Another Orangeman, a farmer named Hobbs, had attracted the wrath of the Shiners, and though he kept clear of Bytown himself, his wife and other women from his household on a shopping expedition were attacked in their sleigh by a gang of Shiners. After belabouring the women with sticks, the Shiners made off with their horses, which were found next day with the ears and tails cut off, and one with a wound in its side.

This was too much for Hobbs's neighbours, who appeared en masse at Bytown with guns and pitchforks, while the Shiners tried to turn the confrontation into a religious conflict by spreading the word that Orangemen had come to kill all the Corktown Catholics and burn their homes. Even Irishmen who otherwise had shunned the Shiners turned out to repel the Orangemen, and only the arrest of a man named Gleeson, one of those who had attacked Mrs. Hobbs, persuaded the farmers to retreat without a bloody conflict. A few nights later when Aylen heard that Hobbs could be found at the home of James Johnston, he summoned sixty Shiners and surrounded the house. When Johnston, armed with two pistols, confronted them, they scattered, coming back later to shoot out his windows. Writing to the

Lieutenant Governor at York, Johnston complained that Aylen "neither respects himself, nor fears God or man. The laws are like cobwebs to him. There are now several warrants out for his apprehension, but there is not a constable in Bytown who will undertake to arrest him." At least forty deaths had been attributed to Shiner attacks, and the *Brockville Record* called the Shiners "demons in human shape."

Aylen, charged with starting three riots, was bound over to keep the peace, but this still did not stop him from ordering his Shiners to attack the Orangeman who had dared oppose him. Three Shiners caught Johnston one snowy afternoon, shot at him, fractured his skull with a rock and would have done worse had they not been driven off by passing citizens. The attackers were arrested and jailed at Perth, where Shiners broke in and freed them.

In attacking people like Johnston, instead of their usual victims, French-Canadian lumberjacks, the Shiners had gone too far and from that time on their power began to wane. Citizens banded together into the Bytown Association for the Preservation of Peace, which consisted of 200 armed men prepared to patrol the night streets. John Egan, alarmed at the bad name the Irish and the lumber trade were getting, formed the Ottawa Lumber Association to lay down rules for the industry and control the men being hired for the camps. Martin Hennessy was killed in a brawl; others were jailed or hanged or drifted off to the United States like less notorious Irish emigrants. Aylen, his grab for power thwarted, sold his house, moved across the river to Aylmer and there, surprisingly, became known as a pillar of the community, an Ottawa Valley Dr. Jekyll and Mr. Hyde.

One event in 1837 that broke the power of the Shiners was the very thing the authorities feared might incite them to greater violence. That was the insurrection that autumn of the French-Canadian *Patriotes* under Louis-Joseph Papineau in Quebec and of William Lyon Mackenzie's democratic reformers out to topple the Family Compact in Upper Canada. The outbreaks brought troops to Bytown, but the

Corktown Irish had no intention of joining the short-lived rebellion, whatever their anti-English activities in their native land. Some, like Irish Catholics elsewhere in the colonies, joined with Protestant Orangemen in the militia to put down the rebels.

"There was something remarkable and most honourable in the whole bearing of the Irish population throughout these troubles," commented John Beverley Robinson. "They seemed not only to acknowledge promptly their obligation to support their government and the laws, but they discharged their duty with an eager forwardness, and a fine, hearty warmth of feeling that was really quite affecting to witness. It did honour to Ireland, and it showed that whatever may be the vices and errors of the Irish peasantry, hatred of their Sovereign and ingratitude to their Government were not among the number."

For once, Catholics and Protestants, the Green and the Orange, had found common cause, something that had hardly seemed possible. Since the Ballygiblin Riots in 1824, Orangemen such as Alexander Matheson of Perth, who played such a part in that sad affair, had been using Catholics as bogeymen to drum up support for a network of Orange lodges. He was aided in this process by Catholic attacks on the annual 12th of July parades celebrating the Battle of the Boyne in which Presbyterians, singing "The Sash My Father Wore" or "The Protestant Boy," turned out behind "King Billy" on his white horse to march to the lilt of the flutes and the beat of the big lambeg drum. In Kingston in 1827 when fifty Orangemen paraded on "the Glorious 12th," despite a magistrate's warning not to do so, they marched into an ambush of a hundred Catholic Irish canal workers and several were injured. Though both Protestants and Catholics were arrested, the Catholics were found to have struck the first blows and a jury headed by an Orangeman put them in jail. Fights became an annual event in Kingston and were common in Toronto, Montreal and Saint John. The quarrels of Ireland had crossed the Atlantic, and Orangemen taunted their foes with the ditty

Titter totter, holy water
Slaughter the Catholics everyone.
If that won't do
We'll cut them in two
and make them live under the Orange and Blue.

"Such exhibitions can now, and in this country, serve no good," wrote Dr. John Hutchinson in Peterborough, "but on the contrary lead to perpetuate the religious feud which has so long destroyed the peace of the native isle. For heaven's sake why transplant the rancorous party feeling to this peaceful country?" The government, though Protestant, deplored the Orange lodges, but stopped short of suppressing them despite efforts to pass anti-Orange laws. Dr. William Baldwin, an Irish Protestant from Cork, declared that "no party ever cultivated greater animosity, or exhibited a greater degree of hostile distinction from the rest of their fellow subjects than the Orange Societies."

As more Catholic emigrants arrived, sectarian violence had grown, though the Orange Lodge stressed its fraternal and social aspect in public pronouncements. Its purpose, the Perth lodge maintained, was to "cherish that kind of intercourse of friendly feeling which should exist among brethren ... to raise a fund for the relief of friends in distress, and to inculcate in the minds of one another, brotherly love, morality, religion and loyalty...." Membership in an Orange Lodge was a Protestant emigrant's guarantee of getting a job.

It was the arrival of Ogle Robert Gowan, a twenty-six-year-old journalist from County Wexford whose father had been a founding member of the Irish Grand Lodge, that ensured that the Orange order would endure as a powerful force in Upper Canada. Establishing himself with his family on a farm at Brockville, Gowan called a meeting of Orangemen in 1830 which formed the Grand Lodge of British North America. Running on a moderate platform, which championed Catholics as well as Protestants, Gowan became a member of the legislative assembly for Leeds County, whose population was one third Irish. A document issued by the Grand Lodge stated its disapproval of religious persecution. "Holding in detestation every species of intoler-ancy," it said, "we admit no man into our brotherhood whom we do not believe to be incapable of injuring or persecuting any person on account of his religion, and for whose moral rectitude we have not received the most solemn pledge." In 1833 there was a network of 100 lodges throughout Upper Canada with a membership of 13,000.

Gowan declared that despite religious differences the Protestants and Catholic emigrants had much in common. George Tully from Tipperary, an Orange organizer in the Ottawa Valley, said, "We are ready at all times to give the right hand of fellowship to our Catholic fellow subjects and, free from those aspersions some falsely impute to us, to love them as men, though we cannot admit them as master." There were efforts to unite Irish Protestants and Catholics and talk of renaming the Orange Lodges the United Lodges, prompting the Hamilton *Gazette* to editorialize on the occasion of the 12th of July, 1836: "Among the Irish, petty jealousies, party feuds and religious dif-ferences were thrown over-board with common consent and hearty good-will." Unfortunately, this phase of goodwill was hardly typical of relations between the Green and the Orange, which were to harden as more Catholics flowed into Protestant Upper Canada. Lord Durham, whose sympathies lay with the Catholics, found it "somewhat difficult to understand the nature and objects of the rather anomalous Orangeism of Upper Canada." In his report on the state of the colo-nies in the late 1830s, he said the Orangeman's desire to uphold the Protestant religion was at odds with his profession of tolerance.

In townships pioneered by Ulstermen, such as Mono in the hills northwest of Toronto, Catholics were unwelcome, which presumably did not bother them much since a surveyor said the township was swampy and hilly and not fit for settlement. On the other hand, Catholics who sought land in Cavan Township, in Newcastle District west of Peterborough, which had been settled by Ulstermen, were dis-couraged by a gang of Orange bully boys calling themselves the Blaz-ers. No magistrate would issue warrants against the Blazers, but John

Huston, an Orangeman who lived in Cavan and as government surveyor had helped Peter Robinson get the emigrants settled around Peterborough, did a great deal to promote peace, and complemented the Catholics for refraining from disturbing the annual 12th of July parades.

Distances were shrinking in the Newcastle District with the building of roads and the appearance of two steamboats on Rice Lake and the lower reaches of the Otonabee. Peterborough had grown into a community of Irish, Scots and English, and was a thriving district capital in the late 1830s with 150 houses, four churches, a school, post office, bank, government office, circulating library, two inns and two distilleries. John Langton, one of several English gentleman farmers like the Stricklands, found Peterborough a "very pretty, picturesque, thriving village." Among his neighbours were three Irish university men, including the son of a mayor of an Irish town.

John Richards, a government agent, visited thirty or forty Irish families and found them doing well. It was rare to find a farm with less than thirty cleared acres, and sometimes they had twice that amount. Abraham Groves, son of the widow Margaret Groves from Wicklow, had forty acres under cultivation in Emily Township and owned four cows and two horses. William Mulcahey had cleared fifty, and in Asphodel Township John Reardon had sixty productive acres and a profitable sideline in timber.

Prejudice, as always, died hard. There were those who disdained the Catholic "bog Irish," though it was obvious that even families described by the doctors on the ships as lazy or fractious were as hardworking and successful as anyone in the settlements. There were those who considered Peter Robinson's migrations a failure but the emigrants themselves were clearly not among their number. Richards was accompanied on his visit by Peter Robinson and said, "The manner in which they met him was quite affecting; it was more to bless him as a benefactor than to receive him as a visitor."

Lieutenant Charles Rubidge, the one-legged pioneer of Woodland

Cottage in Otonabee Township, had once been inclined to criticize the Irish, saying they would benefit from being scattered among English and Scottish settlers rather than being left on their own. But now this criticism had turned to praise. "They are generally perfectly independent," Rubidge said, "having fine farms well stocked with cattle, sheep, pigs, etc.; and many of them keep horses with conveyances both for summer and winter. Their families are all settled about them on farms purchased by their own industry. There is not one instance of any member of these families asking charity from anyone. If any of them were addicted to crimes in Ireland, they are now free of them, and placed above necessity, are as peaceful and loyal a body of people as we have in the province."

FACED IN THE 1830s with feeding large numbers of evicted and unemployed whose presence was a rebuke to the conscience and a hindrance to farm modernization, landowners in Ireland had begun to look to emigration as the alternative. Since the government had no intention of taking a hand, certain landowners began to fund emigration themselves.

The cost of sending a family to Canada was half the cost of maintaining them at home for a year, and one of the first to recognize this was St. George Caulfield in County Roscommon. His lands had become so divided, overworked and worn out that he feared his tenants would starve to death in 1831, a year of partial famine. That spring he made them an offer: those willing to surrender their leases would be given free passage to Canada. His offer was accepted by thirty-six families, who were described by his agent as a "set of ragamuffins in appearance, but with wit, bone and sinew worthy of a better fortune." When they arrived in Quebec City, the Emigration Agent, A.C. Buchanan, suggested they go to Peterborough but their spokesman, Peter Bly, replied that the landlord had given them only their passage and they had no money. Caulfield later disputed this, claiming he had given them money to get started as well; but whatever the truth, once they were in Canada they were dependent on government help and Buchanan aided them as he did so many others, including 153 woollen workers who arrived from Kildare. Their passage to Quebec had been paid by subscription raised by magistrates who did not want to support them at home. They were in such pitiable condition that the governor, Sir James Kempt, complained to London that people were being sent out "perfectly destitute among strangers." Land was provided in townships west of Montreal, though we do not know under what conditions; they were so poor that Montreal boatman took them up-river at no charge, out of charity.

William Hickey, who published a book of advice to emigrants in 1832, said "much distress was experienced last spring at Quebec by a crowd of Irish emigrants who arrived there penniless; their unfeeling landlords having paid their expenses no further than that port, instead of furnishing them with the means of proceeding to the upper provinces where abundant employment awaited them." By 1833, landowners had assisted emigrants from fifty parishes, but few made provisions to take them farther than Quebec City.

By the late 1830s there were 70,000 Irish living in Upper Canada, 8,000 in and around Toronto and the rest scattered throughout the colony. There were 40,000 in Lower Canada, almost half of them in Quebec City and Montreal, and of every ten immigrants arriving at Quebec City, six were Irish. Though Presbyterians and Anglicans, the minority in Ireland, had long been the majority of the emigrants, the balance was changing, with Catholics coming in large numbers, a mixture of farmers, artisans and labourers seeking jobs on such projects as the St. Lawrence Canal, which was hiring 2,000 men. A sampling of the weekly logs of the Emigration Agent for 1836 and 1837 shows that some were destitute but others had some little means:

1836, Week ending June 4: Complaints against the Captain of the *Belisle* from Dublin. Passengers complained of shortage of water and what they had was too bad to use and two passengers died of dysentery.

Week ending June 18: The greater part of the emigrants who arrived this week were very destitute and were forwarded to Montreal by the Emigrant Society. They were principally from the west and south of Ireland.

Week ending August 6: The emigrants arrived this week consisted principally of tradesmen, farmers and labourers, of whom very few remained in Quebec; the majority are Irish and have all proceeded up to Montreal; very many are induced to go to the United States, owing to the exaggerated accounts of wages given them on the numerous railroads and canals at present in construction.

Week ending August 13: The great proportion of emigrants arrived this week are from Ireland, with 231 English Pauper emigrants....Very many of the Irish have gone to the States, and many have obtained orders for employment on the St. Lawrence Canal.

1837, Week ending May 20: All the emigrants arrived this week are of a very respectable class, and having with the exception of a few, gone to Upper Canada. Some of the passengers in the *Recovery* from Kinsale have gone to the United States, notwithstanding the unfavourable accounts received from there, and the utter impossibility of persons of the working class obtaining employment.

Week ending May 27: Among the emigrants who arrived this week is Captain Cotter and family in the *Arabella* from Cork. He has brought out several poor families with him, and intends settling in the neighbourhood of Toronto. A very large proportion of the arrivals this week are from Ireland, and particularly the south.

Week end June 10: The emigrants arrived during the past week are principally from Ireland and in good health, and appear well supplied with means.

The rebellions in Upper and Lower Canada in the autumn of 1837 frightened off emigration, and it dropped to hardly more than 2,000 people, the lowest since the end of the Napoleonic Wars, but in 1839 it started to climb again. One of the Emigrant Agent's entries for the week ending July 6 was particularly noteworthy:

The emigrants arrived during the past week are, with the exception of fifty-nine, all from Ireland; and among them thirty-four families, numbering 181 souls, sent out by Col. Wyndham from his estates in Clare and Limerick, under the superintendence of Lieut. Rubidge, R.N. They all landed in excellent health, and proceeded immediately on their route to Upper Canada. Their destination is the Newcastle District, where I understand arrangement has been made for their reception, and to furnish them with employment on arrival. These people were amply provided with everything necessary for their comfort during the voyage, and had a large surplus stock of provisions on hand for their health and comfort during the voyage, and it fully proves that, by a little care and attention on the part of the captain or person in charge of passengers, all the sickness and misery which many of the emigrants on vessels to this port are subject might be avoided.

Rubidge, who had given up farming to become Emigration Agent for the Newcastle District, had been hired by Colonel Wyndham to shepherd his contribution to this new wave of assisted emigrations, funded not by government but by landowners. Wyndham had inherited 44,000 acres and was anxious to reorganize his estates, but unlike many landlords shied away from simply evicting his tenants. Instead he adopted the practice begun by his father, George O'Brien Wyndham, Lord Egremont of Petworth in Sussex, who had for several years been funding the emigration of his English tenants and settling them between Lake Erie and Lake Huron – the Huron District – with the cooperation of Wilmot Horton at the Colonial Office. To this end he sponsored the Petworth Committee, which, determined to avoid the distress and overcrowding common to 19th-century emigrations, chartered its own ships so it could control steerage space and shipboard rations. This was the model that Colonel Wyndham set out to copy for his estates around the Shannon estuary in the counties of Clare and Limerick.

Wyndham's aim was to clear his estates of tenants holding less than twenty acres, and he offered two choices to those willing to leave their land: if they agreed to vacate but wanted to remain in Ireland he offered two pounds an acre; if they agreed to emigrate he would pay their passage. Early in 1839 he organized a committee under James M. Brydone, a ship's surgeon who had headed five Petworth emigrations, and issued the following notice at Ennis, County Clare:

The Committee acting for Col. Wyndham are authorized to offer free passage to Canada to all tenants or labourers, their wives and children, being occupiers of small portions of land on the Irish estates of Col. Wyndham, now out of lease.... Col. Wyndham will give assistance in fitting out the families for the voyage, but that only when the family are ready to embark.

"Getting rid of the surplus families by paying them a trifle in money would certainly be a much cheaper plan for the Colonel than sending them to Canada," said Brydone, "but would fall infinitely short in beneficial effects for these poor people." Nevertheless 200 of those approached opted to take the two pounds per acre and remain in Ireland. Brydone was a newcomer, and when asked if the Wyndham tenants included troublemakers, or "bad and idle people," he admitted that neither he nor Wyndham knew much about them "excepting that they held portions of land and were very poor."

As on many estates, the farms leased out by Wyndham and his predecessors had been so divided and subdivided over the years that land once expected to support two or three families was now expected to support eight or ten families. Conditions varied greatly. Some, such as young widow Bridget McNamara, who was trying to raise two sons, had only a cabin and no land at all. John Murphy, on the other hand, had fifteen acres, though he had fallen ill and was in arrears. Murphy got full compensation when he agreed to move off his land, but the widow Malarky, who was fifty years old and had only a cabin, had to make do with only two pounds ten shillings for leaving her house, which was then torn down. Patrick Curtaise, fifty-two, had such a large family that Brydone questioned whether it would be too expensive to send him to Canada, but in the end he was sent anyway because "he is an exceedingly troublesome fellow." In some cases, Wyndham's agents followed the practice of landlords in other areas and ordered forced evictions, but in the Aghorina townland, thirteen families successfully defied all eviction efforts.

Daniel Browne, who fought a losing battle to remain on his ten acres, which had been split up among neighbouring farmers, wrote, "Dear Sir, I wish to let you know how I am greatly regretting being turned out of my holdings at Knockmeal, part of the lands of Lissifen, which I had well prepared with a field of clover and four acres of soil well manured." He said while he farmed it there had not been a "spot of land in the parish yielding such crops" but consolidating it with the neighbouring farms had simply resulted in trouble and "wrangling every day."

Having selected 230 people for Upper Canada and hiring Lieutenant Rubidge to shepherd them, Brydone chartered the ship *Waterloo*, but as the date of departure drew near he found that people were starting to back out, fearful that "Colonel Wyndham was sending them out that they would be made slaves to cultivate his land in Canada." Brydone patiently explained that in Canada they would be free citizens and moreover that Colonel Wyndham owned no land in Canada.

On the 22nd of May, 1839, [wrote Rubidge] I embarked on board the *Waterloo* in the River Shannon and made arrangements for the reception of people, stores and provisions. On the 24th at 5 p.m., ninety-three of Colonel Wyndham's tenants came on board. A boiler full of potatoes was in readiness, besides which one pound of biscuit was served out to each of them. From prejudice and ignorance they would not eat the potatoes because they had not been boiled in soft water, and the biscuit they disliked so much they would not consider it good wholesome food.

On Saturday the 25th of May, at half past 5 p.m. about 120 more of the people were received on board from Limerick City, and also some more provisions, stores and water. A few of the people on board, as well as some of the last received, appeared to be infected with a discontented, bad spirit, which was very difficult to counter with them.

The husbands of three of the women failed to appear, and they set up such a wailing they had to be taken ashore. By sailing time on May 28 only 181 of the original 230 were willing to sail, and it was not until the *Waterloo* was out in the Shannon estuary that "all repining and discontent ceased." The doctor found some of them "infected with itch, and swarming with vermin." As a precaution against ringworm, Rubidge said that "with threats and kindness I got the children's hair cut close." There was remarkably little sickness during the voyage. Daniel Clancey, an old man, kept to his bunk with a feverish cold, and Mrs. Cornelius McMahon "suffered a miscarriage from fright in a mild breeze we had one night." Two children were born.

There was more than enough space and food for all, and the weekly ration consisted of five and a half pounds of oatmeal per person, seventeen pounds of potatoes, twelve ounces of butter, one and a half ounces of tea, and some salt pork, herring and biscuits. "I have endeavoured to make myself acquainted with the likes and dislikes of this class of person," Rubidge said, "and have come to the decision that the only proper food agreeable to them is such as they have been accustomed to use." They clamoured for more potatoes, scattered biscuits around the deck and threw their cheese overboard.

On the June 30, after a fast, easy voyage of thirty-three days, the *Waterloo* anchored off Grosse Isle, where Rubidge mustered the people on deck to make sure they had washed themselves and wore clean clothes to make a good impression on the quarantine officer. "I also took this opportunity to warn them against listening to the stories they might be told of high wages or the advantages of the United States, as they would be sure to be deceived. At the same time, I told them that, far from putting any restraint on them, they might go when and where they pleased." Because the vessel was clean and the people looked healthy, the *Waterloo* was allowed to proceed to Quebec City the same day, and the emigrants arrived at Montreal by river steamer on July 2.

Colonel Wyndham had paid their way as far as Cobourg, where Rubidge had undertaken to get them jobs, and their journey into Upper Canada was vastly different from that undertaken by Peter Robinson's emigrants. They were taken up the Ottawa River to Bytown in barges towed by a steamer, and from there down the Rideau Canal to Kingston and Cobourg. Three of the men, including Cornelius McMahon, whose wife had suffered a miscarriage, accepted jobs along the way. At Cobourg, the emigrants received a warm welcome, and Rubidge had prepared four houses to receive them.

"As soon as our arrival became known," said Rubidge, "farmers of the country came from all directions to hire them. It will be pleasing to me to be able to assure Col. Wyndham that the general good conduct of the people, both on the voyage out and in going up the country, was very praise worthy for sobriety, obedience and peaceable demeanour. They assured me they were quite content and happy with Col. Wyndham for sending them out, and said they would write home to urge their friends to come out.... I regret we had not a larger number aboard, everything has gone so well."

Rubidge had learned from Peter Robinson the value of favourable emigrant letters in coaxing relatives to follow, and at his prompting several wrote home soon after their arrival at Cobourg. James and Mary Davis assured their mother in County Limerick "we are all seemingly in a way doing better than we could expect at home." Ellen Gleeson, who went to work as a servant for Rubidge's daughter in Peterborough, said she had plenty to eat and drink, and did not want her friends at home to think she had been sold into bondage. "I wish my friends to realize we are not slaves, but allowed to do as we please."

"My Dear Edmund," wrote Catherine Quinn to her cousin, Edmund Ryan, "we got plenty of provisions while we were on board, a pound of bread and a pound of meat four times a week. We had nothing to want for while we were at sea. Dear Man, let my mother know we have landed safe and I will send her something as soon as I can." Catherine Burns assured her widowed mother, "This is a fine country from all appearance. I wish my brother to come out as soon as possible."

To Lord John Russell, the Home Secretary, Wyndham's project was a model to be followed by all landlords. "The prosperous condition in which these persons have been placed by the well-directed generosity of Colonel Wyndham," he said, "will probably induce many other landlords, especially in Ireland, to imitate his example." He said the emigrants' letters should be well publicized and urged Lord Sydenham, Governor of the United Provinces of Canada, to encourage emigration, adding that "want of funds" precluded active government participation. Lord John Russell's enthusiasm for the scheme was premature. When, toward the end of the year, he sought to discover how the Wyndham project was going, Rubidge was strangely silent. When others were queried, in the absence of any answer from Rubidge, the reason became clear. Despite Rubidge's solicitude, most of the emigrants had gone to jobs on the canals and railways in the United States. John Brown, a merchant at Port Hope who had hired thirty men – two thirds of the men in the group – reported, "They were not content although I paid them five pounds a month. They all left for the United States with the exception of three." He added that unless the government was prepared to grant land, as had been done up to the 1820s, many more would desert to the United States.

Lord Durham, in his report on British North America, estimated that 60 per cent of all emigrants were leaving Canada for the United States. Among reasons given were lack of public works projects and the fact that Canadian farmers wanted single men whom they could pay by giving them board, having no place to house whole families. A.B. Hawke, Emigration Agent for Upper Canada, believed that emigrants had been encouraged to expect too much. "It too often happens that emigrants on their arrival set too high a value on their services," he said, "and refuse wages which they would gladly accept after a longer residence in America ... indeed it is notorious and has been the subject of frequent regret, that for some time the emigration from these provinces to the States has been very considerable. I am of the opinion that it is less at present than at any former period since the spring of 1837; and if we could manage to start any of our public works, many who have left would immediately return to the province."

Colonel Wyndham was not discouraged. During the next decade he was to send out 220 families – 1,419 people – in small groups, though without the amenities enjoyed by the people on the *Waterloo* or the generous guidance of Lieutenant Rubidge. Instead of chartering a ship, he would send them on random emigrant vessels, a practice followed by many landowners.

11

"Shovelling Out the Paupers"

*B*Y THE 1830s living conditions of country people in Ireland had suffered such a grievous decline that a government commission concluded that people had lived better in the 1770s than their grandchildren did now. Well over two million, a third of the population, subsisted on the verge of starvation for eight months of every year, getting enough to eat only in the four months following harvest. The commission established to investigate the "State of the Poor in Ireland" deplored the dependence on only one source of nourishment, the undependable potato. It criticized the system whereby landowners gave their labourers no money but paid them off with a scrap of land on which to throw up a hut and plant a potato garden. With no money except what little could be earned from the sale of a bit of produce now and then, or perhaps a pig, they were tied to a landlord's service, unable to leave.

The commission heard a wide range of reasons for the woes of the poor: the enormous increase in population from five million to eight million since the turn of the century; religious differences; political extremism; absentee landlords; lack of investment; the prevalence of alcoholism; and the passing of the Act of Union in 1800 which united two nations without uniting their peoples. Canon Sheehan, a respected churchman, blamed the "whole ghastly genealogy of Irish history, and particularly the Act of Union…. The Union begat outlawry, and outlawry begat Whiteboyism; and the Whiteboyism begat informers and judicial murders, and judicial murders begat revenge."

Barely a quarter of the population lived past the age of forty, and because of the high rate of infant mortality the average age at death in the poorer regions was nineteen. The number of homeless was increasing as landowners, caught between debt and shrinking rent rolls, evicted tenants in the scramble to reorganize and modernize farmland before they went bankrupt. When Francis Spaight, the Limerick shipowner, purchased a property near the Shannon River, he found it swarming with an "immense number of widows and poor persons and paupers." Most had paid no rent for years. "I found it totally impossible," said Spaight, "to make any progress in improving the estate while I had such a dense population of poor creatures upon it."

Lord Charles Midleton, a cabinet minister, was considered to be a progressive landlord, but when the English author William Cobbett visited his estate near Cork City, he found the tenants in great poverty. "I went to a hamlet near the town of Midleton which contained about fifty hovels in all, consisting of mud huts with a covering of rafters and straw. One was twenty feet long and nine feet wide, no table or chair. The smoke went out a hole in the roof. I sat on a block of wood. Nothing but a pot and a shallow tub for the pig and the family to eat out of. No bed or mattress. Some dirty straw and a bundle of rags were all the bedding. The man had five small children, and the mother, thirty, was worn into half ugliness by hunger and filth." Midleton's agent, who ran the estate in his master's absence in London, had ordered that 560 acres, occupied by seventeen families, "should be laid down to pasture and kept as sheep walks. All the tenants under notice to quit, in consequence of their bad management and non-payment of rent ... all the miserable cabins shall be destroyed."

There were thousands of evictions in the counties of Cork, Tipperary, Limerick, Clare and Leitrim. "Families were totally expelled," said Father Patrick Fitzgerald at Dunkettle, County Cork, "or located on spots of barren black mountain to drag out a miserable existence, not one of whom ever committed a political act calculated to give offence to their landlord...." Gerald Griffin in County Limerick said, "You never know the moment they may pounce on you, ruin you, and throw you out." A witness at the Poor Inquiry said, "Ejectment is tantamount to a sentence of death by slow torture."

"It was the most appalling sight I ever witnessed," reported a Galway correspondent for the *Freeman's Journal*, "women, young and old, running wildly to and fro with a small portion of the property to save it from the wreckage – the screaming of the children, and the wild wailings of the mothers driven from their home and shelter. In the first instance the roofs and portions of the wall only were thrown down. But that Friday night the wretched creatures pitched a few poles slantwise against the walls, covering them with thatch in order to procure shelter of the night. When this was perceived, the next day the bailiffs were dispatched with orders to pull down all the walls and root up the foundations in order to prevent the poor people from daring to take shelter amid the ruins."

Eviction was easy. The landlord would post a notice that arrears must be paid on a certain date, "otherwise summary steps will be taken to recover same." As for the tenants who had no lease – "tenants at will" – a landlord could get rid of them as he wished without compensation, even if they had improved the property. The government did not find this outrageous. "You might as well propose," observed

Lord John Russell, then the Home Secretary, "that a landlord compensate the rabbits for the burrows they have made."

Evictions followed a well-worn pattern. On the appointed day a bailiff would appear with hired men called "destructives," professional wreckers bearing crowbars and ropes. If trouble was expected there might be a policeman, or perhaps some soldiers, though most redcoats, many of them Irish, hated such work. Surrounded by weeping women, frightened children and sullen men, the bailiff would read the notice, empty the house and set the wreckers to work. A gang of half a dozen "destructives," many themselves victims of eviction doing this dirty work to feed their families, could pull down a dozen houses in a day, for the simple cabins were pathetically easy to destroy. They tied a rope to the roof beam and led it down through the house and out the door. When the beam was broken with a few blows, a strong pull on the rope brought the roof crashing into the house, and all that remained was to level the walls with crowbars.

Landlords who showed no pity could expect none from the Ribbonmen, Captain Rocks and other rural terrorists, whose activities flared again in the 1830s. Described euphemistically by an Irish writer as a "vast trade union for protection of Irish peasantry," they fought evictions, and the payment of tithes to the Protestant church, with intimidation, arson and sometimes murder. "There exists to the most frightful extent a mutual and violent hatred between the proprietors and the peasantry," said Lord Anglesey, the Lord Lieutenant of Ireland.

Eviction was not only dangerous for the landowner, who could expect retaliation, but was often futile. As often as not a family would turn up again, squatting in a makeshift shelter in some out-of-the-way corner of the estate, for there was nowhere else to go. Having found 600 people trying to make a living on 400 acres he owned in Limerick, and clearing half of them off, Lord Stanley, Secretary of Ireland, had to provide food to keep them from starving.

In 1836 the Poor Enquiry Commission released its long-awaited report, a tome of half a million words that recommended a comprehensive and expensive scheme of national improvement – better education, a public works program, land reclamation, and controlled and subsidized emigration. In a pervading atmosphere of thrift and *laissez-faire,* the report was rejected by the government. To formulate a simpler, cheaper solution, an English Poor Law Commissioner, George Nicholls, was sent to Ireland.

"Ireland is now suffering under a circle of evils, producing and reproducing one another," Nicholls wrote. "Want of capital produces want of employment; want of employment, turbulence, misery and insecurity; insecurity prevents the introduction and accumulation of capital, and so on. Until this circle is broken, the evils must continue and probably increase."

He hacked at the branches rather than the roots, and while his solution was no panacea it was what the government wanted to hear. London's concern had been less the well-being of the Irish than the well-being of the English. There had long been protests about the number of destitute Irish coming every year to the ghettos of Liverpool, Manchester and London, to seek work, or failing that, shelter within England's Poor Law, which had no equivalent in Ireland. Nicholls proposed that the Poor Law be extended to Ireland, and in the summer of 1838 an "Act for the more effectual relief of the Poor in Ireland" was passed. Ireland would be divided into 130 districts, called unions, each with its board of guardians composed of magistrates and gentry. Assistance would be given only to those so poor they were prepared to give up their normal lives and become inmates of the workhouses; to discourage malingering, regulations were deliberately harsh. "With one hand they offered the poor an alms, and with the other they opened a prison," said the French traveller Gustave de Beaumont.

The Poor Enquiry Commission, its report ignored, declared the act would never work, that the Irish would never enter the workhouses. The aging Daniel O'Connell, his power long gone, said the law would "tend to diminish self-reliance, to paralyze industry, to decrease economy, and above all to damp and extinguish the generous feelings of nature towards parents, children, relations and friends." Landowners opposed it because they would bear the brunt of extra taxation necessary to build and operate the workhouses.

The workhouses were great, gaunt buildings, usually built to a standard design, that loomed over the countryside and can still be seen in Ireland, though the system ended early in the 20th century. Families were broken up and segregated by sex and age. Life was regulated by bells and supervisors, the able-bodied men kept busy on institutional chores or breaking up rock, the women engaged in cooking, cleaning, spinning and knitting. Children were given some schooling, the girls taught sewing and domestic service, and boys instructed in carpentry, shoemaking and tailoring.

At Fermoy in the Blackwater, where the workhouse was a disused military barracks, men were issued with a uniform of corduroy trousers, cap, shirt, jacket and shoes, and the women with gown, petticoat, shift, cap, apron and shoes. Meals were taken in silence, as in a monastery, and consisted mostly of oatmeal, potatoes and buttermilk. As the Poor Commissioners said in an annual report, all efforts were directed to "awaken or increase a dislike to remain in the workhouse." Disobedience, swearing, bad conduct and even the most trivial of offences were punished by confinement, reduction in rations, or beatings, as the records of the Poor Law Union of Armagh show. One entry says: "Punishment authorized: Patrick Monaghan and five others for leaving their work to search for onions on the grounds; to receive six stripes three times next week. Patrick Mallone, Daniel Kane, Bernard Fox; exchanging shoes with each other; buttermilk to be taken from them for supper for four days. James McKinney, neglecting his work; no supper for a week and twenty-four lashes; James McLaughlin; burning his shoes; to be flogged by school master when out of hospital." Life in a workhouse was a last resort, and people committed petty crimes so they would be sent to prison instead of the workhouse.

George Nicholls, who drafted the Irish Poor Law and served as its Chief Commissioner, prophetically admitted its most tragic weakness. Since at no time was it envisaged that workhouses and the Poor Law could handle more than 100,000 people at a time, he recognized that a general famine would be "above the powers of the Poor Law to provide for." He hastened to reassure the government – with unfortunate optimism, as events proved a decade later – that total famine was highly unlikely, "as habits, intelligence and forethought of the people improve with the increase of wealth and the progress of education."

To lighten the burden on the workhouses, the legislation permitted local Poor Law Guardians to borrow money against rates (local taxes) for emigration purposes, but few did so until the crisis years of the famine in the late 1840s. When the Poor Law Union at Belfast tried to send inmates to Canada, the Guardians were baulked by ratepayers who argued it was too late in the year to send poor people to a "cold grave and a snowy winding sheet." When the Union at Cork City tried to get government help to assist emigration, they were refused on grounds that paupers made poor settlers.

One of the effects of the Poor Law, intentional or otherwise, was to stimulate landowners to pay for emigration, which was cheaper than keeping hundreds of paupers in the workhouses. A landowner near Mallow in the Blackwater, John Dillon Croker, estimated that Poor Rates consumed 40 per cent of his income, and his neighbours insisted they would be bankrupt. The result was a drive to clear lands of unproductive tenants, tear down taxable hovels and bundle the unwanted, whether they would make good settlers or not, off to North America, where, it was hoped, someone would look after them. This was politely referred to as the "removal of redundant population" or more crudely as "shovelling out the paupers." Some managed to send people to Canada with humanity, though a government report in 1843 said most landlords cared little for the misery their actions caused. The worst cases usually involved the estates of absentee landowners who left the "shovelling out" to agents.

Lord Darnley's foray into emigration was a fiasco. His agent supplied 400 tenants with food for twenty-three days and sent them to Quebec with a promise of a pound per family on arrival. The voyage, as the agent might have expected, took almost twice as long, and the people were half starved on arrival. Nor, so far as is known, did they ever get the promised pound, which was little enough in itself to start a new life. Cases like these caused Lord Sydenham, the Governor of Canada, to exclaim: "To throw starving and diseased paupers under the rock at Quebec, ought to be punishable as murder."

Colonel C.B. Wandesforde of Castlecomer in the coal-mining region of County Kilkenny sent out a group of 120 that was "absolutely destitute" upon arrival at Quebec, though others he sent – and there were thousands – arrived in good health and spirits. A great deal depended on the owners and masters of the ships, and since there was poor passenger legislation and poorer supervision, conditions varied greatly at sea.

Colonel Wyndham sent out tenants year after year, and although they were not as well cared for as his first group, most were well treated. But apparently not all. When he despatched his second contingent of 230 people in 1840, he sent them in groups on five different ships at a cost of three pounds fifteen shillings a head, having given up chartering vessels. He outfitted them with clothes, but apparently gave them no money, because an official at Quebec complained of their poverty in a letter to Lord John Russell, adding diplomatically, since Lord John spoke highly of Wyndham, "I am confident, however, that it would not have been his intention to throw these people on the charity of the government."

Among the emigrants themselves, or at least those who wrote letters, there seem to have been no great hardship on the Wyndham ships, although two children died during the voyage. An emigrant called John Russell wrote home to his mother that there had been plenty to eat during the voyage, "with free access to the stores of potatoes, water, meal and herrings." He noted there were 3,000 emigrants

looking for work in Quebec that spring. "Persons who do well here are single men and women, persons who are willing to work pretty hard for their bread." William Collins wrote that whiskey was selling at a shilling a gallon "and all kinds of eating and drinking in proportion to that, and if any of you could come here you could never live at home as well."

During the next two decades, dozens of landowners paid to have unwanted tenants shipped to Canada and New Brunswick. When the Colonial Association of Ireland, incorporated in 1839 and intent on colonizing land in New Brunswick and the southwestern region of Lower Canada in Beauharnois Country, sent agents through southern Ireland to encourage emigration, they found landowners interested in assisting people to go. Lord Fitzwilliam sent 300 families – 1,600 people – and would have paid the passages of more but they refused to go. Lord Stanley, who sent several groups, commented, "The warm attachment of the Irish peasant to the locality where he was born and brought up will always make the best and most carefully conducted scheme of emigration a matter of painful sacrifice to the emigrant." Viscount Midleton of Cork, Richard Eaton of Kilkenny, who sent 1,050 in two years, Sir Lucius O'Brien, Judge Pennefather, Sir Robert Gore Booth, Lord Palmerston, Sir Francis Spaight of Limerick and many others sent emigrants. The Marquis of Clanrichard spent £551 on emigration in 1841, a considerable sum at the time, but whether he did so from charity or fear of terrorists was not clear.

Over the years, landowners paid for the emigration of between 50,000 and 100,000 people, but this was a small number compared with the vast majority who paid their own way or, more likely, were assisted by relatives. Family loyalty, more than anything else, transported hundreds of thousands of Irish across the Atlantic. Up to the 1830s, the typical emigrant had been a "small farmer" with a bit of money. Now, with the help of uncles, cousins, neighbours, a family sought to scrape up enough money to send one or two healthy young family members to the New World. Soon, often in remarkably short

time, the travellers would remit money home so relatives could join them until the whole family, and often neighbours as well, were brought out in a chain migration. In this way many more Catholics were coming.

Sending money home was a moral duty, like attending Mass. Thomas Garry, a Sligo professional beggar who stowed away on a ship bound for Saint John, New Brunswick, leaving a wife and children behind, wrote to assure them he would look after them. "I don't delay in Relieving youse," he wrote, "as it is my duty encumbered on me by the laws of Church and I hope God will Relieve me." The last act of Michael Foley, taken mortally ill on the brig *Trafalgar* bound for the same city, was to ask that his life savings of four pounds be sent to his family in Killarney.

They sent home surprisingly large sums, in the post or through banks or shipping companies. The Board of Emigration Commissioners estimated remittances at half a million dollars a year in the early 1840s, and the figure climbed four-fold in the 1850s, including remittances from both the United States and Canada. In 1834, shipping agents in Londonderry said relatives in British North America paid half the emigrant passages that year and bought most of the food taken aboard the ships. In 1844, a witness told one of the innumerable parliamentary inquiries into Irish affairs: "On board one vessel, the bark *Anne* of New Ross, out of sixty-four passengers I was assured by the master that only one family had paid their passage money before leaving, all the others having come out in the manner just described," that is, with remittances from relatives abroad.

Relatives slow to send money were sharply reminded of their duty by those depending on them. "It is out of the young men's power to save money in this country," said James Nolan, an unemployed Wexford miller, in a letter to kinsman in Nova Scotia. His brother, John, added that no true Irishman would "shut himself up in a distant nation without showing his love for his friends." Wills Anstil, a Cork County farmer and part-time weaver, appealed to a brother in New

Brunswick for aid, saying, "The weavers in Bandon are in a state of beggary and many of them have turned to beggary entirely."

Economic depression and the rebellions in 1837 in the colonies, combined with the new government policy of assisted emigration to Australia, slowed Irish emigration to British North America to a trickle in the late 1830s.

Standish O'Grady, a graduate of Trinity College, Dublin, and an impoverished Protestant clergyman unable to collect tithes to support his family, had homesteaded near Sorel on the St. Lawrence in Lower Canada. "A poor person with a large helpless family has no business here," he wrote. "Lodgings come dear, and what with the sundry necessaries of life it is scarcely in the power of an individual to supply the wants of a family. I would recommend that those with young families remain patiently at home for a few years…." But O'Grady suffered severely from the Canadian cold and took a jaundiced view of his Promised Land, nor did he like the French Canadians among whom he lived. In a poem called "The Emigrant," he wrote:

Thou barren waste; unprofitable strand
Where hemlocks brood on unproductive land,
Whose frozen air on one bleak winter's night
Can metamorphose dark brown hares to white!
Here forests crowd, unprofitable lumber,
O'er fruitless lands indefinite as number …

The flow of Irish emigration resumed – 24,000 in 1840 and a similar number in 1841. During the next five years, until the Great Famine turned the flow into a flood, 180,000 came. How many stayed in the British colonies was difficult to tell. Lord Durham, in his report on the Canadas estimated in 1839 that more than half were going on to the United States, but in 1840 the Emigrant Agent in Quebec claimed only one sixth were doing so that year. To confuse matters, some of these came back after short stays in the States, and new arrivals came up from Boston or New York through border points where no check was kept.

193

There had been some improvement during the 1830s in conditions aboard emigrant ships, but most were unsuitable for the conveyance of people, and the Passenger Act was weak and poorly enforced. Emigrants were expected to bring their own rations aboard, and as they were often misled as to the length of the voyage, supplies were often exhausted before a ship reached port. Excerpts from the weekly logs of the Chief Emigration Agent at Quebec said the emigrants were the usual farmers but also a number of poorer people sent by landlords, family and friends, or their local parishes.

1840. Week ending May 2. The emigrants arrived this week are in good circumstances and come from Ireland. They consist chiefly of labourers and small farmers and most possess sufficient means to proceed upcountry. I am happy in being able to state that among those there are comparatively few going to the United States.

Week ending June 6: The emigrants sent out this week are principally of the labouring class and mechanics; the latter class of people find no difficulty in getting employment, with the demand here for carpenters, masons and tailors, with good wages. In the *James Cook* there were twenty-eight families of 126 souls assisted to emigrate by Col. Wyndham's estates in County Clare; these people received a free passage to the country and were supplied with provisions for the voyage; many of them, however, are widows and penniless, and not likely to obtain employment here which will support them. They were to proceed to the Newcastle district, where they state they have friends who were sent out last year; but cannot for want of means. Eleven families numbering fifty passengers arrived yesterday in the brig *Balfour*, sent out under similar circumstances; they do not appear altogether so destitute as the others. There are some very respectable and wealthy families in the *G. Wilkinson*, Liverpool, and *Thomas Gilson* and *Chieftain*, Belfast, their routes are chiefly to Upper Canada, where many have friends.

Week ending June 13: The emigrants arrived during the past week are chiefly labourers and farmers; their destination is, with few exceptions, Upper Canada. From the *Nicholson* from Sligo, a few families of about thirty persons have gone to their friends in the township of Rawdon, Lower Canada. The passengers in the *Quinton Leitch* from Newry were respectable farmers and labourers; several families were in great distress on their arrival here, owing to being short of provisions; they were fifty-four days at sea, and had to purchase from the

captain at exorbitant prices. It appears that masters of vessels in many instances lay in a stock of provisions, which they dispose of at a large profit to those who may run short during the voyage.

The ship *George,* with 377 passengers, arrived this morning from Liverpool; she has been a week at Grosse Isle; the passengers are in great distress, having suffered from want of provisions; they have been fifty-seven days on the voyage, and purchased from the captain and their fellow passenger so long as their funds lasted.

Week ending June 20: Among the arrivals this week are many families possessing capital, and who are anxious to purchase lands in Upper Canada. I have furnished them with the necessary instructions how to proceed, and to whom they should apply for direction and advice. The emigrants per *Eliza* from Sligo are going to their relations settled in the township of Cavan, Newcastle district. There has been several families in the *Emerald* from Sligo; the *Mary Coxon* from Cork, and *Leander* from Liverpool in great distress for want of provisions during the voyage. Constant applications are made for assistance to enable families to proceed to their friends in different parts of the province. There are now about 250 emigrants, most of whom go up in the steamer this evening.

Week ending June 27: The emigrants arrived this week are chiefly labourers and a few tradesmen. Those in the *Lively* from Cork, *Edwin* from Killala, *Doris* and *Thetis* from Limerick were in great distress. Ten families numbering thirty persons were sent out by Colonel Wyndham in the *Thetis,* who assisted them with provisions and a free passage to Quebec. Mr. Brydone writes me that these people, he considers, have no further claims on Colonel Wyndham after their arrival here.

Week ending August 22: The emigrants arrived during the past week are Irish and Scotch and consist of labourers and tradesmen; the majority of them are in good circumstances. The brig [name crossed out] with 142 passengers arrived after a passage of seventy-three days; they suffered great distress from lack of provisions.... The master appears to be intemperate, and on his arrival here he was taken up by the police and his conduct was so bad that the magistrate sent him to common gaol to hard labour for ten days.

Week ending September 5: On the *Mariners Hope* from Londonderry were seventy-three, all in good circumstances and possessing small capital; they proceeded immediately to Toronto, furnished with every information necessary for their guidance, in purchasing land from The Canada Company in the Huron tract. Among the emigrants this week were ninety persons assisted by their respective parishes.

In the spring of 1841, a month after the opening of the season, Lord Sydenham, was relieved at the favourable reports he was getting from emigration agents. "Notwithstanding the unusually large number of emigrants, scarcely any sickness has prevailed among them" he said, "nor has there been so many cases of destitution."

Sydenham regretted that emigrants had been given unrealistically high expectations of wages they could make in Upper Canada. As a result, they refused work on the roads around Quebec City or Montreal, preferring to push on west where, however, there was no work for unskilled labour until harvest time. "Accordingly the emigrants on arriving here find that they have exhausted all their means procuring conveyance to a place where their labour is not wanted and where they are only likely to become a burden on the public."

Failure to keep emigrants informed was apparent in 1842, when 33,000 arrived, expecting work on canal improvements. The work had not materialized and thousands were destitute. In Quebec City, shipmaster William Mitchell, in a letter to his wife, reported, "The times is very bad in these parts, even worse than in Ireland." A.C. Buchanan warned that sending large bodies of emigrants without first preparing to settle them or providing work, could entail "serious distress and misery, and result, perhaps, in a materially injurious effect on our future emigration." Since 1838 there had been a new Chief Emigration Agent at Quebec City, though this was sometimes overlooked because his name was the same as that of his predecessor, who was his uncle. In an effort to avoid confusion, the new agent sometimes signed himself Alexander Carlisle Buchanan, Junior. He had helped his uncle in the immigration office, and at the age of thirty, when the older man became ill, he took over full responsibility. A member of a well known Ulster shipping family, he was born in County Tyrone and had come to North America at an early age when his father, James Buchanan, was appointed British consul in New York City.

Sydenham spent the final months of his term as Governor urging an adequate Passenger Act. "You will observe," he told Lord John Russell, "that of the emigrants who proceed to Canada, a large proportion, even when they embark, are insufficiently provided with clothes, with bedding and provisions ... it is evident that a great part of these evils are caused by the fraudulent practices on the part of passenger-agents, by the rapacity of the ship charterers, and by the misconduct of officers during the voyage." He called for greater control at ports of embarkation, limits on the number of people crowded into ships' holds, and stricter enforcement of regulations to ensure that emigrants did not arrive in near starvation.

During the previous twenty-five years, emigration had grown in such haphazard, chaotic fashion it was surprising the death toll had not been greater. Except in atypical years such as 1817, or 1832 and 1834 when there had been serious famine, or the cholera epidemics, fatalities had averaged less than 1 per cent. But few years went by without horror stories, and in 1842 the government passed a Passenger Act which it believed would put an end to much of the misery on ships that compared unfavourably with the slavers the English prided themselves on having abolished earlier in the century.

12

Emigrant Ships

*F*OR SHIPOWNERS and their captains, the emigrant trade began as a grudging afterthought, a means of making profit on the westward run to load timber in New Brunswick and Quebec City. Emigrants, however inconvenient, were more profitable than ballast of sand or bricks.

Few emigrant ships had been built to carry passengers. Most were aging cargo vessels, three-masted barks and two-masted brigs, the workhorses of the North Atlantic, vessels of 350 tons or less with holds so shallow and wide that unless they were well loaded with ballast they rolled like a drunk in the slightest seaway. Some were ancient East Indiamen that had once carried tea or silk from the Orient under their mahogany decks, or superannuated frigates with cut-down masts, worm-eaten planking and ports cut into the bows to receive forty-foot baulks of timber. No matter how leaky and decrepit these coffin ships, a cargo of timber, it was hoped, would keep them afloat long enough to get home.

Once a ship discharged its timber, loose boards were laid over the bilges as temporary flooring and rows of rough berths little bigger than dog kennels were fitted in place and covered with straw for bedding. A couple of rickety wooden privies nailed to the foredeck scuppers completed the transformation from timber drogher to emigrant ship, where hundreds of women, men and children were fated to live for at least a month and a half, and sometimes as long as three months if contrary winds blew a ship off course. Even in fine weather with the hatches off there was little light or ventilation, but in rough weather with hatches battened the steerage was like a dungeon lit with smoky kerosene lamps and filled with a fog of sweat, spilled chamber pots, rotting scraps of food, and the vomit of seasick humanity. All around lay luggage, bags, sacks and boxes. No effort was made to segregate unmarried women from men until the 1850s.

The evils began before a ship left port. Speculators chartered steerage space at the cheapest price they could and sent commission agents into the countryside to recruit as many emigrants as possible to fill the space. These men, paid by the number of emigrants they could produce, spun fanciful yarns of shipboard facilities, often claiming the vessels were twice as big as they actually were, and glibly assuring potential passengers that the voyage would be short, three weeks at most, and a kindly captain would look after their needs like a father. Passage could be engaged inclusive or exclusive of provisions, and in the latter case a master was required to furnish nothing but water and a berth. If an emigrant's small stock of food – potatoes, oatmeal and perhaps some bacon or salt herrings – ran out on the voyage, as it usually did, there was nothing to do but buy whatever the captain had to offer at exorbitant prices. There were complaints that the captain's cheese was so old it was fit for boot soles and sugar was sand and sawdust.

There were complaints of ships failing by as much as a month to meet their advertised departure dates, which meant emigrants had to exhaust whatever savings they had put aside to start their new lives. They got no compensation, and some after waiting for weeks were forced to return home penniless. "Make your bargain for your passage with the owner of the ship or some well-known respectable broker or shipmaster," warned A.C. Buchanan. "Avoid by all means those crimps that are generally found about the docks and quays near where ships are taking in passengers. Be sure the ship is going near where you contracted for, as much deception has been practised in this respect."

A government committee was told that the Irish showed "great ignorance and gullibility." Many could neither read nor write and spoke no English. Dr. Joseph Skey, a medical health officer at Quebec City in the 1830s, reported:

A pauper emigrant on his arrival in this Province is generally either with nothing or with a very small sum in his pocket; entertaining the most erroneous ideas of his prospects here; expecting immediate and constant employment at ample wages; entirely ignorant of the nature of the country, and of the place where labour is most in demand, and of the best means by which to obtain employment. He has landed from the ship, and from his apathy and want of energy has loitered about the wharfs, waiting for the offer of employment; or, if he obtained employment, he calculated upon its permanency, and found himself, at the beginning of winter, when there is little or no employment for labour in this part of the country, discharged, and without any provision for the wants of a Canadian winter. In this way emigrants have often accumulated in Quebec at the end of summers, encumbered it with indigent inhabitants, and formed the most onerous burthen on the charitable funds of the community.

Innocent of geography, people who thought they were bound for New Brunswick found themselves in Quebec City. One group arrived at Charlottetown, Prince Edward Island, under the impression they were in Charleston in the Carolinas. The worst confusion was to be found in Liverpool, the former headquarters of the English slave trade, which became a major point of departure for the Irish. It was cheaper to pay a few shillings to cross the Irish Sea and depart from Liverpool than to take a ship from Cork City or Dublin, though the risks and discomfort were greater. Crossing the Irish Sea by steamer, they were obliged to remain crowded on deck in all weathers or were jammed into the hold amid livestock and their seasick companions. An official who observed the arrival of a coastal steamer from Ireland wrote, "The people were positively prostrated from the inclemency of the weather, seasick all the way, drenched from sea and rain, suffering from cold at night." He called the conditions "disgraceful, dangerous and inhuman."

"Of all the seaports in the world," wrote the American author Herman Melville, "Liverpool perhaps most abounds in all the variety of land sharks, land rats and other vermin which make the helpless mariner their prey." Down by the docks, Waterloo Road swarmed with "man catchers," the touts and runners employed by speculators to fill the ships, by kidnapping if need be. When Irish emigrants were not robbed outright on the streets, they were overcharged for lodging and food. "Sometimes agents take payments from emigrants for the passage," warned a Colonial Office circular, "and then recommend him to some tavern, where he is detained from day to day under false pretences for delay, until before the departure of the ship the whole of his money is extorted from him." The mayor of Liverpool told the Colonial Office that the plight of emigrants was "painful to witness." A local doctor condemned the typical "lodging cellar ... an underground cave, in which drainage, light and ventilation were utterly unattainable, where every exhalation rolled in volumes of pestilential mist round the apology for a ceiling." Dr. George M. Douglas, a Canadian quarantine officer based at Gaspé and later at Grosse Isle, reported, "From these places the emigrants embark on board vessels, bringing with them in their foul clothes and bedding the seeds of disease." With twenty ships leaving Liverpool for North American every day, from docks spread over an area of three miles, emigration officers were too few to enforce the law, and the death rate on Liverpool ships was higher than on those from other ports.

There were nine separate Passenger Acts during the first half of the 19th century and while most were toothless or impossible to enforce, the first, passed in 1803, was enlightened and many years ahead of its time. Its enactment followed shocking reports of conditions on ships carrying emigrants from Scotland and Ireland in the 1790s when people were cooped into half the space required for slave ships, or slept in the hold atop cargoes of bricks or stinking green hides. On one Irish ship, half the passengers died at sea, and thirty bodies still lay on deck when the vessel made port like a ghost ship in a tale of maritime horror.

The Passenger Act of 1803, which stipulated no more than one adult for every two registered tons of vessel, required emergency rations in case the emigrant's own supply ran out, a medicine chest and, on ships carrying more than fifty passengers, a doctor. Since there were still few emigrants – barely 1,000 from Ireland in 1803 – the act was ignored. Had there been the will and the administrative machinery to enforce it, the 1803 act might have saved misery and many thousands of lives. Whereas slavers had a vested interest in getting their human cargoes from Africa to American plantations in working condition, Irish emigrants were regarded as "free agents" and were left to fend for themselves once their fares were collected. In 1815 the Governor of Newfoundland protested the "loss of life and misery which has been sometimes produced by the manner in which, shocking to humanity, passengers have been brought from Ireland."

The 1803 law was replaced with a watered-down version in 1817 which in two respects was worse than no law at all since it implicitly legalized overcrowding and starvation at sea. It condoned overcrowding by permitting one adult (or three children) for every ton and a half of registered tonnage, whereas an American act passed in 1819 allowed no more than two passengers for every five tons. It condoned starvation by permitting ships' masters to carry no emergency rations if passengers agreed to bring their own food.

American law required ships flying the Stars and Stripes to carry 100 pounds of breadstuffs, 100 pounds of salt meat and 60 gallons of water per passenger; there were heavy fines if a ship carried more passengers than the law allowed. This drove up the cost of passage to the States and had the effect of diverting, for years to come, the flow of Irish emigration from the States to the British colonies. People found it cheaper to go to Quebec City or New Brunswick and travel south from there, and in some years two thirds of all emigrants to the British colonies followed this route.

In 1823 the British tried to emulate the Americans and tighten regulations, which provoked the shipowners' lobby to complain that stricter laws would discourage emigration completely or drive emigrants onto American ships. Attacking a regulation requiring ships to carry food rations, John Ostle, a Dublin shipowner, told the Colonial Office: "The emigrants from this country, being mostly poor Catholics, are not accustomed to beef and biscuit and do not like it. In fact they are not able to purchase it if they did." Appearing before the emigration committee in 1826, John Uniacke, the Anglo-Irish Attorney General of Nova Scotia, argued against the comforts of the 1823 act: "The Irish emigrant, before he comes out, knows not what it is to lie on a bed. If you put him in a bed and give him pork and flour, you make the man sick; but when a man comes to Newfoundland he gets no more than his breadth and length upon the deck of a ship, and he has no provisions but a few herrings, and he comes out a healthy man and he has no doctor."

In an era of free enterprise, the government dropped passenger regulations completely in 1827. The results were disastrous. William Todhunter, a Cork City Quaker campaigning for humane conditions, told the Colonial Office he saw overcrowding that "nothing in the annals of the slave trade could equal." A naval officer who had been active in suppression of the slave trade had seen emigrant ships at St. John's, Newfoundland, "that beggared all descriptions of the state of captured African slave ships."

When the brig *James* from Waterford arrived at Halifax with sixty cases of "ship fever," a lethal combination of typhus and dysentery, an official blamed it on "scanty nourishment during the voyage and the

crowded and filthy state of the ship and want of medical assistance."
John O'Flaherty, a Waterford man writing from Halifax, said Irish
emigrants had arrived on the *Bolivar, Cumberland* and *Cherub* suffering great misery, "partly from the hardships suffered on the voyage and
partly from contagion." Eight hundred people caught typhus and, as
O'Flaherty said, many died: "Whole families have been consigned to
an untimely grave, some lost parents, others children."

The brig *William Henry* arrived in Saint John with 250 passengers
in "dreadful state" from lack of food and water. The brig *Eleanor*
brought so much sickness to Chatham, New Brunswick, that the
frightened town officials turned some old sheds on Middle Island into
an isolation hospital and buried victims at night so as not to alarm the
town.

"It is notorious," declared the Secretary of the New Brunswick
Agricultural and Emigrant Society, "that many of the poor emigrants
were deluded from their homes by false but specious statements of
brokers and shipmasters whose sole object in prosecuting the inhuman traffic appears to be that of collecting as many large cargoes as
possible of their unsuspecting fellow subjects; and as the passage
money is paid in advance, it is of little consequence to them in a pecu-
niary point of view whether the helpless victims of their cupidity perish on the voyage or live to spread disease and death among the people
on whose shores they may be landed."

If anything proved the need for state intervention, it was the disastrous migration of 1827; an alarmed government, whose civil servants had tinkered so ineptly with human lives, sought help from a
man who knew the emigrant trade first hand. This was Alexander
Carlisle Buchanan, member of a family of Londonderry shipowners,
whose brother, James, Consul General in New York, had dispatched
thousands of Irish emigrants to Upper Canada a decade earlier.
Buchanan had come to Canada as an emigrant himself, establishing a
farm and mill at Sorel on the St. Lawrence and acting from time to
time as a consultant to the Colonial Office.

Buchanan's proposals were neither radical nor impossible to administer, but bore little relation to the act the government produced in 1828 and which governed emigration for the next seven years. Instead of a limitation of two passengers for every three tons as he suggested, the ratio was increased to three for every four tons, which worked out to no more than two square feet of space for every adult passenger. The emergency ration he proposed was cut by one third, which he found inadequate for sustaining health, and he complained people were not given food they were used to. "If you give an Irish peasant beef and biscuits and salt pork and coffee," he said, "they will be all over scurvy before they get to North America." His proposal that passengers and food be inspected at point of departure was ignored.

The new attempts at regulating emigrant traffic, even if the laws had been faithfully enforced, were inadequate to control the migration of 41,000 people to British North America in 1831, twice the number of the previous year. Ships unfit for Atlantic crossings were pressed into service without inspection. "The ships selected for this purpose were old vessels especially taken up for the occasion and never used again," said Edward G. S. Stanley, Secretary for Ireland. "They were crammed with human beings, badly provided with necessaries, and the consequences were disease and death. The persons who carried on this system were left to play the game over and over again with fresh victims."

Many ships reaching Quebec City in the summer of 1831 carried more passengers than permitted by law, but their only penalty was to be listed as offenders in the newspapers. Ships like the *Ulster* had 500 people crowded into space big enough for half that number. "I had great trouble," said Buchanan, "with captains and their passengers in disputed cases; and unless some satisfactory plan can be adopted, I anticipate a great increase in existing abuses."

Even at Saint John, where port regulations were stricter, there were frequent abuses. The 156-ton brig *Billow* from Kerry came in with 148 people, thirty-seven more than allowed by law and many of them ill. Her case was unusual only in that her master, Alexander Elder, was fined. More usual was the case of the *Eleanor*. Though she carried an illegal number of passengers, her captain, who had a relative on the jury, was acquitted.

Disease, overcrowding, dirt, lack of food and clean water, these were common complaints year after year. One man wrote that he found himself "shut up in a dark hold without a ray of light and almost no air." Another compared the smell to the "stink of a dung heap." Frederick Sabel, who ran one of the few honest lodging houses in Liverpool, told a government committee that conditions on the ships are "worse than can be imagined.... It was like a regular dungeon. When we opened some of the hatchways under which the people were, the steam came up, and the smell was like the smell of pigs. The few beds they had were in dreadful state; for the straw, when once wet with water, soon decays; besides which, they used the between decks for all sorts of filthy purposes."

People refused to use the flimsy toilets nailed in the bows because the little huts were too dirty and dangerous. "It was mere humbug to call them water closets," said a witness. "The first sea that comes washes them down, or an ill-disposed man can knock them down with one blow, and the whole is left open." Doors burst open in rough weather exposing the squatting inmates to the view of the forecastle crew, and people took to relieving themselves in the darkness of the hold, for there were never enough chamber pots, and often none at all.

The Times of London described the cramped steerage – no more than twenty-five feet wide and fifty or sixty feet long on the brigs – as a "noisome dungeon, airless and lightless, in which several hundred persons of both sexes and all ages are stowed away on shelves two feet one inch above the other, three feet wide and six feet long, still reeking from the inevitable stench left by the emigrants of the last voyage." Others compared them to dog kennels or the Black Hole of Calcutta.

A passenger on the *Thomas Elson*, which carried 500 passengers from Londonderry to Quebec City, said there were tiers of berths on

both sides and a row down the centre which left hardly any passage way, and that was filled with luggage and barrels. "The passengers were thus obliged to eat in their berths. In one were a man, his wife, his sister, and five children, in another were six full grown young women, while that above contained five men, and the next eight men." He said the only thing that made the voyage barely tolerable was the good weather, which permitted the hatches to remain open, providing some light and air.

The equally large emigration of 1832 was turned into a shambles by the cholera epidemic. Some 20 per cent of emigrants from Limerick, 500 people, died at sea. Ships from Liverpool were badly infected with cholera and when the *Brutus* sailed from that port inspection had, as usual, been sketchy and she was nine days into her voyage when cholera was detected. "The ravages of the pestilence then rapidly increased, the deaths becoming numerous in proportion to the cases," reported *The Times* on June 15. "The greatest number of deaths was twenty-four in one day. The captain had no intention of returning to port, until the disease began to attack the crew. He then saw that to continue the voyage was to risk the lives of himself and the survivors, as well as the property entrusted to his care. Under these circumstances, his vessel a lazarhouse, and men, women and children dying about him, he resolved to put back to Liverpool." By the time he reached Liverpool the death toll was eighty-three.

As a result of that disastrous season, Edward Stanley, who had left the post of Secretary of Ireland to become Colonial Secretary, took one of the most effective actions to date. He appointed a small corps of officers whose sole duty was to police emigration ships at major ports of departure. The first of these was Lieutenant Robert Low, a half-pay naval officer, who took up his appointment in Liverpool early in 1833 and found that the customs officers previously entrusted with emigrant ship inspection had done very little, being busy with revenue matters. There were never enough emigration officers, but their presence did have some effect on overcrowding, lack of sanitation and

seaworthiness of vessels at a time when hardly a season went by without its toll of shipwreck.

One cause of shipwreck was drunkenness. When the *Lancaster* was caught in the ice off Newfoundland in 1833, a passenger claimed that the master was so drunk he had to be restrained while more sober officers worked the ship free. Another cause was faulty navigation, since officers used the ancient system of dead-reckoning their course and distance, checking their position at noon with a shot of the sun, which on the Newfoundland Banks was often hidden by fog. Navigation error was the reason for the wreck of the *Hebe*, which had brought the Robinson people in 1823. The *Hebe* hit a ledge off Cape Ray, Newfoundland, but all were rescued, which one passenger found miraculous given the quality of the crew, "a set of the most vile, abandoned wretches I have ever met with."

The *James*, the same ill-fated brig that brought typhus to Halifax in 1827, sailed from Limerick on April 8, 1834, with 267 people bound for Quebec City and Upper Canada. Half way through her voyage, the *James* was crippled by a storm that ripped out the mainsail, carried away the topmast and broke two booms. Leaking and disabled in a westerly gale off the Newfoundland Banks, the *James* began to sink. Dr. Henry Downes, one of the few survivors, set down an account in his journal:

On Sunday, the 25th, at six a.m., they set about pumping the ship, but were not long engaged before the pumps were found to be choked with the passengers' potatoes, which, from the rotten description of the bags in which they were kept, went adrift about the hold, filling the pump wells and preventing the possibility of working the pumps, which were hoisted on deck and a great quantity of potatoes brought away with them.

Finding the water to increase to an alarming extent, and a gale from the N.W. springing up, with a heavy sea, the ship straining very much, we had recourse to the expedient of baling her out from the fore hatch with buckets; but the water casks, which were floating about there, excited the apprehensions of the people, and one passenger, Henry Morgan, getting three of his fingers broken between two of them, the attempt was abandoned.

About four o'clock p.m. she shipped a sea which carried away the bulwarks, and was soon after struck by a second still heavier, with the force of which she listed, canting her ballast, and never returned to an erect position. The water having reached the between-decks, and no chance of saving her presenting itself, the Captain, at five o'clock, ordered the longboat and skiff to be lowered, as a sail tacking to the southward make its appearance. The passengers crowded into the skiff while she was in the longboat, and by this means made it difficult to lower the latter, which when drawn from the after-chock came against the stanchions; after which they did not seem inclined to take further trouble with her. At half past six we lowered the jollyboat, in which eleven of us were picked up by the *Margaret* of Newcastle, Capt. Wake, to whose kindness and humanity since we are indebted to our preservation.

Before abandoning ship, the captain urged passengers to disentangle the skiff from the longboat so they could both be launched, "but their answer was, the sea is so rough we are sure to be drowned, and may as well die on board as in the boats." The rescue vessel tacked up and down through heavy seas all night but found no trace of her boats, or 256 passengers.

The *Aberdeen* from Belfast sank in the Gulf of St. Lawrence with the loss of 315. Some of these tragedies, such as the wreck of the *Lady of the Lake,* which hit an iceberg with the loss of all but fifteen of her 250 people, had ballads sung about them:

> Our ship was split asunder
> As you may understand
> And left our bodies floating
> On the Banks of Newfoundland

One of Samuel Strickland's neighbours at Peterborough survived shipwreck twice. Returning to Stangford in Ulster with his wife and two children, he sailed late in the year in a timber ship that ran into a terrible gale and began to sink. During the twenty-day ordeal that followed, his wife and two children died of exposure though he was saved by a passing ship and reached Stangford ill and penniless. Some time later when he sailed back to Canada, he was shipwrecked again. "My ill luck still attended me," he told Strickland, "for owing to the dense

fogs we experienced on the Banks of Newfoundland we got out of our course and our ship struck the shore near Cape Ray; fortunately the sea was smooth and the weather fine; so that when daylight broke we were able, without much difficulty, to be landed on that most inhospitable shore."

Lying in his bunk one night, Henry Johnson from Dungonnel in County Antrim was "awakened by cries and shouts of 'the ship's lost, the ship's sinking!' I started up and such a sight: men, women and children rushing to the upper deck. Some praying, crossing themselves, other with faces as white as a corpse. On deck they were gathered like sheep in a pen, crying to the captain to save them." The ship was a timber drogher and one of the bow ports cut to receive tree-length timber had sprung open, admitting streams of seawater that threatened to sink the vessel.

Johnson was one of forty Protestants in a passenger list of 500, mostly Catholics. He complained that the Catholics would not man the pumps. "They would do nothing but sprinkle holy water, cry, pray, and all sorts of tom foolery instead of giving a hand." When the man in the next berth died of dysentery at the height of the storm, the ship was pitching so badly that his wife, daughters and the corpse were all thrown on Johnson in a heap. "The corpse, boxes, barrels, women and children all in one mess were knocked from side to side for about fifteen minutes." Johnson had brought a ham with him but it went rotten and the voyage took so long, eight weeks, that he was obliged to subsist on the five pounds of biscuits and two pounds of salt meat doled out each week by the mate. Pigs wouldn't eat such biscuits, he said. "So for the remainder of the passage I got a right good starving."

Like Johnson, Patrick Finan, was awakened by commotion on deck. "The wind howling dreadfully, the sea roaring in a terrible manner." When he tried to help the sailors he was knocked into the scuppers by a wave. "The women in the steerage who heard the waves striking against the ship, and flying down among them, and supposing at the instant that she was sinking, sent forth piercing and heart-

rending shrieks and cries. A very few moments elapsed when another wave, greater than the first, came dashing in, which caused them to redouble their shouts. 'O mamma, mamma!' cried a little boy. 'Kiss me before we go!'" Dawn found the vessel battered but intact.

To people from inland parishes who had never seen the ocean, the storms were fearful. Annie Griffin, a middle-aged Catholic, wrote that she fully expected "to die of fear." An Ulsterman recalled the "yell of water" in his ears and another wrote: "As we sat listening to the moans of the sick and the dying, the whistling of the wind among the creaking rigging, and the melee of rats which chased each other from hole to hole, and falling out, sometimes raised a tremendous squeaking – while to crown the picture, wave after wave broke like thunder at our ear, shaking the vessel from stem to stern."

In 1834 sixteen vessels were lost. The bark *Astrea* was wrecked off Louisbourg, Nova Scotia, the brig *Edward* foundered on an iceberg and the ship *Fidelity* sank, the death toll on these three being 700. The *Rob Roy* from Belfast hit a reef and lost seventy-seven people. News of this spate of disasters reduced the flow of emigrants in 1835 to 10,000, or a third of the previous year's total. An Ulster woman wrote, "All could not induce me to go. If it was any place I could travel by land, I would not mind it so much, but I feel a kind of terror of the sea."

An emergency meeting in Quebec blamed the "common avarice" of shipowners. "The desire for gain prevailing over every other condition," said A.C. Buchanan, "has led many captains, owners and agents of worthless vessels, more particularly in the seaport towns of Ireland, into a most horrible traffic in human life, that should be immediately arrested by the urgent voice of humanity and the strong voice of power. In an endeavour to make a profitable voyage by the embarkation of the greatest number of passengers, no expedience for deception appears to them too shameful."

Supported by emigration officers in Liverpool and Ireland, Buchanan was successful in introducing improvements into the 1835 Passenger Act. Emigrants were to receive slightly more space, though still not as much as in American ships, and lists of emigrants were to be sent ahead by fast mail packets to be checked against arrivals to detect overcrowding by emigrants slipped aboard in the last confused moments before a ship sailed. "These may be seen arriving in flushed and panting detachments," said one witness. "It so often happens that the gangway has been removed upon their arrival, in which case their only chance is to wait until the ship has reached the dock gate, in which case their boxes, bales, barrels and bundles are actually pitched into the ship and men and women and children have to scramble up into the rigging amid a screaming, swearing and shouting perfectly alarming to listen to, while frequently a box or barrel falls overboard and sometimes a man or a woman, but is speedily saved by men in a small boat which follows for that purpose."

The law was inadequate and enforcement was sketchy. The *Kingston* and the *Celia* arrived at Quebec City in 1836 with passengers suffering from lack of water, and the clumsily fitted berths on another ship collapsed, killing several children. But conditions were improving, which Buchanan said "may be attributed in a great measure to the appointment of emigration agents in the principal ports in the United Kingdom."

Since most of the horror stories stemmed from particular years of famine or epidemic, in normal years the bulk of the emigrants, as letters and diaries suggest, found the voyage more uncomfortable and tedious than horrendous. Seasickness was a serious matter because it was so debilitating and dehumanizing in the cramped confines of the airless steerage, but once past that, some emigrants even enjoyed the novel journey. Younger men and women recalled fiddles and singing and dancing on deck, and the shanties of sailors as they set the sails to the wind.

"The hold was full of people, mighty snug and decent," wrote Bridget Lacy, a young Catholic servant from Wicklow bound for Upper Canada. "Most of them Protestants, that found home growing too hot for them; and that they had better save their four bones, and their little earnings, before it was too late; and sure enough, I believe they're right. There are mighty good people among them, and mighty pretty girls, that when they aren't sick, sing psalms in the evening, very beautiful."

Bridget's only fear was the "whillaloo" of a storm that lashed the ship with a cracking of masts and ropes. "We were all knocked of a heap, and then if you were to hear all around you, as I did, groaning, and raching, and willy wombing, and calling for water, nobody to bring them a sup, and wishing themselves at the bottom of the sea; in troth you would have pitied a dog." During the voyage a child was born, a girl choked to death on a potato and an old woman died, "and the captain, long life to him, put the old woman in a coffin, saying that *sherks* would have a mouthful of sawdust before they got at her old bones."

Much has been written about bucko mates and bullying captains, but there were also masters who displayed kindness. When Edward Talbot came over on the *Brunswick* in 1818, he had great praise for the captain. "From the moment of our embarkation at Cork to the night of our departure from his ship, his attention, not only to the cabin passengers but also to the humblest individual in the steerage, evinced a disposition highly creditable to himself and honourable to his profession. He was to all a friend, an attendant, and a physician and constantly solicitous of our health and welfare."

John Anderson of Balinree, Ulster, who sailed on the brig *Symmetry* from Belfast to Quebec, said, "We had as good a captain as ever sailed the sea. He was never seen intoxicated." He did, however, get into difficulties in the ice, and his ship had to be pumped day and night all the way to Quebec. "For two days and nights we had to walk the deck with oars and other pieces of timber to defend the vessel," said Anderson. "We had to let down logs of timber with chains and ropes around the vessel to keep her from being wrecked in the ice."

Samuel Craigy, who sailed from Belfast on the *Rienze*, found the captain a "pleasant man, as was the first mate, a little agreeable fellow and a good dancer." The emigrants had brought two flutes, two accordions, a bugle, fiddle and fife. They ate salt beef and potatoes boiled in seawater, and a goat provided milk for the children. Sometimes people ate better than they had done at home, but cooking was a problem on the little brick hearth on deck. Craigy, whose humour ran to slapstick, described "amusing cooking scenes" when the vessel rolled and tumbled. "Some were thrown headlong from the fires up against the bulwarks, scattering their saucepans with the contents about the deck. One man spilled his dinner three times in succession coming up the companion ladder. Another tumbled from the top of the ladder with a saucepan full of gruel, and alighted between the shoulders of a proud skipjack young man besmearing his clothes, all of which was a source of merriment to the rest of the passengers."

Craigy made the trip in August when days that the sea was "as smooth as a fish pond" alternated with storms when the waves were "uphill on all sides." There was cholera aboard but it was diagnosed as dysentery, and lives might have been saved, Craigy believed, had there been a doctor. There were several deaths, the bodies being stitched into shrouds of canvas with an iron weight at the foot before being slid into the sea. Describing the sea burial of an old man, Craigy wrote: "The night is setting in dark and stormy with heavy rain. Sea running very high and the ship steering NE with scarcely a stitch of canvas unfurled. The funeral tonight was a very frightful and solemn scene. After a hurried prayer was read over the body below, it was with some difficulty hauled up on deck, the ship at the time pitching very much; and as we committed it to the deep, the foam-crested billows boomed by, flashing like illuminated winding sheets in the flickering lamp light, which rendered more fearfully dense the pitchy darkness. There is no doubt the body was devoured by sharks."

Shipwrecks, though fewer than in the 1830s, were still common enough to cause alarm. In 1841, the 300-ton brig *Minstrel* bound from Limerick to Quebec struck a reef and only eight of her 141 passengers survived. A third of the victims were children. There had been no previous legislation to cover shipwreck, but the Passenger Act of 1842 required ships, for the first time, to carry lifeboats for steerage passengers. Though it did not address all abuses, it was the best law, at least on paper, since that of 1803, and decreed there should only be two tiers of bunks and ceilings should be six feet from the floor so that adults could stand upright. Each passenger was to have ten square feet of space between decks. Water was to be carried in clean containers so it would remain drinkable throughout the voyage. Though most emigrants were expected to bring their own rations as an insurance against starvation, each passenger was by law to be given seven pounds of breadstuffs or potatoes each week. There was to be no sale of liquor, on pain of a fine of £100. Brokers and agents were licensed, and emigrants were to be reimbursed one shilling a day if the vessel did not sail on the promised date. There was no requirement to carry a doctor, however, and there would be no regulation until the late 1840s to ban unseaworthy vessels or eliminate the cramming of unmarried young women and men into the same space. The 1842 act, though adequate in normal years, was the legislation in force during the chaotic years of the Great Famine when 20,000 died during the voyage or soon after.

It was not until fast, dependable steamships replaced sailing ships, and dishonest speculators were pushed out of business, that abuses began to disappear in the second half of the 19th century. In 1853, the annual report of the government's Colonial and Land Emigration Commissioners was still concerned with abuse. "We would recommend," it said, "that free emigrants should be treated at least as well as convicts in transport ships."

13

"The Song of the Black Potato"

The Potatoes that failed, brought the nation to agony,
The poorhouse bare, and the dreadful coffin ship,
And in mountain graves do they in hundreds lie,
By hunger taken to their beds of clay.

Anon

No VEGETABLE has been more crucial to a nation's survival. Though the potato accounted for hardly a quarter of Ireland's total agricultural production, it had gradually replaced oat bread and meat until by the 18th century it was virtually the sole sustenance of a third of the rural population. Like rice in Asia, the potato held power of life and death.

An acre of the "poor man's crop" contained as much nourishment as three acres of grain. Potatoes were easy to grow and flourished on wet, boggy wasteland or rocky hills, where they were planted in "lazy beds," broad ridges of earth thrown up by a spade over layers of sod or seaweed. "Lazy beds" were so called because they were self-draining, and planting was simply a matter of thrusting a narrow-bladed spade into the ridge, dropping in the seed potatoes and covering them with earth and a little manure.

Of the many varieties cultivated since Elizabethan travellers brought the potato from Virginia to Ireland in the late 16th century, the potato of the poor was the Lumper, or Horse Potato, coarse, white, watery, but prolific; like its fancier cousins it contained enough starch, sugar, nitrogen, vitamin C and minerals to provide a healthful diet, when eaten with a little protein in the form of milk or butter. Moreover, unlike other root vegetables such as the turnip, it was bland enough to be eaten day after day for months on end without palling. The Irish not only depended on the potato – they enjoyed it.

A pot of boiling water, a basket of Lumpers, and the family had a cheap, quick meal, so easy to prepare that Father Theobald Mathew, the temperance preacher from Cork, complained that Irish women had lost the art of cooking anything else. When milk was available a saucer was placed on a stool and the potatoes were dipped in it – "a dab at the stool" it was called. It was fashionable among country people to grow one fingernail long, the better to peel off the potato skin.

"Mark the Irishman's potato bowl placed on the floor," wrote Arthur Young, "the whole family upon their hams around it, devouring a quantity almost incredible, the beggar seating himself to it with a hearty welcome, the pig taking his share as easily as the wife, the hens, geese, the cur, the cat and perhaps the cow – and all partaking of the same dish. No man can often have been a witness of it without being convinced of the plenty, and I will add the cheerfulness, that attends it."

Young believed that the potato diet of the Irish compared favourably with the bread and cheese of the English farm worker. "When I see people of a country, in spite of political oppression, with well-formed vigorous bodies, and their cottages swarming with children; when I see their men athletic, and their women beautiful, I know not how to believe them subsisting on an unwholesome diet."

A healthy worker might eat ten to fourteen pounds of potatoes a day, with milk and sometimes an egg or, if near the sea, some herring.

Potatoes left over might be made into *fleatair*, potato cake. Children took boiled or roasted potatoes to school and gave one to the teacher, as other children might give an apple. Oats, wheat, barley, beef and pork produced in the midland and eastern counties went largely for export though oats remained the staple diet among the Scots-Presbyterians in eastern Ulster.

Though the potato's nourishing properties were credited in part for the incredible growth in Irish population, particularly in the west, the potato was a treacherous friend. When the potato crop failed in Canada or England it was no great tragedy, for there were other foods, but in Ireland potato failure was disastrous. Few regions were entirely free of wet rot, dry rot or the fungus known as "curl." The Irish census for 1851, analyzing past famines, blamed the crop failure of 1821–22 on an unusually cold summer followed by unusually heavy rain through much of the winter.

It was scarcely possible, and generally unprofitable, to dig out the potato crop – it soured and rotted in the ground; and although a sufficiency was obtained in the dry and upland districts to support human life for some months, it was expended early in the ensuing spring; and then destitution, famine, and pestilence in quick succession followed. Fortunately these effects were not generally throughout the kingdom, but occupied a district which might be defined by a line drawn from the bay of Donegal, upon the north side, at the junction of the counties of Sligo and Leitrim, to Youghal harbour, where the counties of Cork and Waterford border on the south – thus including the whole western seaboard of Sligo, Mayo, Galway, Clare, Limerick, Kerry, and Cork; all exposed to the full force of the Atlantic, the influence of which though mild is moist.... The year 1829 was wet, and the month of August particularly so; the crops were beaten down by heavy rains and severe storms, and in all low grounds the water overran the potatoes, and so remained for many weeks; thus a great quantity of the potatoes was lost this year also....

In 1830 we read that "violent storms and heavy rains brought upon the West of Ireland another failure of the potato, with its usual accompaniment of famine and pestilence," but it was principally confined to the coasts of Mayo, Galway, and Donegal. This blight was common to parts of America, and to Germany, where it continued for two years. In 1832, and for several years following in succession, an epidemic attacked the potato throughout Ireland. In 1833 it presented not only the appearance of the "curl" but likewise attacked the potatoes in pits.... A partial failure of the potato was observed in several parts of Ireland in 1836.... We have no recorded account of any special failure of the potato crop in Ireland in 1838, which was also a wet year, but the "inherent constitutional weakness" of the esculent was observed, and the deterioration in the best kinds of the potato formed the theme of public remark at the time. In 1839 there was an unmistakable failure of that crop, attributed to the incessant rains.... The year 1839 was characterized by an amount of moisture unparalleled, according to modern observations; the quantity of rain that fell near Dublin being nearly 10 inches beyond the average; and the potatoes failed throughout the western and midland counties. Part of 1840 was likewise characterized by excessive moisture; although there was less rain than in the previous year; yet it came down in an unpropitious period – the potato crop failed again in Leinster and Munster; and upon both occasions great distress followed.

None of these regional crop failures had brought general famine through the whole country, but in 1830 the Duke of Wellington, an Anglo-Irishman from County Meath, had predicted that sooner or later there must be another great famine equal to that of 1740, in which 300,000 had died. The population – increased from five to eight million since the turn of the century – was too great for the potato to sustain. As the Poor Enquiry had found in 1835, two and a half million went hungry for several months each summer before the new crop was ready to eat.

In 1844 western Ireland produced so many potatoes that it was common to find them used for fertilizer or to fill the gaps in stone fences. The hot, damp summer of 1845 seemed well on the way to producing another such a crop when, on July 23, the *Freeman's Journal* declared, "The poor man's property, the potato crop, was never before so large, and at the same time so abundant."

Reports of a new disease invading northern Europe, apparently carried in ships from the Atlantic seaboard of North America, raised little concern, nor did an item on August 16 in the *Gardener's Chronicle*, an English publication, which spoke of potato infection of "unusual character" on the Isle of Wight. Readers were asked if they knew what it was.

Despite heavy rain and thunder and lightning in Ireland in August, the crops flourished. "The growth of the potato plant progresses as favourably as the most sanguine farmer could wish," said the *Freeman's Journal* of August 20. Three days later newspapers reported crop failure in Belgium and Holland, and spreading blight in southern England. "As for a cure for this distemper," concluded the *Gardener's Chronicle*, "there is none."

Once it reached Ireland, appearing first in counties Wexford and Waterford, the blight spread quickly with eerie effect. "A mist rose up out of the sea," wrote a Sligo man, "and you could hear a voice talking near a mile off across the stillness of the earth. You could begin to see the tops of the stalks lying over as if the life was gone out of them. And that was the beginning of the great trouble and famine that destroyed Ireland."

"We regret to state," said the *Freeman's Journal* of September 11, "that we have had communications from more than one well-informed correspondent announcing the fact of what is called 'cholera' in potatoes in Ireland. In one instance the party had been digging potatoes – the finest he had ever seen – from a particular field and a particular ridge of that field up to Monday last; and on digging in the same ridge on Tuesday he found the tubers all blasted; and unfit for the use of man or beast."

The first symptom was a faint spot, followed by others until a green leaf turned purple. When tubers were dug they seemed healthy, only to collapse into "wet putrefaction." The potato is apparently sound when dug," said the *Cork Southern Reporter*, "but on examination small round spots are found running round the tuber and having each the appearance of a running sore or cancer." Not knowing that the disease was caused by a tiny spore carried by the wind, people ran into the fields to chop off infected leaves. Confused and contradictory reports sent in by constables led to hope this crop failure might be partial, and no worse than others in the past. One cause of confusion was the way the fungus spread in a chequerboard pattern, one field turning black with rot while its neighbour remained green. Dry, upland regions were the last to be infected, and crops other than the potato flourished.

In some regions potatoes did not seem in great risk as late as September 29, when the *Ballyshannon Herald* of Donegal reported: "Almost all the wheat in the country is reaped, an average crop. The barley is reaped and more than average crop. Turnips look well. The potato crop looks luxuriant, but some are complaining that a disease has prevailed to a partial extent." On the other side of the country, however, a priest in Kills, County Meath, said, "In this most fertile potato-growing locale, one family in twenty will not have a single potato left on Christmas day next." In County Sligo holy water was sprinkled on the fields. Some blamed the thunder and lightning. The people at Downpatrick Head in County Mayo said it was the work of malignant fairies.

Three scientists, including Dr. John Lindley, professor of botany, founder of Kew Gardens in London and editor of the *Gardener's Chronicle*, were commissioned to investigate. Unfortunately they failed to find the cause, attributing the outbreak to damp, which was only a contributory factor. Normally farmers stored potatoes by simply burying them in a pit, a primitive version of a root cellar. Now farmers were advised to choose dry and airy sites and provide ventilation, leaving holes in the top of the pit and a channel at the bottom for air to pass through. If the potatoes were kept cool and ventilated, it was believed, fermentation would be arrested and even slightly diseased potatoes could be saved. But when these pits were opened the potatoes were rotten. "These learned men," scoffed the nationalist author John Mitchel, "prepared so valuable and large a book that if it had been eatable the famine had been stayed."

To do the scientists justice, no one else knew the cause, which was identified seven years later as *Phytophtora infestans*, a parasitical fungus that thrives on damp and is carried by wind and deposited on leaves. It attacks the tuber after being washed down into the soil by rain, which accounts for the fact that sometimes the leaves are killed without the tuber seeming to be infected. The antidote was to elude scientists for another thirty years before a spray of copper sulphate and lime proved effective.

By late October the blight had spread through seventeen counties from Waterford to northern Ulster. "The rot is making frightful ravages even in the potatoes which about eight days ago were intact," reported a County Mayo correspondent in the *Freeman's Journal.* "The country hereabouts is in a most melancholy state; despondency and tears are to be seen in almost every face." Writing from his estate near Limerick, Lord Monteagle, a former cabinet minister, told Prime Minister Sir Robert Peel that he could recall no failure "being anything near so great and alarming as at present." The Earl of Clare said farmers with substantial holdings could "struggle through the year," but what, he asked, of the "unemployed multitude whose store of provision for the next ten months is gone, and who have not a shilling to purchase food?"

Sir Robert Peel, who had served six years as Chief Secretary for Ireland and organized relief during the partial famine of 1816, had acted early in November to meet an apprehended crisis. Peel knew from experience that when the potato failed, hunger and sickness must follow. The worst problem in earlier crop failures had been getting emergency food to the people and providing them with cash to buy it, so Peel authorized the Irish Board of Works to start up a program of road building, whether roads were needed or not, and employ as many as possible at a wage sufficient for survival. To provide a cheap alternative to the potato, he ordered shipments of maize, or Indian corn, from the United States. Peel did this without waiting to consult parliament, or even his Treasury Board, and when questioned reportedly said, "Good God, are you to sit in cabinet and consider and calculate how much diarrhoea and bloody flux, and dysentery, a people can bear before it becomes necessary for you to go and provide them with food?" Maize was the cheapest food on the international market and had been brought in at least twice before in time of shortage. "Many people like it well," wrote Humphrey O'Sullivan in his diary for 1827. "It will keep down the cost of living for the poor." Peel saw maize as a last defence against starvation and ordered it issued from government depots at less than cost price only when it became absolutely necessary to do so. Meantime he put his faith in local relief committees. "Our main reliance," said Peel, "must be placed on the cooperation of the landed gentry."

A relief organization was set up in Dublin under Sir Randolph Routh, a senior commissariat officer who had experience in feeding masses of people. His superior in London was the civil service head of the Treasury, a thirty-eight-year-old Cornishman, Charles Edward Trevelyan. Intelligent in most things, hardworking, conscientious in his own fashion, Trevelyan was a poor choice as virtual czar of Irish relief because of his dogmatic belief in a free market and opposition to government hand-outs. "You cannot answer the cry of want," Routh told him in a moment of exasperation, "by a quotation from political economy."

Crops other than potatoes had flourished, and oats, wheat, barley, beef, pork and butter were allowed to be exported as if no threat of famine existed. Even potatoes were exported, but they were rotten by the time they reached Holland and Belgium. Daniel O'Connell condemned such exports when Ireland was going hungry, protesting that the English were treating his nation like a "foreign farm" and if Ireland still had its own parliament "the grain would be preserved in Ireland and the inhabitants would be saved from hunger." Peel made no move to halt exports, though he did use the threat of Irish famine as one reason to repeal the English Corn Laws, which had kept grain prices artificially high through protective tariffs against imports. English landowners and merchants who supported the Corn Laws declared that Peel was exaggerating the seriousness of the Irish potato failure merely to excuse his repeal of these tariffs, and that he was killing for all time the prosperity of the English farmer. In this way the Irish famine became caught up and submerged in a domestic English debate over the future of English agriculture.

Meantime, the full impact of potato blight was slow in manifesting itself. For a while it even seemed that potatoes must be more abundant, as Irish farmers hastened to sell their harvest before it went rotten before their eyes, but by mid-November reports from the various counties left no doubt about the extent of the damage, or the futility of the instructions of the scientists who had sought an antidote.

"The disease has spread extensively in the pits," said a report from Tipperary. "A large portion of the potatoes pitted as sound three of four weeks ago being now bad and in some instances unfit for any use. On the lowest calculation, one third of the entire crop is diseased; and though the produce this season is considered to be from one sixth to one seventh greater than that of last year, there must be a great deficiency. The people seem very regardless of the advice circulated – more particularly the poorer class whose crops are the most affected."

Kildare reported: "Since the fall of rain, the crop is rapidly running to decay. The poorer class of people are beginning to despair." From Rathdowney, Queens (now Laois) County, a constable wrote: "Nearly one third of the potatoes dug are more or less affected. The potatoes pitted have not been generally attacked, but in some instances large quantities of them have been lost. Sufficient caution is not used in selecting the sound from the unsound." From Glaslough, County Monaghan: "With very few exceptions, the inhabitants of this district pay no attention to the Commissioner's instructions, which have in many instances been torn down or defaced immediately after posting."

A third to half of the national crop had been lost by the end of 1845, and though the destruction had followed an erratic, unpredictable pattern, touching nearly all counties, those that suffered most at that time were Waterford in the south, Clare in the West, and Monaghan and Antrim in the north. Limerick, Kilkenny, Kerry and east Cork lost nearly 50 per cent, and pockets in the west of Cork were even harder hit. The counties that got off relatively lightly were those in the central midlands from Queens to Tyrone.

The relief commission, which had expected that the inevitable famine would not appear until the following spring, perhaps in April or May, were caught unprepared when appeals for aid began to come in by mid-January. The first came from the village of Killarty near the mouth of the River Shannon. No Indian corn had yet arrived from America, so the commission sent money, oatmeal and some three-year-old biscuits salvaged from an army depot. By the end of February, a hundred calls for help had come in from west coast communities that stretched from Skibbereen in the south to the fishing village of Belmullet in the Barony of Erris in County Mayo. People were eating rotten potatoes or whatever they could get their hands on, and Lord Monteagle said people in County Clare were eating food so rotten "they were obliged to leave the doors and windows of their cabins open." There were reports of the reappearance of typhus, never far below the surface in the 19th century.

"It is utterly impossible for us to adopt means to prevent cases of individual misery in the wilds of Galway, Donegal or Mayo," Peel admitted. "In such localities the people must look to the local proprietors, resident and non-resident." Many of the local committees were failures from the beginning, and landlords willing to help preferred to concern themselves with their own tenants rather than the whole countryside.

The ships with Indian corn began to arrive at Cork Harbour in the last week of January, but because of the government policy of reserving it until all other measures were exhausted, it came in such secrecy that the press learned about it only two weeks later. The *Freeman's Journal*, pointing out that people were starving, called government policy "positive cruelty," but by the end of March only three food depots had been opened, at Cork City, Clonmel in Tipperary and Longford in the northern midlands, and maize distribution was too little to prevent food riots.

At Carrick on Suir, Tipperary, troops had to be called in to break up violent demonstrations. At Mitchelstown, hundreds of women and children stormed government carts and made off with two tons of maize. On April 15 the *Freeman's Journal* reported, "There have been attacks on flour mills in Clonmel by people whose bones protrude through the skins which covered them – staring through hollow eyes as if they had just risen from their shrouds, crying out that they could no longer endure the extremity of their distress. As we pass into summer, we pass into suffering. Every week develops the growing intensity of that calamity."

Famine at first was worse in the countryside than the towns, at least until starving people began to congregate in the towns looking for food; those most afflicted were cottiers and labourers though thousands of tenant farmers were also suffering. The mayor and a deputation from Limerick City went to Dublin to warn the central relief commission that work, wages and food must be provided soon to avert a revolt.

Landlords received threats from the secret societies, as they had in the famine of 1821 and the tithe wars of the 1830s. "I do hereby require of you," said a notice at Ballingary, Tipperary, "to set on work in your neighbourhood, or if you will not you will feel the displeasure of me and my brethrens – signed Captain Starlight." Another said, "I do hereby require of you to set on work in your neighbourhood or if you will not I will not bear hunger no longer while there is beast in the field. And I do bleam you for the whole of it that you would not exert yourself like all gentlemen in the country. I give you Three Days Notice. When you are not a penny out of pocket, it appears to me that you are betraying the Neighbours. I am as well Die by the rope as Die by the Hunger."

The militant nationalist journal the *Nation* declared, "Tipperary is in insurrection. Clonmel in a state of siege. Government bayonets deployed. The peoples' food locked up. Hill tops covered with thousands of strong men, livid with hunger. Provision boats boarded, mills and stores ransacked."

By the end of June, a dozen depots had been opened and were selling hundreds of tons of Indian corn every week at cost price, but even at a penny a pound there were many with no money to buy it. Public works projects had begun but the 25,000 people employed were a small fraction of the needy. In Craughwell, County Mayo, eighty-one labourers petitioned the Lord Lieutenant in Dublin: "Our potatoes are nearly run out, with some of us already exhausted. Petitioners humbly pray that Your Excellency may order that an immediate supply of Indian Corn Meal be sent to this district and sold to us at prices our wages can reach." Earnings for road work varied from four pence to ten pence a day, never enough to feed a large family.

People had trouble with the Indian corn. When Peel had ordered the shipments from America in November someone had failed to make clear that processed meal was needed rather than the flint-like dried corn in the grain. The first shipments consisted of kernels that required special milling, which was lacking in Ireland, and when people boiled the kernels they were still hard and irritated their empty stomachs. There were riots when corn was introduced into workhouses, so the government issued recipes on how "Peel's brimstone" should be cooked "to get rid of much of the raw taste which has been objected to." One recipe called for five pints of boiling water to one pound of meal, the meal to be boiled for an hour. "The weight will be increased six-fold; that is to say, seven pounds of Indian meal will produce at least 42 pounds of substantial porridge." One pound of maize daily was deemed sufficient to keep adults alive, and half a pound for children. Whatever its shortcomings, maize saved thousands of lives.

No deaths specifically due to starvation had yet been reported, and people lived in hope that the 1846 harvest would end their misery, for they believed crop failures never struck in successive years. Emigration increased that spring, though many were turned away because they did not have the three pounds for a passage. The first ships at Quebec City, which arrived in late April, brought "well clad and respectable looking people" such as those on the *Lord Sydenham* that carried Johanna and Oliver Kelly from Newtown, Tipperary. Writing to her father from Pine Grove, Vaughan Township, in Upper Canada, Johanna said she survived the six-week voyage in good health and, apart from homesickness, "we are as comfortable as we can wish to be." The potato crop had failed in Canada, as it had in Ireland, but this mattered little as there was plenty of other food at low cost, "and every day is like Christmas Day for meat," She urged relatives to come and promised to send money. "Hoping to see youse all again," she concluded, "and if not, to meet youse all in Heaven."

Logs kept by A.C. Buchanan at Quebec City showed immigration much as usual that spring. An excerpt for May 23 said:

The emigrants arrived during the week ending this date have landed in good health. 154 passengers by the *Lively* from Galway are from the counties of Clare, Galway, and Mayo. Six families brought out capital, and intend settling in Canada West. The remainder are stout, able young men and single females; some going to their friends, and others seeking employment. They were all able to pay their way, with the exception of three families, eight adults and twelve children, who received a free passage.

The emigrants from the ports of Limerick, Cork and Youghal, 483 in number, are mostly young single men and women. They are chiefly labourers; a considerable number, at least one third, of whom are going to their friends in the United States. A few are employed here and the remainder have gone to different stations of Upper Canada.

June was the same, although the return for the week ending June 20 noted there were a few more cases of "fever" than usual among the emigrants. Most were young people seeking work, and most were Irish, though there were English, Welsh, Scots and Germans as well. The log for the week ending June 27 said, "4,588 emigrants have landed at this port during the past week, chiefly agriculturists. A number of pensioners were sent out by Her Majesty's Government from Cork. They are all proceeding to Toronto, and will be put under stoppage until they repay the cost of their passage to that port. As they were totally destitute on landing here, and no orders having been received by the Commissariat, they were sent forward to their destination at the expense of this department."

IN IRELAND, where 8,000 tons of Indian corn had been distributed by the end of June, supplies were sinking fast, but since there was every expectation the new crop of potatoes would be adequate, no plans were made to import more corn, and the relief commission was ordered to close its depots by mid-August. On June 26th the *Freeman's Journal*, unaware that the warm, damp weather was precisely the condition most favoured by potato blight, saw "every appearance of an abundant harvest." The one concern was that people had eaten so many potatoes meant for seed that only a third of the normal planting had been done.

"The limited distress which Sir Robert Peel was called upon to meet he provided for fairly and fully," said the *Freeman's Journal*, normally no friend of government. "No man died of famine during his administration, and it is a boast of which he might well be proud." Unfortunately, Peel's Conservative government was forced out of office by the powerful agricultural interests in England that had elected him, enraged now at his repeal of the Corn Laws that had brought them high profits. The *Freeman's Journal* declared this removed one of the few men capable of mitigating the Irish famine, for whereas crop failures might be the act of nature, famine was the act of man.

Just how much Peel could have done is questionable since the cause of Ireland's tragedy lay in centuries of abusive colonialism and a social system that suppressed the rural population. But there can be little doubt that the policies and actions of Peel's successor, the Whig Prime Minister Lord John Russell, failed dramatically. Though Russell had always been regarded as better disposed toward the Irish than Peel had been, and Russell's father, the Duke of Bedford, had once been Irish viceroy, he lacked Peel's experienced and pragmatic grasp of Irish affairs. Russell was also a prisoner of the Whig belief in free trade at any price, and failed to contain the extreme free trade policies of such civil servants as Charles Edward Trevelyan, who as chief executive at the Treasury had dictatorial power over Irish relief. And though there is nothing to suggest that Trevelyan was personally more anti-Irish than most Englishmen of his time, his power and influence far exceeded his experience and his narrow point of view, in which protecting the English exchequer was the priority. Trevelyan still believed that the law of supply and demand, left to operate without interference, would gradually correct Ireland's trouble.

"The only way to prevent the people from becoming habitually dependent on the government," Trevelyan told Routh, "is to bring operations to a close." On July 8 he turned back the last shipment of Indian corn from America and closed down food depots as well as many public works projects, which now employed 100,000 people. Because of lack of organization, the projects had not been a success in any case, and the people who had flocked to road-making were needed to harvest the new potato crop.

This was the state of affairs in mid-July 1846, with the harvest soon to begin, when the blight struck again. "The reports of the new potato crop are very unfortunate," Routh reported on July 14. "All letters and sources of information declare the disease to be more prevalent this year than last in the early crop." In the hills of Kings County (now Offaly), William Steuart Trench, whose plantation employed 200 people, encountered blight for the first time:

On August 1st of that calamitous year I was startled hearing a sudden and strange rumour that all the potato fields in the district were blighted; and that a stench had arisen emanating from their decaying stalks. I immediately rode up to visit my crop, and test the truth of this report, but I found it as luxuriant as ever, in full blossom, the stalks matted across each other with richness, and promising a splendid produce, without any unpleasant smell whatever. On coming down from the mountain I rode into the lowland country, and there found the report to be true. The leaves of the potatoes in my fields I passed were quite withered, and a strange stench, which I had never smelt before, but which was a well known feature in the blight for years after, filled the atmosphere.

The next day I made further enquiries, and I found the disease was fast extending, and on rooting up some of the potato bulbs under the withered stalks I found that decay had set in, and that the potato was rapidly blackening and melting away. In fields having a luxuriant crop the stench was generally the first indication of disease, and the withered leaf followed in a day or two afterwards.

In less than a week the blight crept up the mountainside and attacked Trench's crop. "The luxuriant stalks soon withered, the leaves decayed, the disease extended to the tubers, and the stench from the rotting of such an immense amount of rich vegetable matter became almost intolerable. I saw my splendid crop fast disappearing and melting away under this fatal disease." On August 7, Father Theobald Mathew, the temperance preacher, said he had ridden from Cork to Dublin and seen "this doomed plant bloom in all the luxuriance of an abundant harvest." Returning home a few days later, "I beheld with sorrow one wide waste of putrefying vegetation. In many places the wretched people were seated on the fences of their decaying gardens, wringing their hands and bewailing bitterly the destruction that had left them foodless."

In mid-August a black stain polluted the green fields of Ireland. "All is lost and gone," wrote Sir James Dombain, the Coast Guard chief, on the west coast. On August 17 the new Prime Minister told parliament, "The prospect of the potato crop this year is even more distressing than last year – the disease has appeared earlier and its ravages are more extensive." *The Times* spoke of a "total annihilation" of the potato crop and, to make matters worse, grain crops were poor throughout Ireland, England and most of the Continent. Instead of ending relief as announced, the government introduced other "extraordinary measures" to combat the result of two crop failures in succession, but the most notable aspect of these measures was their inadequacy. By the end of August it was clear the crop failure was universal, but the government saw fit to provide less help than Peel had secured for a considerably lesser crisis the previous year. Common sense fell prey to economic dogma, to the inadequacies of a distant government, and to civil servants accustomed to treating the Irish less as people than as specimens to be observed in an administrative laboratory.

The government announced it would provide jobs, but otherwise the Irish must work out their own salvation, whatever the Act of Union said about two nations being one. Gone was Peel's policy of importing corn and selling it cheap, a measure that had impeded inflation and profiteering and saved many from starvation. The Whigs, in their new-age economics, feared such intervention would destroy the market economy, failing to understand there was no such thing as a market economy in most of rural Ireland. "We do not propose to interfere," said Lord John Russell, "with the regular mode by which Indian corn and other kinds of grain may be brought into the country." Supply would be left to merchants, though Routh, for one, warned that while this might work in England, there were many parts of Ireland that had no shops at all.

"I cannot make my own mind up entirely about the merchants," said Lord Bessborough, the viceroy. "I know all the difficulties that arise when you begin to interfere with trade, but it is difficult to persuade a starving population that one class should be permitted to make 50 per cent by the sale of provisions while they are dying in want of them." Even *The Times*, notorious for anti-Irish sentiments, questioned why the government had refused to issue cheap food with the "extensive failure of the year's potato crop staring them in the face."

One of the government's few concessions to common sense was to retain depots in the most destitute western regions, though even there food was sold at market price and only when private dealers ran out of provisions. On August 24, a week after the government measures were announced, the west Cork village of Unionhall near Skibbereen was invaded by gangs of hungry men demanding food and chanting, "We will not be starved."

Having opted for jobs rather than food depots, the government ordered the revival and expansion of public works projects, mostly road building, that had been the basis of government policy during lesser famines in the past. Since necessary roads had already been built, the make-work projects were often pointless – side roads that led nowhere, miles of stone walls that served no purpose, heaps of stone broken up and never used. The idea was that jobs, however pointless, would provide money with which to buy food from merchants who would import more, but however sane this theory seemed in London it made little sense in Ireland. While the Irish Board of Works fumbled with the cumbersome machinery of renewing abandoned projects and starting new ones, people were starving.

In October, tens of thousands were still without aid, and with prices double their spring level even those with work were hard pressed to feed their families. "Why this delay in starting the public works?" asked the *Freeman's Journal,* while people transferred their hatred of landlords to hatred for works officials. There were riots at work sites, which compounded the chaos because clerks were reluctant to go there to administer the wages. At Ennis in County Clare a works foreman was shot and severely wounded while walking home, but his neighbours did nothing to help him as he crawled bleeding to his house.

In an effort to explain their plight to an obtuse government, eighty-six labourers at the village of Rattibarren, County Sligo, drafted a long petition. "From the Poor Irish to the Right Honourable Lords Temporal and Spiritual," it began, and was addressed to Lord Monteagle, chairman of the Committee of Colonization:

We thank ye and our Gracious sovereign and the Almighty for the relief we had, though one pound of Indian meal for a full-grown person, which has neither milk nor any other kind of garnish, is hardly fit to keep life in them; but if we got all that, we would be thankful. But if we have reason to complain, there is others has more reasons to complain, for the Parish of Townagh they are getting but half a pound, and several of them are not able to buy one pennyworth of milk. I fear the curse of the Almighty will come heavier on this country, the way they are treating the poor, but distress stares us in the face more grim than ever, for we have no sign of employment, for the farmers is not keeping either boy or girl or workmen they can avoid, but are doing the work by their families, though they are not half doing it.

In times past the poor of this country had large gardens of potatoes, and as much conacre as supported them for nearly the whole year, and when they had no employment from the farmers they were working for themselves, and when they had no employment they had their own provisions; but now there are thousands and tens of thousands that had not a cabbage plant in the ground; so we hope that ye will be so charitable as to send us to America, and give us land according to our families, and anything else ye will give us (and we will do with the coarsest kind). We will repay the same, with the interest thereof, by instalments.

At Skibbereen there was not a loaf of bread or pound of meal to be found in the shops; the local depot was open but the demand was so great and stocks so small it was closed again. At Schull, Crookhaven and north to Tralee there was little food and no money, the people literally penniless. Nor were things much better in the more prosperous county of Waterford, where people were seen eating nettles and cabbage stalks. At Loughous Bay, County Donegal, a mountainous district that had grown only potatoes, the coast guard defied orders and opened a corn depot though there was only enough to feed a third of the people. On the road from Doneraile to Mallow hundreds marched in protest, led by a man "bearing in his hand a wand with a tainted potato on top, emblematic of their blighted prospects."

At Ennis, near Colonel Wyndham's estate, agitators demanded that the poor be given work, food or emigration. "Every man of rank and property, person or priest," wrote a local landowner, Sir Gaspard le Marchant, "are afraid to do or say anything that may be contrary to the wishes or feelings of the mob." Nothing maddened people more than the sight of grain being shipped away. Three armed men injured a farmer on the assumption he was exporting food when in fact he was carting it to the local relief committee. "Fifteen millions worth of food is annually taken away from Ireland and eaten in foreign countries," said the *Nation*, which blamed the "foreign government" for "an artificial famine." "Every nation, except a nation of slaves," it said, "takes care that the food raised on its own soil shall feed its own people first."

At Youghal, crowds rampaged through the streets hijacking grain carts and boarding ships to protest export of grain, frightening longshoremen into refusing to load. On Friday, September 25, the *Cork Examiner* reported an "immense number of people" gathered on the hills, "determined to sack and pillage the town." After three days of looting, they were dispersed by the priest and the arrival of troops. At nearby Dungarvan two men were killed and many wounded when troops opened fire on a mob plundering shops.

Though Trevelyan in London stubbornly maintained that "perfect free trade is the best course," Routh, his agent in Dublin, called grain exports a "most serious evil." If even a portion of the Irish-grown food exported that year had been distributed to the starving it would have saved lives, if only by bridging the lengthy time lag between the exhaustion of the maize reserves and the arrival of new supplies from America. The order had gone out so tardily, and there was so much demand for maize in Europe, where the crops had also failed, that it was late in the year before badly needed supplies arrived in Ireland. "I tremble," said Routh that autumn, "when I think of the number of empty depots we have to fill." When Trevelyan was asked to divert grain intended for England and Scotland to Ireland, he refused on grounds that this would mean simply transferring famine from one country to another.

There were only enough jobs on the roads for 150,000, nor was road work proper employment for the weak and the starving. "Unless actually seen," said the an engineer at Borris-in-Ossory, a one-street village in Queens County, "it is difficult to form a correct conception of the wretched state in which labourers and many of the poor farmers are. It is not a very unusual thing for men, who have been only a few days on our works, to work all day without eating a morsel." To buy food, they had to work, and they could not eat until they were paid, though pay frequently was delayed. Women were expected to work like men. "They were employed not only in digging with the spade and pick," said a Quaker relief agent, "but in carrying loads of earth and turf on their backs, and wheeling barrows like men, and breaking stones, while the poor neglected children crouched in groups around bits of lighted turf." The overseers – former policemen or soldiers – were hard men, disliked and feared.

On the Caheragh road near Skibbereen, 800 people shouldered their tools and marched into town in search of food. Shopkeepers barred their doors, the local army unit of seventy-five men took up positions at the crossroads by the Court House, and serious trouble was expected. After a four-hour stand-off the magistrate, Michael Galwey, persuaded the men to return to work, issued them with biscuits and got them to join in "three cheers for the Queen and plenty of work tomorrow."

Eleven days later one of those men, Jeremiah Hegarty, dropped dead on the road, the first starvation death. A coroner found death due "to want of sufficient sustenance, occasioned by his not having been paid his wages on the public works for eight days previous to the time of his death." The second death at Skibbereen was much the same, Denis McKennedy having "died of starvation caused by the gross neglect of the Board of Works." Having received no wages for a fortnight, McKennedy, his wife and five children had eaten nothing for a week but two pints of flour, one cabbage and twenty-one pounds of potatoes donated by a neighbour. McKennedy must have given most of this to his wife and children, for when the coroner examined his stomach it contained nothing but a bit of undigested raw cabbage.

As October slipped into a chill and rainy November, reports came in of deaths and hunger worse than 1822. "I see hundreds of women and children going through the stubble fields," said a magistrate in County Mayo, "striving to get an odd stalk of potato." In Lismore,

County Waterford, a coroner's jury found that "death was caused through negligence by the government in not sending food into the county in due time."

Starvation, and the "famine fever" that followed, came not with a rush, but slowly, first among pockets of destitute in remote areas. In the Finn River valley, County Donegal, William Forster, a Quaker who came to set up soup kitchens, found people who could scarcely walk, "destitution and suffering far exceeding that which had been at first supposed." Near Carrick-on-Shannon, County Leitrim, he saw children "like skeletons, their features sharpened with hunger and their limbs wasted so that there was little left but bones, their hands and arms in particular being much emaciated, and the happy expression of infancy gone from their faces, leaving the anxious look of premature old age."

Though other communities in the west were suffering as badly, Skibbereen, because it was only sixty miles from the city of Cork, attracted so many journalists, clergy and philanthropists it became synonymous with famine. The terrible starvation in the market town on the banks of the Ilen became a focus for protests for generations to come when it was commemorated in a ballad:

> O father dear, the day will come, when vengeance loud will call,
> And we will rise with Erin's boys to rally one and all.
> I'll be the man to lead the van beneath the flag of green,
> And loud and high will raise the cry, "Revenge for Skibbereen."

Nicholas Cummins, a Cork City magistrate who owned land near Skibbereen, bought a supply of bread and set off for the town of 5,000 people on December 15, "to investigate the truth of several lamentable accounts that had reached me."

At the Skibbereen Workhouse, 200 had died, many of them children who had contracted dysentery, the "bloody flux." There was no way of knowing how many had died in their cabins in the countryside. A woman was seen burying a naked child under a pile of rocks. Seven people were found in a hut huddled under one blanket. "One had been dead many hours," wrote Cummins, "but others were unable to move either themselves or the corpse." Not far from town he came to a hamlet which seemed deserted.

"I entered some of the hovels to ascertain the cause, and the scenes which presented themselves were such that no tongue or pen can convey the slightest idea of. In the first, six famished and ghastly skeletons, to all appearances dead, were huddled in a corner on some filthy straw, their sole covering what seemed a ragged horse cloth, their wretched legs hanging about, naked above the knees. I approached with horror, and found by a low moaning that they were alive – they were in fever, four children, a woman, and what had once been a man … in few minutes I was surrounded by at least 200 such phantoms, such frightful spectres as no words can describe, either from famine or from fever."

William Steuart Trench, who had seen his own potatoes wither and die in Kings County, recalled that "dark whisperings and rumours of famine in its most appalling form began to reach us, but still we could scarcely believe that men, women and children were actually dying of starvation in thousands. They died in their mountain glens, they died in the fields; they wandered into towns and died in the streets; they closed their cabin doors, and lay down upon their beds and died of actual starvation in their houses. To us, even at the time, it appeared almost incredible that such things could be. But a cry soon arose from the west, and especially from the districts of Skibbereen and Schull in the county of Cork, which left no further doubt." The *Cork Examiner* of December 20 said:

A terrible apathy hangs over the poor of Skibbereen; starvation has destroyed every generous sympathy; despair has made them hardened and insensible, and they sullenly await their doom with indifference and without fear. Death is in every hovel. Disease and famine, its dread precursors, have fastened on the young and old, the strong and the feeble, the mother and the infant, whole families lie together on the damp floor, devoured by fever, without a human being to wet their burning lips or raise their languid heads; the husband dies by the side of his wife, and she knows not that he is beyond the reach of earthly suffering; the same rag covers the festering remains of mortality and the skeleton forms of the living, who are unconscious of the horrible contiguity; rats devour the corpse, and there is no energy among the living to scare them from their horrid banquet; fathers bury their children without a sigh, and cover them in shallow graves ... without fuel or gruel, bed or bedding, whole families are shut up in naked hovels, dropping one by one into the arms of death.

Father Richard Henry, a parish priest near Castlebar, the county town of Mayo, told of 500 people seeking employment on the roads where there was no work to be had. "The tears of agony and despair gushing from the eyes of hardy and aged men," he said, "gave evidence of the intensity of their sufferings. Should employment be given to them now even the bulk of the people will, I fear, be unable to avail themselves of it. Their strength is enfeebled, their spirits and hopes broken; they become gradually unable to go abroad; they pine within the cabin and may expire there unknown to all, forgotten and unrecorded."

Nevertheless people were leaving. Normally emigration dwindled away in the autumn, but in 1846 it increased, and the arrival at Quebec of the *Elizabeth and Sarah*, a sixty-year-old ship from Killalla, County Mayo, was a harbinger of what was to come. She was decrepit and leaky and carried 276 people – sixty-four more than allowed by law – and a third less drinking water than the law permitted, and that in foul barrels. The master also broke the law by failure to serve out the statutory breadstuffs. There were only thirty-two berths, those on the starboard side having collapsed, so most slept on the floor. The voyage took eight weeks during which forty-two people died, and once in the St. Lawrence she had to be towed up to Grosse Isle. Buchanan described the emigrants as being "in a most wretched state of filth and misery brought on by the crowded state of the vessel, want of cleanliness, bad water, and starvation." Three ships were wrecked that spring, the barks *James and Mary* and *Hebe* and the brig *Brilliant,* but by the end of the season 100,000 Irish had crossed the Atlantic, a third more than the previous year. At least two thirds went directly to the

United States, and the rest to Quebec City or Saint John. Upwards of 1,000 were sent out by landlords, some, such as those sent by Colonel Wandesforde of Kilkenny, being "absolutely destitute" on arrival at Quebec City. Colonel Wyndham sent forty-six families, tenants who had earlier refused to leave their land whom Wyndham now aided "out of kindness."

The cost of passage – between two and half and three pounds per adult – was beyond the reach of most who wanted to go, and Lord Monteagle, who sent tenants on his own account, urged state-assisted emigration as part of famine relief. But the new Colonial Secretary, Lord Grey, turned a deaf ear, stating that the cost would be too great and that government involvement would do more harm than good. Although he had once supported state-aided emigration in general, and had approved of it for Australia, he feared the greater demand for passage to North America would prove overwhelming. Many years later he sought to justify this view, on political if not humanitarian grounds, in a book entitled *Colonial Policy of Lord John Russell's Administration.* "As it was," said Grey, "there were great complaints as to the description of emigrants that went to the North American Colonies, and it was only by showing that the Government had neither the power nor the right to interfere as to the selection of emigrants, that these complaints were met. If the emigrants had been sent out by the Government, it would have been universally felt that the Government could not possibly repudiate the responsibility of providing for them on their arrival in the Colonies."

Nor was the government receptive to innovative ideas like that advanced by Samuel Cunard, the Nova-Scotia-born founder of the steamship line. To the horror of the Admiralty, he proposed that the navy's new steamships, which were engaged in exercises off the coast, be pressed into carrying thousands of emigrants, arguing that the cost would be moderate and the steamers could cross the Atlantic from Ireland in a third the time taken by sailing ships. Had Cunard's plan been adopted it would have saved much suffering.

"Talk of the power of England, her navy, her gold, her resources," said the *Cork Examiner* of November 2, 1846, "oh yes, and her enlightened statesmen, while the broad fact is manifested that she cannot keep the children of her bosom from perishing by hunger. Perhaps indeed Irishmen may not aspire to the high dignity of belonging to the great family of the Empire; they may be regarded as Aliens. But when the Queen at the coronation swore to protect and defend her subjects, it is not recollected that in the words of the solemn covenant there was any exception made with regard to Ireland. How happens it then, while there is a shilling in the Treasury, or even a jewel in the Crown, that patient subjects are allowed to perish with hunger?"

Those with no money were doomed to stay home and starve. "For God's sake take us out of poverty, and don't let us die with the hunger," wrote Mary Rush in Adnaglass to her father, Thomas Barrett, who had emigrated from Sligo a few years earlier to an Irish settlement near Carrillon on the lower Ottawa River. Barrett's only asset was his little farm in the bush, and cash was so rare in the backwoods settlements he had none to send his daughter and asked the colonial government to help, with what results we do not know.

By October 30, when Dr. George Mellis Douglas, superintendent at Grosse Isle, completed his last report for the season, 40,000 emigrants had arrived in British North America, most of them Irish. Some settled in New Brunswick, Quebec City or Montreal, about one third went on to the United States, and the rest went to Upper Canada. Most were poor but in reasonably good health, and though the migration for most of the year had been much as usual, the last ships to arrive carried a portent of what was to come. "A large number of those by *Rockshire* from Liverpool," reported Douglas, "had left their homes at this late season in consequence of the failure of the potato crop, fearing that if they should delay until next year they would not then have the means of paying their passage. As it was they landed here quite destitute, and required assistance from this department to enable them to proceed to their friends."

On November 20, as reports of mounting famine in Ireland trickled into Quebec City, Douglas added: "I am persuaded that next season the number of sick will exceed that of any other year, pouring upon our shores thousands of debilitated and sickly emigrants." His warning was largely ignored, as was the warning issued by the Prime Minister in London, Lord John Russell, who said in December, "Those eager for emigration on a larger scale should recollect that the colonies cannot be prepared at once to receive large masses of helpless beings, and there is no use sending them from starving at Skibbereen to starve at Montreal."

14

Black '47

*I*N THE TERRIBLE WINTER of 1846–47, blizzards swept down out of northern Europe, blocking Irish roads with snow and ice. It was impossible to transport emergency supplies and the organization of soup kitchens for the hundreds of thousands of hungry was seriously delayed. To death from disease and starvation was added death from exposure on the roads and in the fields. "The people sink," wrote Alfred Bishop, a relief worker in Erris, County Mayo. "They have no stamina left. They say, 'It is the will of God' and die."

It was now six months since the potato crop had failed, and starvation and disease, starting among the chronically destitute, had crept like a slow tide up the social scale to embrace small farmers and the artisan class. Due to the poor communications, reports of the crisis appeared in the press in bits and pieces, but a compilation of the many little items tells a story of fearful suffering.

"It is scarcely possible to exaggerate in imagination what people will and are forced to do before they die from absolute want of food," said a census report when the famine was over. "The actually starving people lived on the carcasses of diseased cattle, upon dogs and dead horses, but principally upon the herbs of the field, nettle tops, wild mustard, and water cresses, and even in some places dead bodies were found with grasses in their mouths."

Charles Edward Trevelyan, whose narrow economic dogma had contributed so much to the disaster, finally admitted defeat. The famine in Ireland, he told Lord Monteagle privately, had now passed "beyond the power of man." To his agents in the field he wrote, "We deeply sympathize with you who daily have to witness scenes of heart-rending misery without being able to give effectual relief but, as justly observed by you, we must do all we can and leave the rest to God."

The workhouses, built to hold 100,000 people, were overflowing with 110,000, and thousands were being turned away daily. "Two cart loads of orphans, whose parents had died of starvation, were turned away from the workhouse yesterday," said a report from Leitrim. But even the people who thought they had found a refuge in the work-houses were not safe, for they had become a focus of "famine fever," with 2,000 cases reported in February. The government had been slow to acknowledge the spread of disease, but now there could be no doubt.

"A pestilential fever is now raging through the house, every room of which is so crowded as to render it impossible to separate the sick from the healthy," said an entry in the Minute Book of the Fermoy Board of Poor Law Guardians. "The weekly admissions are chiefly confined to the sick and dying." At Scariff Workhouse in County Clare 250 were ill, and at Lurgan, a linen manufacturing town in County Armagh, ninety-five had died in one week. "Many diseases are now prevalent in the country," said the Lurgan medical officer, "and the great majority of new admissions are, when brought into the house, at the point of death, in a moribund state, many having been known to die on the road." At Clonmel in County Tipperary people were "so completely paralyzed that they have more the appearance of ghosts than of living human beings." A letter from Macroom, County Cork, said, "Persons of all ages are dropping dead," whereas formerly the deaths had been among the very young and very old.

Though most of the thirty-two counties reported some degree of distress, the worst were as usual in the west: Kerry, Tipperary, Clare, Leitrim, Mayo, Galway, Limerick, Donegal, Cavan and Cork. At Schull, in west Cork, an English naval officer wrote in mid-February of passing 500 people "half naked and starving," waiting for a soup kitchen to open. "Not a single one you now see will be alive in three weeks," a doctor told him. Of the 18,000 people in the parish of Schull, fifty were dying each day, as the officer wrote to his family in England:

Fever, dysentery, and starvation stare you in the face everywhere – children of ten and nine years old I have mistaken for decrepit old women, their faces wrinkled, their bodies bent and distorted with pain, the eyes looking like those of a corpse. Babies are found lifeless, lying on their mothers' bosoms. I will tell you one thing which struck me as particularly horrible: a dead woman was found lying on the road with a dead infant on her breast, the child having bitten the nipple of the mother's breast right through in trying to derive nourishment from the wretched body. Dogs feed on the half-buried dead, and rats are commonly known to tear people to pieces who, though still alive, are too weak to cry out.... Instead of following us, beggars throw themselves on their knees before us, holding up their dead infants to our sight.

"Why should these things be?" asked William Steuart Trench. While it was true the people had been dependent solely on the potato for food, and the potato had failed them, this was the 19th century; Ireland was not, like India, isolated from the western world; and there was ample grain, cattle, sheep and pigs, particularly in eastern Ireland, that continued to supply the export trade. By February emergency food was flowing into the country from America, along with large sums of money from overseas Irish. Some came from unexpected places. Soldiers in Calcutta who had relatives in western Ireland sent their contributions, as did seventeen lumberjacks in New Brunswick's Miramichi region who clubbed together to send £21. The Catholic Archbishop of Quebec collected £4,000, and one of his parish priests, Father Bernard O'Reilly of Sherbrooke, said, "I got thirty or forty dollars in cash – it was all they had. But there is not a man who is not selling some article to give his mite."

Meanwhile, tens of thousands were dying, 50,000 before the coming of the spring. In an effort to answer the question "why?" Trench's cousin, the Rev. Fredrick Trench, travelled to Skibbereen and Schull from Cloughjordan, County Tipperary, and observed that while there was food in the countryside, sometimes only a dozen miles from the scenes of fatal misery, it was not getting to the people who needed it, a common problem in famines to this day in Africa. "In near proximity to plenty," said William Steuart Trench, "the people were dying by the hundreds of actual dire starvation, merely for want of someone with sufficient energy and power of organization to bring the food and people together."

Guided by the local priest, Father James Barry, Fredrick Trench visited nine homes at Schull and Ballydehob, from whence so many Fitzgeralds and O'Driscolls had migrated to the Miramichi a decade earlier. At Patrick O'Driscoll's home he found a man's body by the smouldering peat fire, and half the family of eight down with fever. At Paddy Ryan's next door one child had died and eight were ill, and not far away Phil Regan and three of his children had died and his widow was "awfully swelled" with famine dropsy. At the home of "Mr. Barry, a decent farmer," three children had eaten nothing all day, and probably not the previous day. At the home of a man who had died in the act of gathering turf for the fire, "the mother buried one child (as they said) 'off her back,' meaning that she carried the child on her back to the grave, and I saw three others apparently dying." In the ninth house he visited, that of Charles Regan, only three of the family of eleven had survived. "I have within a fine young man of nineteen years of age," Mrs. Regan told him, "and you could carry him in the palm of your hand." When Trench looked in he saw a bundle of skin and bone, naked and partly wrapped in an old blanket. "I did not see a child playing in the streets or on the roads. No children are to be seen outside the doors but a few sick and dying."

He saw coffins fashioned with trap doors in the bottom, held in place with hinges and a hook and eye, so that dozens of bodies might be buried from the same box. "In these coffins the poor are carried to the grave, rather to a large pit, which I saw at a little distance from the road, and the bodies dropped in it ... the majority were taken to the grave without any coffins and buried in their rags. In some even the rags were taken from the corpse to cover some still-living body."

Horror succeeded horror. Elihu Burritt, a philanthropist from New Britain, Connecticut, had a nightmare journey to Skibbereen that began soon after he left Cork City in the mail coach. "The road was lined with apparitions of human misery, strangely contrasting with the green fields which indicated the fertility of the soil," he said. For almost a mile a little girl ran behind the carriage calling, "A ha'penny, a ha'penny, buy a piece of bread, for the love of God." At Skibbereen he was taken on a tour.

As soon as we left the house a crowd of haggard creatures pressed upon us, and, with agonizing prayers for bread, followed us to the soup house. A man with swollen feet pressed closely upon us, and begged for bread most piteously. The soup house was surrounded by a cloud of these famine-spectres, half naked, and standing or sitting in the mud beneath a cold, drizzling rain.... Among the attenuated apparitions of humanity that thronged this gate of stinted charity, one poor man presented himself under circumstances that even distinguished his case from the rest.... His cheeks were fallen in, and his jaws so distended that he could scarcely articulate a word. His four little children were sitting upon the ground at his feet, nestling together and trying to hide their naked limbs under their dripping rags....

We entered the graveyard, in the midst of which was a small watchhouse.

This miserable shed had served as a grave where the dying could bury themselves. It was seven feet high and six in width, and was already walled around on the outside with an embankment of graves, half way to the eaves. The aperture of this horrible den of death would scarcely admit the entrance of a common-sized person. And into this noisome sepulchre living men, women and children went down to die – to pillow upon the rotten straw – the grave clothes vacated by preceding victims surrounding them. Here they lay as closely to each other as if crowded, side by side, on the bottom of one grave. Six persons had been found in this fetid sepulchre at one time, and with only one of them able to crawl to the door to ask for water. Removing a board from the entrance of this black hole of pestilence, we found it crammed with wan victims of famine, ready and anxious to perish. A quiet, listless despair broods over the population, and death reaps a full harvest.

People were reduced to eating "famine food" – seaweed, nettles, hedgehogs baked in clay, soup made from dogs, turnips stolen from a farmer's field, and stolen farm animals as well. Farmers who had hoarded seed potatoes to plant in the new year buried them under their floors, as if they were gold, and guarded their fields at night with loaded guns.

Newspapers in the early weeks of 1847 were filled with strange and terrible stories. The Reverend Curran, writing in the *Freeman's Journal* from Westport, County Mayo, reported, "At this moment I am beholding a scene of distress at which Nature herself must recoil. The eyes and nose of a poor man, who died of starvation, eaten away by rats in a wretched hovel where he lay dead two days." The Reverend Patrick Fitzgerald of Kilgiver, County Mayo, wrote, "I shall never forgive the impression made on my mind a few days ago by a most heart rending case of starvation – a poor mother with five in the family sending her poor little children, almost lifeless from hunger, to bed and despairing of ever seeing them alive, she took her last leave of them. In the morning her first act was to touch their lips to see if the breath of life still remained. These fears were not groundless, for not a breath of life could she feel. That day she buried them in the Night of Eternity."

The Mayo correspondent of the *Freeman's Journal* found a family named Kelly in the village of Kilbegwills living on the remains of a horse that had died some days before and been gnawed by dogs. "I visited the village and met the wife, a horrible, famine-stricken spectacle with her bones protruding through her skin. I returned with her to her cabin in which nothing could be seen but a wad of half-eaten straw, that seemed a bed for the whole family who were covered at night with nothing but the tattered rags they wore during the day. 'Sir,' said she, as the tears ran down her worn cheeks, 'look here,' pointing to her six helpless children. These did not take a morsel of food for four days. Three of them, we felt, were dying, and hearing that Makum's horse had died, brought home a basket full of it, which was all the dogs had left. We ate it for a whole week, and the Lord only knows what I will do now it is gone.'"

Richard O'Grady, the coroner in Mayo, held inquests on the bodies of four people who had been living for three weeks on boiled watercress and salt. A correspondent at Ballydehob said a man had died in his pig sty and lain for several days with no one to cover the remains. "Death is fearfully on the increase here," he reported. "Coughlan of the Board of Works was crawling home a few nights ago when hunger and exhaustion seized him near his house where he was found next morning. I have just learned that in the neighbourhood of Crookhaven they are buried within the walls of their huts. They have in most cases forgotten the usual ceremony of interment. The living are so consumed with famine they are unable to remove the dead."

A correspondent of the *Cork Examiner,* writing from Skibbereen on January 14, said, "Yesterday, Joseph Driscoll, the Schull Poor Rate Collector, went to Drishane in the parish of Schull East to collect poor rates and on coming to the house of a man named Regan the door was shut. He repeatedly knocked on it to no effect. He then pushed in the door and what was his astonishment to find three men dead in the house. He also told me that in Drishane in the same parish there is a woman named Neal dead since the 6th instant and not buried yet.

Three children of hers died, one boy and two girls. The father had died earlier."

Fatalities in County Cork, as in other western counties, were three times their normal rate, and so many reports of death by starvation and "famine fever" were flooding in that the *Cork Reporter* announced in February that the "limits of our space do not admit of their publication." Famine deaths were no longer news. "On my too bended knees," wrote a woman named Mrs. Nowlan to her son in the colonies, "I pray to God that you nor one of yours may never know nor ever suffer what we are suffering at present."

"Famine fever," also known as "road fever" – and "ship fever" when it struck emigrants – was usually not one but two or more diseases, including typhus and relapsing fever. Typhus, which had been endemic in Ireland for as long as anyone could remember, was the more deadly, attacking blood vessels and nervous system, crippling the brain until the patient appeared dazed, a condition that gave the disease its name, which is Greek for mist. It was more lethal than relapsing fever, which often accompanied it and which struck more quickly and returned to plague the victim again and again. That both these diseases were carried by lice was not realized at the time, nor was the contagion of the diseases understood by the starving people who huddled together in cabins and under hedges for warmth. Nor was it necessary to be lousy to catch the diseases, for the excrement of lice, which dried to a light dust, was blown by the wind and could infect a healthy person through the nose and mouth or cuts on the skin, which accounted for a large number of deaths among the gentry as well as the peasantry.

There were four other major famine diseases. "Frightful and fearful is the havoc around me," wrote the Reverend Robert Traill, the Anglican minister at Schull, who himself was to die of typhus that year. "The aged, who with the young – neglected perhaps, amidst the widespread destitution – are almost without exception swollen and ripening for the grave." Such swelling was caused by famine oedema, or dropsy, in which water accumulated in the tissues. "I had seen men at work on the public roads," said Elihu Burritt, "with their limbs swollen almost to twice their usual size." A woman showed him a boy of twelve whose body was swollen to "nearly three times its usual size ... and a thin-faced boy of two years with clear, sharp eyes, that did not wink, but stared, stock still at vacancy, as if the glimpse of another existence had eclipsed its vision."

Whereas typhus took its heaviest toll among the elderly because of its effect on the heart, epidemic dysentery, spread by flies and contaminated food, afflicted the young, as did ophalemia, a blindness caused by starvation in which hundreds of children lost sight in one or both eyes. Scurvy was also common, for the potato had previously provided the vitamins that kept it at bay.

Under these conditions the tradition of charity was breaking down. Charity had been the Irish way for centuries, and though it had dealt with the results of deprivation rather than the causes, it had sustained millions over the years, but now people were turning their backs to save their own families. William Forster, a Quaker relief worker on the west coast, wrote: "Like a scourge of locusts the hunger daily swamps over fresh districts, eating up all before it; one class after another is falling into the same abyss of ruin. There is now but little difference between the small farmer and the squatter. We heard in Galway of little tradesmen secretly begging for soup. The priest cannot get his dues, nor the landlord his rent."

Though all regions suffered, the central midlands, eastern Leinster and northeast Ulster suffered less than the west. In County Wicklow, wrote Elizabeth Smith, a landowner's wife, families with large farms were actually profiting from inflated grain prices and the brisk export market. The smaller farmer was facing bankruptcy, however, for as she said, "He must sell his corn, sell his stock at an unseasonable time because he has no fodder, and therefore leaves himself penniless for the coming year." The famine had paralyzed a system that had never been strong, and as the Central Relief Committee reported, there were few who escaped its impact:

Prices were so high that those who were still able to maintain themselves and their families could not afford to spend any more money except on food. The small shopkeepers consequently lost their trade. The business of the wholesale dealer and merchant was diminished. The various branches of manufacturing felt the want of demand; many of the work people were discharged. Few houses were repaired or built, and masons, carpenters and other tradesmen connected with building were left unemployed. The demand for clothes, notwithstanding the great want of them, which was everywhere felt, decreased. Tailors, shoemakers and other tradesmen of this class suffered accordingly. The gentry, whose rents were not paid and who had poor rates added to their other incumbrances, reduced their spending.

When Peel had set up relief committees in 1846, they were expected to raise money, which the government would match, channel aid to the needy, and lobby government for public works. But the committees, run by local gentry, had proved disappointing or worse, and nowhere more than in Skibbereen, where the effort had withered away from lack of support. As a result, Skibbereen had received less support from the government than places that needed it less, such as Kilkenny, which had strong committees. Another cause of Skibbereen's plight was the number of absentee landlords. Routh, who sent his own agent, Richard Ingles, confirmed the terrible reports about the place and put much of the blame on twelve landlords, including Wrixon Becher, who owned land in the town, drew the largest rents, but had bankrupted himself in interminable lawsuits with his relatives. Despite the famine, the largest number of evictions that year was in Cork.

Still, there were those who observed the old traditions of charity. Colonel Wyndham fed 10,000 daily in County Clare, only 3,000 of whom were people on his own estates. At Mitchelstown, Big George had died and was succeeded by the fourth Earl of Kingston, who was spending a fifth of his rents on famine relief, though he was virtually bankrupt. The new Lord Kingston opened a soup kitchen in his garden and gave out eighty gallons of soup three times a week, supplemented with meat from his deer park. Father Morgan O'Brien, the priest for the surrounding Brigown parish, said that, but for the Earl, Mitchelstown would have gone the way of Skibbereen and Schull. "Strong farmers" such as the Phaidin family in Donegal kept their destitute neighbours alive on "yellow buttermilk, barley bread and rye porridge" and their name has been blessed ever since in the folklore of the county.

But given the immensity of the crisis, private charity was snow on the sea. At Clonfad, near Carrick-on-Shannon, County Leitrim, the local Poor Law Guardian reported that thirty-two people had died in a fortnight, "three unfortunate creatures found in the fields dead, not having strength to reach their miserable dwellings." His money was exhausted, and he had nothing left with which to buy coffins, having received contributions only from the Anglican minister, "my mother, and two other humane persons."

All over Ireland, the relief apparatus was breaking down. *The Economist*, the influential London journal that reflected the views of English merchants, considered the situation hopeless. "Under such a calamity, what can a government do to alleviate it? Extremely little. A government may remove all impediments which interfere to prevent people from providing for themselves, but beyond that they can do little."

Thousands begged at the entrance to the workhouses, but these were already grossly overcrowded. Like refugees in wartime, great crowds fled the barren mountains and boglands of the west, and Father Mathew, who opened a soup kitchen in Cork City, called them a "living tide of misery." "They wait on the outskirts of the town till dark, when they may be seen coming in droves," reported the *Cork Constitution*, the "bedclothes strapped to the shoulders of the father, while the children carry pots, pans, jugs, old sacks, and other articles. On the average about 300 of these miserable creatures come into the city daily, who are walking masses of filth, vermin and sickness." On one occasion 600 men stormed the breadshops and were turned back with bayonets.

The Board of Works, having spent hundreds of thousands of Irish tax money, was in a shambles. At Ennis, the official in charge said all his assistants were quitting in fear and frustration. "I cannot undertake to prevent many deaths for want of food," he said. Although half a million people had signed on to work on the roads, wages were not being paid with regularity, and thousands were too weak and ill to break rock or shovel gravel.

Food was so dear and wages were so low that a government agent in County Clare reported seeing "women returning home from Ennis, crying with grief at their inability to purchase, the price being too high." Realizing too late the depths of its error and the degree of its blindness, the government early in 1847 had no choice short of genocide but to scrap its relief policies and devise others. "We have arrived at a very important crisis in our operations," said Trevelyan, who to give him some credit was working night and day and had moved into a hotel to be near his office. "The tide of distress has for some time been steadily rising and appears now to have completely overflowed the barriers we endeavoured to oppose to it." Lord John Russell, describing the Irish disaster as a "famine of the 13th century acting upon a population of the 19th century," announced on January 27 a new policy, the third in the eighteen months since the famine began.

Roadworks, having been a failure, were abandoned and people were encouraged to return to their fields to plant crops for the new year with seed supplied by the government. The hungry were to receive sustenance, either free or at little cost, from temporary soup kitchens organized by the Relief Commission and supervised by the Poor Law Unions. The government, which had previously resisted calls for free food, agreed to advance funding, but expected to recoup it from the poor rate.

Ireland, it seemed, was to be saved by soup, though as the Reverend Trench pointed out: "Soup may be anything, everything, or nothing; it may be thin gruel or greasy water and I have tasted it of both descriptions; or it may be the essence of meat, and very wholesome where there is some substantial food taken with it." In some areas, soup kitchens had been running for months, established by the Quakers, who had experience running soup kitchens in England. In November 1846 the Quakers organized a large relief effort in Ireland, setting up offices through most of the country to monitor the spread of the famine and organize relief supplies. The London-based British Relief Association, a private organization which had received a large donation from Queen Victoria, also did good work and the success of these efforts had impressed the government.

With its lack of sense when it came to Ireland's needs, the government commissioned a famous French chef, Alexis Soyer of London's Reform Club, to concoct a suitable potage, though he had little training in nutrition and was more at home creating fancy dishes for wealthy clubmen. One Soyer recipe called for onions, celery tops, turnips, eight ounces of flour, two ounces of rendered fat, half an ounce of brown sugar and four ounces of beef in two gallons of water. It was more notable for its cheapness, less than a penny a quart, than for its nutrition, but the government introduced Soyer to the high society of Dublin at a reception where they tasted the thin stuff, and *The Times* called him "Head Cook to the People of Ireland" in an ornate publicity campaign to show the government's concern for the starving.

The English medical journal *Lancet*, having analyzed Soyer's soups, called them "soup quackery" and a salve for the conscience of the rich. "Something more than an agreeable titillation of the palate is required to keep up the manufactory of blood, bone, and muscle which constitutes the strong healthy man," said the *Lancet*. Nevertheless, his soup, which provided a tenth of the calories needed, was fed to thousands who were duly thankful. Mostly it was free, but in some places people had to buy it if they failed to convince the local supervisor they were starving. In Killarney one day 10,000 crowded around the town's one soup kitchen, a huge boiler set up in a shed.

That spring the government dismantled the works projects, which had been meant, in theory at least, to support three million people, counting the dependents of those working on the roads. Since bureaucracy moved slowly and soup kitchens were not available to large numbers until June, there was an increase in deaths. "Eighty per cent of the work people have been dismissed," wrote the Anglican minister in the parish of Cong, County Mayo, which lies at the edge of Lough Corib and the fertile green plain of Moytura. "Yet they can't hope to be under the system of relief for ten days yet. All the relief committee funds are expended. Deaths are increasing ten-fold."

John Mitchel, the radical son of a Unitarian minister and contributor to the nationalist paper the *Nation*, wrote of a "horrible silence" in the Galway countryside. Stopping at the cabin of a young couple who, with their children, had entertained him two years earlier, he shouted his usual greeting, "God save all here!" There was no answer, nor did Mitchel expect one. "We knew the whole story. The father was on a 'public work' and earned the sixth part of what could have nourished his family, which was not always duly paid him. But still it left them half alive for three months, and so instead of dying in December they died in March and the agony of those three months who shall tell?"

Large shipments of maize were now flowing in from America on the spring tides, though distribution was so disorganized the death toll continued to mount. "My hand trembles while I write," said William Bennett on his six-week journey through western Ireland. "The scenes of human misery and degradation we witnessed still haunt my imagination, with the vividness and power of some horrid and tyrannous delusion, rather than the features of a sober reality. We entered a cabin. Stretched in one dark corner, scarcely visible, from the smoke and rags that covered them, were three children huddled together, lying there because they were too weak to rise, pale and ghastly, their little limbs – on removing a portion of the filthy covering – perfectly emaciated, eyes sunk, voice gone, and evidently in the last stage of actual starvation. Crouched over the turf embers was another form, wild and all but naked, scarcely human in appearance. It stirred not, nor noticed us. On some straw, sodden upon the ground, moaning piteously, was a shrivelled old woman, imploring us to give her something – baring her limbs partly, to show how the skin hung loose from the bones. Above her on something like a ledge, was a young woman, a mother I have no doubt, who scarcely raised her eyes in answer to our enquiries, but pressed her hand upon her forehead in a look of unutterable anguish and sorrow."

Visiting Kenmare, Bennett wrote, "The poor people came in from the rural districts in such numbers, in the hopes of getting some relief, that it was utterly impossible to meet their most urgent emergencies, and therefore they came in literally to die in the open streets, actually dying of starvation within a stone's throw of the inn."

Aubrey De Vere, a landowner, told a government inquiry: "Having been absent from this country some years, on my return to it last summer I found it the most miserable scene of distress that ever I read of in history. Want and misery in every face; the rich unable to relieve the poor; the road spread with dead bodies; mankind of the colour of the docks and nettles they fed upon; two or three sometimes on one car carrying them to the graves for want of bearers to carry them; and many buried only in the fields and ditches where they perished. This universal scarcity was ensued by fluxes and malignant fevers, which swept off multitudes of all sorts, so that whole villages were laid waste."

The winter dragged on, and on April 26 a "storm of frozen hail" was reported, and a few days later, a "gale was still blowing and it was fiercely cold." A priest in a western district spoke of "funerals passing and re-passing in every direction, the congregations on Sunday reduced by half, the church yards like fields lately tilled, without a green spot, constantly visited by processions of a few gaunt figures, carrying with difficulty the remains of some more fortunate relative or friend." Death, he seemed to suggest, was more to be welcomed than shunned. An unsigned scrap of document found among the government's Distress Papers for 1847 reads in its entirety: "Oh pity us. Oh what must we do and what will become of us. Pity us here scarce half alive."

By the end of June a staggering number – 2,700,000 people – were finally receiving daily rations of soup and bread. Sometimes the soup was nourishing, with meat, turnips, cabbages, corn meal, onions and carrots. Sometimes it was "poorhouse porridge" consisting of Indian corn meal and water. When Father Mathew appeared before a hearing into famine conditions in June, he was asked to state the process he followed in feeding four thousand a day:

In the City of Cork we had seven soup kitchens, some for gratuitous relief and others for the sale of cheap soup thickened with meal. We tried soup, and found it did not answer, and that dysentery followed from it where it was badly made. I have now got in my hands the supply of the southern part of the city. I have five large boilers constantly at work boiling Indian flour into a mass, what the Americans call mush, and the Italians polenta. At first I obliged the poor to consume it on the premises.... I then thought it a cruelty to keep the poor people fasting till the same hour the next day; and I thought some of them ate too much at one time, and that therefore it was better to give them this food and let them do what they pleased with it. During the last month I gave a pound of raw flour made into this polenta to each adult, and half the quantity to young persons. They take it away with them and eat some of it immediately, and the remainder they take home and broil or bake it for supper.

Commissioner: You stated there were now 10,000 additional paupers thrown upon the town of Cork; do you imagine that such additional number will permanently settle upon the town?

Mathew: I do not think they will permanently remain there. The citizens are adopting every mode they can to get rid of them; they are refusing to put their names on the relief list.

Commissioner: But suppose they get rid of them, where are these unfortunate people to go?

Mathew: They must continue wanderers through the country till death puts an end to their misery, or perhaps some kind person may admit them.

Commissioner: There is no chance of their being able to get back to the place from whence they came?

Mathew: Generally speaking there is no chance of that.

By mid-July the food supply had improved, though the death rate was three or four times the normal in western counties and also above normal in other counties. Death was now more likely to be caused by disease than outright starvation. Though the new planting had been small due to lack of seed, the potato crop was healthy for the first time in two years. Unfortunately, the government used this as a reason to abandon responsibility for relief, throwing the whole burden onto the local Poor Law Unions, many of which were bankrupt from lack of tax support. Under the impression that too many people were getting relief who did not need it, Trevelyan declared: "It is my opinion that too much has been done for the people."

"There is much reason to believe that the object of the Relief Act is greatly perverted," said the Relief Commission, "and that it is frequently applied solely as a means of adding to the comforts of the lower classes, and of assisting the farmers and employers in carrying on their business instead of being, as intended, a provision for the utterly destitute...." The rules were changed for the fourth time, and the soup kitchens were to be shut down by the end of September. The Poor Law Unions were now authorized to provide "outdoor relief" for those who could not find a place in the overcrowded workhouses, but even this was undermined by a proviso that people in possession of a quarter of an acre or more could not apply, which threw thousands into a limbo where they could expect no help at all, the road works being phased out.

John Nowlan of County Wexford, writing to his son, Patrick, in Nova Scotia on September 30, 1847, said, "The people, the young and the old, are dying as fast as they can bury them. The fever is raging here at such a rate that those in health in the morning knows not but in the evening they may have taken the infection.... There is neither trade nor business of any sort going on. Any person that have the means of going to America is either gone or preparing to go there...."

Ironically, in this year of horror the potato fields were green and healthy with no sign of blight. There would be potatoes to eat again, but for hundreds of thousands it was too late, for they were either dead or moribund or fleeing disease and starvation, carrying their misery westward on ships bound for the New World.

15

"The Fearful Mortality"

ON MAY 5, 1847, the brig *Midas*, thirty-eight days out of Galway Bay, ghosted out of the foggy Bay of Fundy and dropped anchor off the city of Saint John. High up in her starboard rigging she flew the flag that told of sickness aboard. She had buried ten of her emigrants at sea, and there was fever and dysentery among the 163 passengers, who were quickly quarantined on Partridge Island just off shore.

Established sixty years earlier, the Partridge Island station was in poor condition that spring, its two little hospitals in disrepair and able to accommodate no more than 100 people. Though the emigration agent, Moses Perley, had warned the government of what might be expected, and the local press had urged the station be renovated, little had been done. Dr. George J. Harding, the only medical officer on the island, cared for the people from the *Midas* and was thankful when the ships arriving at Saint John during the next nine days carried no tell-tale flags in their rigging. However, on the tenth day Partridge Island was swamped by disease and death in the first act of a tragedy that lasted all summer, for the *Midas* was the first of hundreds of emigrant plague ships to reach Saint John and Quebec City in the most lethal year in the annals of emigration.

On May 14 the bark *Aldebaran* arrived, flying the flag of sickness, and fifty-five days out of Sligo, which was one of the towns most heavily afflicted by famine fever. The *Aldebaran* had lost thirty-six emigrants at sea, and a quarter of her 418 passengers were seriously ill. Four days later the *Weekly Observer* warned that worse was to come. "The [Irish] provincial papers appear to be alarmed at the magnitude and character of the emigration from all parts – more particularly from the counties of Limerick, Waterford, Cork and Sligo. Upwards of 3,000 sailed from Limerick within the past months and the tide of emigration is growing...."

During the next two weeks a dozen ships arrived with 3,700 emigrants, 2,000 of whom were quarantined in the dirty holds of the crowded ships or in tents erected on the damp ground to take the overflow from the hospital buildings, "the floors of every ward being completely covered to the very doors." There were no cots in the tents and people slept on spruce boughs or straw. Some, with no covering but their clothes, took the fence around the island's lighthouse to make fires to keep warm on the chill May nights. There was nothing on the twenty-four-acre island but the hospitals – little more than fever sheds – the lighthouse, a signal station and a house or two. Twenty-six bodies from the brig *Pallas,* from Cork, had to be buried during the first few weeks, and eighteen from the brig *Amazon* from Liverpool, the youngest being five-month-old Edward McMullan and the eldest Patrick Lausay, who was forty-five.

John Mullawyn, who came with his sisters Mary and Margaret from Sligo on May 31, wrote to his "Dear and loveing Father and

Mother & Brothers" of his safe arrival. "There is disorder very numerous in this country, what they call the *tipes* fevir, there is thousands of people dieing...." Mullawyn had arrived with 500 other tenants from the Sligo estate of Sir Robert Gore Booth of Lissadell House. Their ship was the *Aeolus*, 817 tons, a new vessel which her master, Michael Driscoll, boasted could not be "classed among the dirty old emigrant hired vessels." Driscoll believed her "superior to any of Her Majesty's transports" but nevertheless twenty-six passengers had died in the five-week voyage to Saint John, "having been weak and destitute before we left home." There were seventeen sick on arrival and seven were buried on Partridge Island.

Early in June Dr. Harding, overwhelmed with work, was authorized to hire his brother, Dr. William S. Harding, and the twenty-three-year-old Dr. James Patrick Collins, who had been born in County Cork. By the end of June, twenty-seven emigrant ships had arrived at Saint John with 5,000 people, 264 having died at sea. More than 500 lay ill on the island, where 154 had died. "The difficulties," said a Saint John official, "hit us like a thunderbolt." But however serious, the events at Partridge Island paled before the disaster unfolding up the St. Lawrence River at Grosse Isle, where the first plague ship arrived May 14 and the first to die was a little girl named Ellen Kane, who was four years and five months old. Her parents had taken her from Ireland to Liverpool, where the teeming lodging houses were breeding grounds for disease. She died in Grosse Isle hospital the day after her ship, the *Syria*, arrived, as did Nancy Riley, twenty-four, Edward Riley, thirty, and Thomas Comer, forty. Nine passengers had died at sea, and forty were to die on Grosse Isle.

Writing to Lord Elgin, the Governor, on May 17, Dr. George Mellis Douglas, the Grosse Isle medical superintendent, said: "All the sick now in hospital are from one vessel, the *Syria*, being the first and only emigrant vessel that has yet arrived. The vessel left Liverpool on the 24th March, having on board 241 passengers, recently arrived from Ireland; many were in weak state when they embarked, and all were wretched and poor. Disease – fever and dysentery – broke out a few days after leaving port, and had gone on increasing until now."

The quarantine station at Grosse Isle had changed little from the time it was built in 1832 – a wooden, 200-bed shed-like hospital, two quarantine sheds, a staff house, a bakery, two chapels, a barracks and some smaller buildings. Before the season began, Douglas had begged the government for £3,000 to repair and enlarge the station, but received one tenth of that amount and a letter saying that the Emigrant Commissioners in London believed him a man of decision, energy and skill who could cope with whatever the season might bring. He had opened the station in late April with his usual staff, the only concession to the emergency being fifty additional bedsteads and twice the usual amount of straw for bedding. Ships were arriving on every tide, and he heard that 10,600 emigrants were already on the high seas and heading for Grosse Isle, where there were facilities for hundreds rather than thousands. Douglas expected there would eventually be 20,000 in quarantine, "the population, in fact, of a large city."

The *Jane Black* from Limerick arrived on May 20 with thirteen dead and six so ill they died in hospital. By May 23 eight ships had arrived with 2,778 people, 530 of them ill. "I did not have a bed to lay them on," Douglas said, adding that he had "never contemplated the possibility of every vessel arriving with fever as they do now." To look after them all, Douglas put two in a bed. With the season barely started, Grosse Isle was already stretched beyond its resources.

By the end of May, forty ships lay at anchor, stretching a mile down river, and there would have been two more but they were lost at sea. The brig *Carricks* was wrecked off the Gaspé coast, only forty-eight of her 167 passengers reaching shore. The *Exmouth* from Londonderry sank with the loss of all but three of her 251 people, causing the *Liverpool Telegraph and Shipping Gazette* to comment: "Another ship has foundered and 248 of our fellow creatures have been launched, unshrived into eternity. Another and another will share the same fate unless a strict and searching inquiry be instituted to ascertain if man is not guilty in some measure of causing so great a sacrifice of human life. A few days and the circumstance is forgotten – it is only the foundering of an emigrant ship – remembered but by relatives."

On Grosse Isle forty people were dying every day, and six men did nothing but dig graves in the shallow, rocky soil. Dismayed at last by the size of the crisis – long predicted but underestimated – the government hastily granted Douglas what he had requested in vain during the winter. A small steamer, the *St. George*, was sent so he could board incoming ships to inspect them. Work was begun on five emigrant sheds, and the government sent four sixty-four-bed hospital tents and 266 bell tents, each with space for twelve beds. Fifty soldiers of the 93rd Regiment, which had been sent to police the island, were pressed into nursing duties due to the difficulty in attracting and holding civilian nurses. Volunteer doctors, priests and Anglican clergymen began to arrive. Captain Edward Boxer from the Port of Quebec set up a commissariat to sell food at cost.

By June 6, 25,000 people had arrived on ships that had already buried 1,097 at sea. With 1,115 of the arrivals detained in quarantine on the island, there was so much overcrowding, confusion and death that Douglas had no choice but to declare the ships themselves as quarantine space though this spread disease. The *Agnes* arrived with 427 passengers and within a short time all but 150 were dead or dying. A medical commission from Quebec City was shocked to find hundreds of sick on the ships, "corpses lying in bed with the sick and dying."

"We entirely disapprove of the plan of keeping a vessel in quarantine for any period, however prolonged, whilst the sick and healthy are congregated together breathing the same atmosphere, sleeping in the same berths and exposed to the same exciting causes of contagion," the commission said. "This year's melancholy experience has in many instances proved that the number attacked, and the mortality of the disease, increased in direct ratio with the length of time the ship was detained under such circumstances." This was true, but clearing emigrants before they went through the two-week quarantine period merely spread disease through the cities and countryside. On June 8 Douglas wrote a hasty, despairing note to his friend A.C. Buchanan in Quebec City:

> Grosse Isle, Tuesday, 9 a.m.
>
> Out of the 4,000 or 5,000 emigrants who have left this island since Sunday, at least 2,000 will fall sick somewhere before three weeks are over. They ought to have accommodation for 2,000 sick at least at Montreal and Quebec, as all the Cork and Liverpool passengers are half dead from starvation and want before embarking; and the least bowel complaint, which is sure to come with change of food, finishes them without a struggle. I never saw people so indifferent to life; they would continue in the same berth with the dead person until the seamen or captain dragged out the corpse with boat hooks. Good God! what evils will befall the cities wherever they alight. Hot weather will increase the evil. Now give the authorities of Quebec and Montreal fair warning from me. I have not time to write, or should feel it my duty to do so. Public safety requires it.

As of mid-June, 6,000 emigrants, brought up-river by three steamers hired by the government, had arrived at the Montreal waterfront, where they sought shelter in the sheds built fifteen years earlier during the cholera outbreak. These were so overcrowded people were forced to lie out on the stone quays without shelter. The Legislative Assembly appealed to Queen Victoria to halt the invasion of the "starving and the sick and diseased, unable and unfit as they are to face the hardships of a settler's life." Bishop Joseph Signay of Quebec sent a letter to the bishops of Ireland warning them of the "dismal fate that awaits the unfortunate children of Ireland who seek relief in Canada." The French-language journal *La Minerve* said the Irish should be sent to the West Indies to take the place of the slaves freed by English planters.

By late June, 5,784 emigrants had reached Toronto, where precautions had been taken that would save the city the high fatality rate suffered in Montreal. A building on King Street was converted into a fever hospital, and the city was taking advice from a man who had come over from Ireland on an emigrant ship and witnessed conditions at Grosse Isle.

His name was Stephen De Vere and he was no ordinary emigrant. Landowner, magistrate, teacher, convert to Catholicism, nephew of Lord Monteagle and member of a respected Anglo-Irish family that lived near Adare in County Limerick, he was also a social reformer. In April he subjected himself to the hardships of a steerage emigrant in order to report conditions to the Colonial Office, whose information was second-hand at best and, when coming from the shipowners, biased. The ship he sailed on was better than most, but his findings were to shock the government into reforming the Passenger Act.

The fearful state of disease and debility in which the Irish migrants have reached Canada must undoubtedly be attributed in a great degree to the destitution and consequent sickness prevailing in Ireland, but has been much aggravated by the neglect of cleanliness, ventilation and generally good state of social economy during the voyage.

Before the emigrant has been a week at sea he is an altered man. How can it be otherwise? Hundreds of poor people, men, women and children of all ages, from the drivelling idiot to the babe just born, huddled together without light, without air, wallowing in filth and breathing a fetid atmosphere, sick in body, dispirited in heart, the fevered patients lying between the sound, in sleeping places so narrow as almost to deny them the power of indulging, by a change of position, the natural restlessness of the disease; by their agonized ravings disturbing those around....

The food is generally ill-selected and seldom sufficiently cooked, in consequence of the insufficiency and bad construction of the cooking places. The supply of water, hardly enough for cooking and drinking, does not allow washing. In many ships the filthy beds, teeming with all abominations, are never required to be brought on deck and aired; the narrow space between the sleeping berths and the piles of boxes is never washed or scraped, but breathes up a damp and fetid stench until the day before arrival at quarantine, when all hands are required to scrub up and put on "a fair face" for the doctor and government inspector. No moral restraint is attempted, the voice of prayer is never heard; drunkenness, with its consequent train of ruffianly debasement, is not discouraged, because it is profitable to the captain who traffics in the grog.

De Vere caught the captain cheating on water rations. The meat was so salty it caused great thirst, and there was not enough fresh water to boil the ration of rice, let along wash. The captain refused to hear complaints, and some of the passengers lay for days in their dark bunks, like animals in a cave, "because they thus suffered less from hunger." Nor were conditions better when the emigrants reached Canada. De Vere said the river steamers were spreading disease with emigrants crowded on to open barges "like pigs upon the deck of a Cork and Bristol packet."

The three large vessels, the *Queen, Quebec* and *Alliance,* that brought tens of thousands of emigrants from Grosse Isle to Point St. Charles in Montreal carried an average of 1,200 each trip but sometimes as many as 2,000. "In almost every boat were clearly marked cases of fever, in some were deaths, the dead and the living huddled together. I have myself, when accompanying the emigrant agent on his duty to inspect the steamer on arrival, seen him stagger back, like one struck, at meeting the current of fetid infection exhaled from between her decks." At Grosse Isle, medical inspection was hasty and superficial. Dr. Douglas walked down a line of emigrants, selected those who looked particularly unwell and ordered them ashore, even when this meant breaking up families. "The ill effect of this haste was twofold," De Vere said. "Some were detained in danger who were not ill, and many were allowed to proceed who were actually in fever."

Father E.J. Horan, one of the volunteers on Grosse Isle, wrote, "The number of sick rose to between thirteen and fourteen hundred. On Friday there were sixty-seven deaths. There are a number of cooks and nurses but never enough. From every side, people are asking for food, and when you see how thin most of these poor wretches are, you have no doubt that lack of food is the principal cause of all this sickness." One of the volunteer doctors, Dr. Benson, who had arrived on the Dublin emigrant ship *Wandsworth* as a passenger, contacted typhus and died.

Two other doctors died in July, both in New Brunswick, both in their twenties. Dr. Collins came down with typhus on Partridge Island while ministering to 900 of his fellow countrymen and died July 2. His wife, Mary, wrote, "On the 1st day of July when all hope for my husband's recovery was given up, word was sent to the city that we (that is myself and his parents) could go down and see him. He was quite conscious when we arrived. He had not been told we were coming and was greatly distressed to see us there in the midst of the awful infection." Some 4,000 people attended his funeral and he was buried in a double coffin, one wood and one lead, because of the typhus.

The same week brought death to Dr. John Vondy, who at twenty-six was the resident doctor at New Brunswick's second quarantine station, Middle Island near Chatham, which contained 350 emigrants, including thirty orphans. His death came shortly after the arrival of the bark *Looshtauk,* which had been bound for Quebec when desperate illness on board forced her master to put in at Chatham. During her seven-week voyage, 117 of her 467 people had died, and forty died on Middle Island, where emigrants were housed in old fish sheds whose sides were open to the weather. The *Looshtauk,* whose home port was Dublin, had sailed from Liverpool and was only a few days at sea when typhus broke out. Captain John Thain did all he could to fight the disease, including removing passengers to the deck while the steerage was fumigated with brimstone and chloride of lime, but on the eighth day the disease spread among the children "who died very fast."

The *Looshtauk* took her survivors on up the St. Lawrence to Grosse Isle, where fever ships were arriving almost daily "reeking with pestilence." On two days, July 11 and 12, four ships with 400 sick anchored off Grosse Isle, the alarming number of 343 having died at sea. One of them, *Erin's Queen* from Cork, brought many bodies to the island for burial and the captain had to bribe crew members with a sovereign for each body hauled out of the steerage. One witness said the saddest sight he ever saw was a glimpse of a young girl's body lying on deck, her blonde hair stirring in the slight breeze.

There were always at least thirty ships lying off shore, their holds full of sick and healthy cooped in together. According to Father William Moylan, vicar of St. Patrick's, Quebec, and a volunteer on Grosse Isle, they were badly treated by fearful, resentful crew members. Moylan said mortality was twice as heavy as that ashore, which must have been bad indeed considering conditions in the island's sheds and hospital tents. "Corpses were allowed to remain all night in places where death had occurred," Moylan said, "even when they had a companion in the same bed." Three new hospital sheds had been erected with space for 360 beds, but this was still far too few. Late in July there were 2,500 sick on Grosse Isle.

There were never enough people to care for the sick; twelve of the seventeen volunteer doctors went down with fever. No nuns had been sent to nurse on the island, but priests and Anglican ministers filled in as nurses when they were not ministering to the dying. Father Moylan brought water to fever patients who had received nothing to drink for almost two days. "I have seen in one day," said Father Bernard McGauran, the island's young chaplain, "thirty-seven lying on the beach, crawling in the mud and dying like fish out of water."

Dr. Douglas, a strongly-built, stocky man, the thirty-eight-year-old son of a Scottish Methodist minister, had the fever himself for a while but kept on limping about the island in conditions that would have broken a lesser man. At the time, Douglas, who was to become the hero of the Grosse Isle tragedy, was probably the most experienced quarantine official in the colonies, having begun his public health career at the small quarantine station on the Gaspé during the cholera epidemic of 1832. Four years later he was appointed superintendent at Grosse Isle, where he married and had seven children and established a small farm where he lived on the east end of the island. He was a respected figure in Quebec City, where he served as secretary of the Literary and Historical Society in 1843, and wrote extensively for medical journals. Little in his career was to prepare him for the superhuman efforts he displayed during the famine migration.

Even by the standards of the age – a few years before Florence Nightingale introduced modern nursing into army hospitals – Grosse Isle was a nightmare. Nurses were afraid to come to the island, and when Douglas tried to enlist healthy women emigrants, offering them high wages, they refused. A great part of the problem was the nature of the disease, for even doctors were "disgusted with the disagreeable nature of their duties in treating such filthy cases," Douglas conceded.

Beginning with aches, chills and fever, the patient took on the stupor that gave the disease its name. On the fourth day dark blotches appeared, the pulse leaped or was feeble by turns, and within a fortnight a climax was reached in which the patient would either recover or die, usually due to heart failure. Treatment consisted of purgatives such as castor oil, doses of laudanum, glasses of brandy as stimulant, and bathing the patient in tepid water mixed with vinegar, though given conditions on Grosse Isle the latter was rarely if ever attempted that year.

"The sick remain lying in their excrement for whole days," wrote Father Jean Baptiste Antoine Ferland. "They complain frequently that they are condemned to go without drinking water for ten to twelve hours. The assistants, if blamed, will tell you that with the best inclination in the world it is impossible for them to carry water from the river to quench the thirst of so many persons." Springs dried up and not enough water was brought from the mainland. "I was eight days on the island," said Father Bernard O'Reilly, who had come down from Sherbrooke, "and during that period I could convince myself that, if things continue as they now exist, very few of those who land on the rocky shores will ever leave them."

Attempts to segregate the sick were sketchy; patients suffering an injury or minor illness were put into the same bed with a typhus patient. That there was some awareness of the contagious nature of the epidemic was demonstrated by the appearance at Grosse Isle of two men claiming to have an antidote. Mr. Ledoyen and Colonel Calvert had convinced Lord Grey at the Colonial Office that they had invented what Grey at first called a "really wonderful" disinfectant, though he was later disillusioned and called Calvert "that pottering blockhead." Douglas was sceptical when he saw them fill a tent with barrels of human excrement to demonstrate the value of their disinfectant. "This was affected," said Douglas, "by M. Ledoyen, who sprinkled the fluid, and waved a wet sheet with the same through the tent for about an hour." Douglas's doubts were strengthened when both men came down with fever and Calvert died.

Two dozen priests and seventeen Anglican clergymen who came to the island at one time or another were infected. The Anglican Bishop of Quebec, George Jehoshaphat Mountain, concerned at the fate of Protestant emigrants who made up 10 per cent of that year's migration, came to Grosse Isle and was touched by the plight of the children. More children arrived than ever before – fifty for every hundred adults instead of thirty-eight per hundred adults as heretofore – and many were orphans sent out by the workhouses. Others, like the child Bishop Mountain saw lying under a heap of rags in a dirty tent, had lost their parents to typhus during the voyage and were dying themselves.

"Although the mortality among children has been very great," wrote Lord Elgin, "nearly 1,000 orphans have been left during the season at Montreal, and a proportionate number at Grosse Isle, Quebec, Kingston, Toronto and other towns." Many were adopted by French Canadians through the efforts of the "priest of the Irish," Charles-Félix Cazeau, Vicar-General of the Diocese of Quebec, and were brought up indistinguishable from Québécois except for their Irish faces. There are records in Quebec City that 619 were adopted. Many families had been split, the children adrift, and it was common to see notices such as one in the Montreal *Transcript*: "Information wanted of Abraham Taylor, aged twelve years, Samuel Taylor, ten, and George Taylor, eight, from County Leitrim, Ireland, who landed in Quebec about five weeks ago, their mother having been detained at Grosse Isle. Any information about them will be thankfully received by their brother, William Taylor, at this office." Another in July said: "Information wanted of Patrick Hurley from the County of Cork who left his wife and two daughters at the Quarantine station about two weeks ago."

The quarantine system was failing and by mid-summer emigrants in their thousands were carrying infection into the countryside and the cities. There were 800 in hospital at Quebec City, with deaths averaging thirty or forty every week. In Montreal, a city of less than 50,000 people, 1,730 deaths were reported and efforts to contain the epidemic had little power. Six fever sheds had been built at Point St. Charles, beyond the Lachine Canal and away from the city, and were described as a "vast charnel house for the emigrants themselves as well as for the physicians and nurses who attended them."

A visitor in mid-summer, when the sheds contained 907 people and sixteen had died during the previous twenty-four hours, found great activity and confusion. "We saw the physician labouring away with generally half a dozen persons speaking to him at once, and two young gentlemen serving out medicines with great activity, while nurses were coming and going in all directions."

"A day scarcely passes without the intelligence reaching us of the death of some valuable and useful clergyman, some public-spirited and humane citizen, or some experienced and skilful captain of a vessel or steamboat," said the *Pilot* newspaper. One of the volunteer workers who lost his life to typhus was John Mills, the popular mayor and former fur trader. Eight priests died, and seventeen nuns who had been given dispensation to leave the Grey Nuns cloister to nurse the sick. Official accounts said 3,579 emigrants and citizens died in and around Montreal before the epidemic was over.

"The panic which prevails in Montreal and Quebec is beginning to manifest itself in the Upper Province, and farmers are unwilling to hire even healthy emigrants," reported Lord Elgin on July 13, "because it appears that since the warm weather set in typhus has broken out among those who were taken into service at the commencement of the season as being perfectly free from disease." A month later he said, "Malignant fever has thus been generated in private dwellings so as might have been expected, under such afflicting circumstances, the sick have been cast back in crowds into the towns, and the doors of the farm houses have been closed against even those who are reported to be free from taint ... every village becomes a station at which the plague-stricken exiles congregate. What is to be done?"

In Kingston, the *British Whig* asked: "What is to be the end of the barbarous policy now pursued of pouring, to the extent of from 80,000 to 100,000 of the famished and diseased population of down-trodden Ireland, into this province in one season we cannot tell." In Bytown, where there were 200 deaths and 1,000 sick, a Dr. Barry proposed that people suspected of carrying disease be driven out of town. A settler's wife at Peterborough wrote, "The typhus fever and dysentery have reached even this remote place. Wherever those wretched immigrants came they brought with them sickness and death. Some of the members of the Board of Health have already fallen under its malignant influence." Officials in Toronto tried to keep out emigrants who had no friends or relatives in the city. An emotional account of the scene on the Toronto waterfront appeared in *The Times* in London: "The quay at Toronto was crowded with a throng of dying and diseased abjects; the living and the dead lay huddled together in horrible embrace. The fever spread with rapid violence throughout Canada and the inhabitants, though they were reduced to great extremity for want of labour, fled from contact with this gigantic intimation of mortality." There was great consternation throughout the city when the Catholic Bishop Michael Power sickened and died after answering a midnight call to administer last rites to a dying woman.

And down the river at Grosse Isle the ships were still arriving. There were 2,000 people on the island, filling the new hospital sheds and tents, and people were lying on the ground under scraps of canvas from the ships. The brig *Ganges* and the bark *Corea* from Liverpool were followed by the barks *Naprima* from Dublin and *Larch* from Sligo, and among them the four ships carried 254 sick and reported 133 deaths at sea. The *Virginius* from Liverpool had lost 158 of her 476 passengers, and the captain, chief mate, steward and nine sailors had died at sea leaving the second mate and two crew members to work the ship with the help of any healthy emigrant willing to help, but it was said only half a dozen passengers were in any fit state to work. She had hardly dropped anchor when another Liverpool ship, the *Naomi,* arrived: "The filth and dirt in this vessel's hold," said Douglas, "creates such an effluvium as to make it difficult to breathe."

A detailed description of one of these vessels was provided by Robert Whyte of Dublin, who published a diary he kept while sailing from Dublin with 110 emigrants sent out from County Meath. Few brought their own food to the brig, and Whyte wrote that many of them seemed too old and infirm to attempt the voyage, which they expected would take three weeks. There were twenty children. The captain was a taciturn man of "uninviting aspect" but his wife, a ruddy sunburned woman of sixty, who came on the voyage, wearing a black bombazine dress and a straw hat, was kindly, as was the mate, who had a wooden leg, black whiskers and was no more than five feet tall. Whyte was the sole cabin passenger and ate with the captain. The brig left Dublin May 30 and by June 6, a Sunday, the usual seasickness having abated, the emigrants were taking their ease in the sun on deck:

The passengers were dressed in their best clothes and presented a better appearance than I expected. A group of young men being at a loss for amusement began to wrestle and play pitch and toss but the mate soon put a stop to this, at which they grumbled, saying they did not think Mr. Mate would be so hard. Very few of them could read, neither did they seem to have much regard for the sanctity of the Sabbath. There were prayers in the hold and they were divided into two parties, those who spoke Irish and those who did not. After their religious exercises they came upon deck and spent the remainder of the day jesting and laughing and singing. We had a clear, beautiful sunset from which the captain prognosticated an easterly wind.

June 7: The passengers elected four men to govern their commonwealth, the principal of whom had the title of Head Committee.... Much to the terror of the little boys who were often uproarious, and to keep them in order he frequently administered the cat. The other duties of this functionary consisted in seeing that the hold was kept clean, preventing smoking below deck, and in settling differences.

June 8: The Head Committee reported that two women were ill. They were accordingly dosed with the best skill of the Mistress....

June 9: ... the shouting of men and the screaming of women was heard on deck, and thinking someone was overboard, judge of our terror when we saw the fore part of the brig in a blaze. All hands having assisted, a plentiful supply of water in a short time subdued the fire. It arose from the negligence of Simon [a young member of the crew] who fell asleep leaving a lighted candle stuck against the boards....

There was always a fear of fire, and great care was taken with the cooking arrangements, which consisted of a "large wooden case lined with bricks about the size and shape of a settee, the coals were confined by two or three iron bars in front." Rations of salt beef and biscuit were issued daily so that a week's ration, which was only seven pounds of food, would not be eaten all at once. Whyte said the fireplace was usually surrounded by quarrelling people trying to get at the fire with their pots, until a crew member put an end to it at 7 p.m. by dousing the fire with a bucket of water, leaving some of the emigrants "half blinded by steam" to go back into the steerage "with their half cooked supper."

June 10: Some more cases of illness were reported. The Mistress was kept busy mixing medicine and making drinks, hoping that by her early attention the sickness might be prevented from spreading.

June 13: The reports from the hold become very alarming; the Mistress was occupied all day attending the numerous calls upon her. She already regretted having come on the voyage, but her kind heart did not allow her to consult her ease. When she appeared on deck she was beset by a crowd of poor creatures, each having some request to make, most of them of a most inconsiderate kind, and few of which it was in her power to comply with....

June 14: The Head Committee brought a can of water to show it to the captain; it was quite foul, muddy and bitter, from having been in a wine cask. When allowed to settle it became clear, leaving considerable sediment in the bottom of the vessel; but it retained its bad taste. The mate endeavoured to improve it by trying the effect of charcoal and alum, but some of the casks were beyond remedy, and the contents, when pumped out, resembled nauseous ditch water. There were now eight cases of serious illness – six of them being fever and two dysentery – the former appeared to be of peculiar character and very alarming; the latter cases did not seem to be so violent in degree.

June 15: The reports this morning were very afflicting, and I felt much that I was unable to render any assistance to my poor fellow passengers. The captain desired the Mistress to give them everything out of his own stores that she considered to be of service to any of them. He felt much alarmed; nor was it to be wondered at that contagious fever – which under the most advantageous circumstances and under the watchful eyes of the most skilful physicians requires the greatest ability – should terrify one having the charge of so many human beings, likely to fall prey to the unchecked progress of the dreadful disease. For once having shown itself in the unventilated hold of a small brig, containing 110 living creatures, how could it possibly be stayed without suitable medicines, medical skill and pure water to slake the patients' burning thirst. The prospect before us was indeed an awful one, and there was no hope for us but in the mercy of God.

June 16: The past night was very rough, and I enjoyed little rest. No additional cases of sickness were reported, but there were signs of insubordination amongst the healthy men who complained of starvation and want of water for their sick wives and children. A deputation came aft to acquaint the captain with their grievances, but he ordered them away, and would not listen to a word from them. When he went below the ring leaders threatened that they would break into the provision store.... In order to make a deeper impression on their minds, he brought out the old blunderbuss from which he fired a shot, the report of which was equal to the report of a small cannon. The deputation slunk away muttering complaints. If they were resolute they could easily have seized upon the provisions. In fact, I was surprised how famished men could so easily bear with their own and their starved childrens' sufferings. The captain would willingly have listened if it were in his power to relieve their distress.

June 17: Two new cases of fever were announced, and from the representations of the mate the poor creatures in the hold were in a shocking state.... Our progress was almost imperceptible and the captain began to grow very uneasy there being but provisions for 50 days. It now became necessary to reduce the complement of water....

June 20 (Sunday): The poor emigrants were in their usual squalid attire; neither did the crew rig themselves out as on former Sundays. All were dispirited and a cloud of melancholy hung over us.

June 22: One of the sailors was unable for duty, and the mate feared he had the fever. The reports from the hold were growing ever more alarming, and some of the patients who were mending had relapsed. One of the women was every moment expected to breathe her last and her friends – an aunt and cousins – were inconsolable about her as they had persuaded her to leave her father and mother and come with them....

June 23: At breakfast I enquired of the mate after the young woman who was so ill yesterday, when he told me that she was dead; when I remarked that I feared her burial would cause great consternation, I learned that the sad ordeal was over, her remains having been consigned to the deep within an hour after she expired. The sick list now amounted to twenty.

June 24: Being the festival of St. John, and a Catholic holiday, some young men and women got up a dance in the evening, regardless of the moans and crys of those tortured by the fiery fever. When the mate spoke to them of the impropriety of such conduct they desisted and retired to the bow where they sat down and spent the remainder of the evening singing. The monotonous howling they kept up was quite in union with the scene of desolation within, and the dreary expanse of ocean without.

June 25: This morning there was a further accession to the names upon the sick roll. It was awful how suddenly some were stricken. A little child, playing with his companions, suddenly fell down, and for some time was sunk in deadly torpor, from which when he awoke he commenced to scream violently and wreath in convulsive agony. A poor woman who was warming a drink at the fire for her husband also dropped down quite senseless and was borne to her berth. I found it very difficult to acquire precise information respecting the progressive symptoms of the disease, I inferred that the first symptom was generally a reeling in the head followed by a swelling pain, as if the head were going to burst. Next came excruciating pains in the bones, and then a swelling of the limbs, commencing with the feet, and in some cases ascending the body, and again descending before it reached the head, stopping at the throat. The period of each stage varied in different patients, some of whom were covered in yellow, watery pimples, and the others with red and purple spots that turned into putrid sores.

June 27: It made my heart bleed to listen to the calls of "Water, for God's sake, water." Oh it was horrifying; strange to say I had no fear of taking the fever which, perhaps under the merciful providence of the Almighty, was a preventative cause.

June 28: The number of patients upon the list now amounted to thirty, and the effluvium of the hold was shocking. The passengers suffered much for want of pure water....

June 30: Passing the main hatch I glimpsed of one of the most awful sights I have ever beheld. Her hand and face were swollen an unnatural size, the latter being hideously deformed. I recollected remarking the clearness of her complexion when I saw her in health shortly after we sailed. She was then a picture of humour and contentment; now how sadly altered! Her cheeks retained their ruddy hue, but the rest of her distorted countenance was a leprous whiteness. She had been nearly three weeks ill, and suffered exceedingly until the swelling set in, commencing in her feet and creeping up her body. Her afflicted husband stood by her holding a blessed candle in his hand, and awaiting the departure of her spirit. Death put a period to her existence shortly after I saw her. As the sun was setting the bereaved husband muttered a prayer over the enshrouded corpse which, as he said Amen, was lowered into the ocean.

On the first of July the brig was feeling its way through fog on the Newfoundland Banks, "our horn sounding constantly." There were thirty-seven sick now, and on July 2 a man died after sending for the mate and giving him a key to open a box and send the money in it to the man's mother. On July 6, almost half the passengers were sick, and, all the spare canvas having been used to wrap corpses, the dead were now placed in meal sacks. One of the dead men left an orphaned son of seven years who, Whyte noticed, was wearing his father's coat. "Poor little fellow, he seemed quite unconscious of his loss and proud of the possession of his scanty covering."

When the brig weaved its way through the islands and ships off Grosse Isle and dropped anchor on July 27, Whyte found the island cool and green and deceptively attractive – at a distance. Rows of white tents shone in the sun like an army encampment, and the huddle of buildings, hospital, chapels and quarantine sheds looked like a snug village. As soon as Whyte stepped ashore the illusion was shattered: "This scene of natural beauty was sadly deformed by the dismal display of suffering – helpless creatures being carried by sailors over the rocks on their way to hospital – boats arriving with patients, some of whom died in transmission from their ships. Another and more awful sight was the continuous line of boats, each carrying the freight of dead to the burial ground and forming an endless funeral procession. Some had several corpses so tied up with canvas that the stiff, sharp outline of death was easily traceable; others had rude coffins constructed by the sailors from the boards of berths, or should I say cribs. In a few, a solitary mourner attended the remains, but the majority contained no living being save the rowers."

The first to board the ship were not doctors, as Whyte expected, but two priests who came in a rowboat, put on their vestments and administered last rites to an old man and woman dying in their bunks. They told Whyte conditions in his brig were much better than in other ships. "In the holds of some of them," they said, "they were up to their ankles in filth, the wretched emigrants crowded together like cattle, and the corpses remaining long unburied, the sailors being ill, and the passengers unwilling to touch them."

The doctor came next morning, wrote a chit admitting six fever patients to hospital and promised to return to inspect the other passengers, after warning the island was already overcrowded with 2,500 people. Whyte saw two German ships come in from Bremen looking clean and well kept, and since there was no illness aboard the Germans were discharged quickly and taken up river. "It was indeed a busy scene of life and death, and to complete the picture the rigging of the vessels was covered over with the passengers' linen hanging out to dry; from the character of which, as they fluttered in the breeze, I could tell with accuracy from what country they came. Alas, the wretched rags of the majority told but too plainly they were Irish."

The doctor came back three days later and lined the passengers on deck before a wooden barrier, all except "one incorrigible family" having cleaned themselves as best they could. The healthy were sent up-river as soon as the fifteen-day quarantine was over; the ill were detained in hospital on the island, including two orphan sisters who were joining their brother in Upper Canada, and a woman "who had attended all her family thru illness; now care-worn and heartbroken she became herself a prey."

Whyte's attention was taken by a man the "very picture of desperation and misery, that increased the ugliness of his countenance, for he was sadly disfigured by the marks of smallpox and was blind in one eye. He walked moodily along the deck, snatched his child from a woman's arms and went down into the hold without speaking a word." His wife had just been buried and a sailor told Whyte what had happened. The man stood at the grave until it was covered, whereupon he snatched two shovels, laid them on the grave in the form of a cross and cried, "By that cross Mary I swear to revenge your death. As soon as I earn my passage home I will go back and shoot the man that murdered you, and that is the landlord." Like most emigrants on Whyte's ship he had been sent out to Canada by a County Meath landowner.

"Ah sir," one of the emigrants told Whyte, "we thought we couldn't be worse off than we war; but now in our sorrow we know the differ; for sure supposin we were dyin of starvation, or if the sickness overtuk us, we had a chance of a doctor, and if he could do no good for our bodies, sure the priests could for our souls; and then we'd be buried along wid our own people, in the ould church-yard, with the green sod over us; instead of dying like rotten sheep thrown into a pit, and the minit the breath is out of our bodies flung into the sea to be eaten up by them horrid sharks."

For three months the state of Irish emigrant vessels had hardened officials so that it took something especially horrendous, such as the arrival of the *Virginius* from Liverpool on August 12, to raise any outcry. She had been chartered by Major Denis Mahon, a cavalry officer who had inherited 2,000 acres near Strokestown, County Roscommon, that were overrun with starving tenants and cottiers who had paid no rent for years and could not feed themselves. Instead of evicting them outright, Mahon offered what he believed was a humane alternative, free passage to Canada; according to the *Limerick Chronicle* of May 26 most were happy to go. He sent them to Liverpool, where the typhus was particularly virulent in the waterfront lodging houses, and by the time they boarded the *Virginius* many of the 476 passengers already had fever. By the time the *Virginius* reached Grosse Isle after an unusually long voyage of sixty-three days, her passengers were in shocking state.

"On mustering the passengers for inspection," wrote Dr. Douglas, "it was found that 106 were ill with fever, including nine of the crew, and the large number of 158 had died on the passage, including the first and second officers and seven of the crew, and the master and the steward were dying. The few that were able to come on deck were ghastly, yellow-looking spectres, unshaven and hollow-cheeked and, without exception, the worst-looking passengers I have seen. No more than six or eight were really healthy and able to exert themselves." Nineteen men, women and children died on the *Virginius* while she was anchored of Grosse Isle, and ninety of her passengers were to die in the sheds and tents of Grosse Isle.

Adam Ferrie, head of the Montreal Emigration Committee and a member of Canada's Legislative Assembly, denounced Mahon in a letter to the Colonial Secretary, but whatever the young officer's sins of commission or omission he paid for them dearly. A month or two later he was shot to death near his home. Some said he was killed by the lover of a girl who had died on the *Virginius*, but the real murderers were two men out to avenge Mahon's eviction of tenants who had refused to emigrate.

Landowners paid the passage of nearly 7,000 emigrants that year, more than ever before. Colonel Wyndham, who had been sending tenants for eight years now, paid for 450 more to go, as did Francis Spaight and many others; tenants who had formerly refused to give up their leases were now eager to go. Sir Robert Gore Booth, who had chartered the *Aeolus* from Sligo to Saint John in the spring, sent a second ship, the 950-ton *Yeoman*, which arrived at Partridge Island August 19. He was at pains to give the people a medical examination at his own home, eight miles from Sligo town; his valet caught fever and died and Gore Booth and his wife contracted the fever but recovered.

The *Yeoman* was a well-founded ship; the master, John Purden, was a qualified surgeon and his wife, a vicar's daughter, came to take care of the young women and children. Writing to Lady Gore Booth, Mrs. Purden said a makeshift chapel had been rigged amidships out of old sails and flags, and there was a fiddler "who makes happy faces and nimble feet all around him." There was a cow to provide milk, and rations consisted of meal, salt fish, salt beef, tea, sugar, coffee, molasses and other food. The ship made fast time and there were only three deaths among 503 passengers, though sixty people were suffering from fever and several died after arrival at Partridge Island. "By all appearances the longer we were kept in quarantine the faster people were getting sick," said Mrs. Purden. The *New Brunswick Courier* of August 28 said that the passengers, while well cared for on the voyage, were then left to shift for themselves, though in truth Captain Purden helped 150 to get jobs.

"They were found to be good men on the roads," wrote Moses Perley, "and the farmers employed them for hay and harvesting." Farmers frequently gave families trudging the roads a night's lodging and a meal, though some complained that it seemed the whole colony was becoming Irish. Some of the emigrants who had arrived from Gore Booth's estate aboard the *Aeolus* in June had jobs, but at least 150, according to the *New Brunswick Courier* were languishing in the city Poor House two months later, where, the paper said, they "subsist chiefly by begging" and were likely to become a "permanent charge upon this community." A doctor described the Poor House as a "factory of disease, in consequence of the filth and destitution of its inmates, many of whom are penniless widows and orphans." Arrangements were made to transfer them to the County Almshouse a mile outside Saint John.

When Richard Yeats, a minister's son who had been among the *Yeoman's* passengers, heard that citizens were resentful at having to support people from the *Aeolus*, he said, "I have no doubt that the passengers brought by this ship [the *Yeoman*] will quite redeem their characters for they are admitted by all who have yet seen them to be of a very superior class, and indeed I must say their appearances have been much improved by the exertions of the captain and Mrs. Purden...."

Letters sent home and preserved by the Emigration Commission support this assessment. Catherine Bradley, writing to "Dear Uncle John" at Lissadell said, "The people I see here are just as we have at home, all trying to live as well as God will allow them.... I do feel most happy and content here, so much so that I sometimes forget old Ireland for a time.... I have seen little of the country but understand that farmers from the Old Country do well here, and soon get on very comfortable and respectable." Owen Boyle, who may have been sent from a Sligo workhouse since he was not a Gore Booth tenant, was described as a "miserable creature" when he left home but seemed to undergo a change in New Brunswick, writing back happily that "this is a good country for smart boys and smart girls." His two sisters had got jobs as domestics and he himself had bought a "new sueat of chloes."

One young man congratulated his parents for staying in Ireland. "I am very glad that you did not come out here," he said. "They are comeing here and dieing in dozens their is not a vessel comes here but the feaver is on board.... Let none of you attempt to come here this season as there are so many here and the feaver in every house almost. It is a good place for young people but there are enough at present until next summer. Tell Andy M'Sarry he would do better here than at home. Let him come next summer. The people are lying out here on the shores under sheads and going to the grave, numbers of them every day.... Larry Runian and wife are on the island and sister ill of feaver. Mrs. Dolan Connor and family are well the husband is in the States. Nor more at present but remains, your son truely, Ference

McGown." Judith Warren, a Protestant who got a position with a family of the same faith who had a farm at Indian Island, said she had been advised to go to New York by her friends, "but it is very sickly there now, the hospitals and poor houses and every place full and it is a very healthy place where I am, and a decent religious family, I do not like to leave them."

Early that season the Americans, whose passenger laws had always been stricter than those of the British, had adopted port regulations designed to discourage famine emigration, and these, as Lord Elgin noted, had the effect of turning the "tide of suffering" toward British North America and away from the States. American laws required a ship's master to pay a bond to ensure none of his passengers would become a public charge, and he faced a year in prison or forfeiture of his ship for carrying passengers above a legal limit. The result, said Earl Grey, the Colonial Secretary, was that "all the poorest and most destitute flocked to Canada, while those who were better off, avoiding contact with such wretched objects, went to the United States."

Despite efforts to exclude ailing emigrants that year, New York City suffered an outbreak of ship fever that killed 1,400 people, and though the mortality was far from the magnitude reached in Canada, emigrants were as badly treated as they were in Liverpool, with "runners" and other petty gangsters preying on every incoming ship. Boston, the other major American port, imposed such heavy penalties on ships carrying sick emigrants that it escaped the worst effects of ship fever, though the *Boston Transcript* reported that "groups of poor wretches were to be seen in every part of the city, resting their weary and emaciated limbs...." Ships with fever aboard were turned away from the port, and in two cases, the *Seraph* and the *Mary* from Cork, emigrants were actually ashore before they were forced back onto the ships. Both were sent to Saint John and of their total of 196 passengers, forty-five were ill and three died on Partridge Island. On September 17 *The Times,* showing an uncharacteristic concern for Irish emigrants, said, "The Black Hole of Calcutta was a mercy compared to the holds of these vessels. Yet, simultaneously, as if in reproof of those on whom the blame of all the wretchedness must fall, foreigners, Germans from Hamburg and Bremen, are daily arriving, all healthy, robust and cheerful."

Nearly 13,000 emigrants had reached Saint John by the end of August, and there were 800 sick and convalescent on Partridge Island and 558 in the Emigrant Hospital and Almshouse outside the city. Several hundred of the poorest emigrants found shelter in sheds on Lower Cove and thronged the streets begging. There was resentment among citizens that the city of 30,000 was expected to care for a total of emigrants equal to half the normal population.

Conditions on Partridge Island reached their nadir in August when Dr. George Harding contracted fever. So many bodies accumulated in the "death house," or makeshift morgue, that forty were buried in a large, shallow pit so near the hospital that a well was contaminated. Rain washed earth off the grave, exposing bits of clothing. Newspapers protested that some of the patients were fleeing the island and spreading contagion in the city. The city's Board of Physicians, which urged improvements on the island, stressed the contagious nature of the fever without being able to explain its cause, but as Patt McGowan, who arrived on the *Yeoman* with his sister Catherine, told his brother Roger in Sligo, some progress was made in the treatment of the fever.

"When I left Ireland I never was stronger or in better health until we were fifteen days on shipboard," wrote McGowan. "Molly Mew died, which lay in the bearth under mine, and I took fevour of her and Bidy Connolly and also Catherine Reilly, and Catherine [his sister] took ill, and neither of us was able to bring the other a drop of drink for nine days.... I took the bowel complaint and it continued with me for three weeks on the ship until we landed at the end of five weeks ... we had to go to Quarantine Island to Ospital and I was given up by the doctor. I passed blood through me for three days and the skin and flesh busted off my teeth and gave blood on my mouth. I was attended

by one Doctor Murfy from County Galway, cured me in six days."
After a long convalescence McGowan got work as a cooper.

Early in September the *Lady Sale* arrived at Saint John, and
though her death toll of twenty-one had not been exceptional, the
state of her passengers exasperated Moses Perley. "This is the fifth season in which I boarded vessels with emigrants," he said, "but I have
never yet seen such abject misery, destitution and helplessness." Perley
was particularly incensed at the number of old people, orphans and
widows, nine of whom had brought fifty-four children. Half the emigrants had come from the Gore Booth estate and the others from the
neighbouring estate of Lord Palmerston, and Perley accused them of
"exporting and shovelling out the helpless and infirm." One old man
on the *Lady Sale* appeared to be the sole support of sixteen ragged
urchins, and it was clear to Perley that the landowners were sending
the least desirable of their tenants to become a burden on the colonies.

Worse was to come before that tragic season was over – events that
heaped blame on the absentee landlords. People surfeited by the sight
of so much misery flooding in on the tide looked for a villain and
chose Lord Palmerston, who as a powerful cabinet minister was in a
position to alleviate distress rather than heap it on.

Henry John Temple, third Viscount Palmerston, known as "Pam,"
was not a man one would automatically cast in a villainous role. He
was admired for his battles against slavery and injustice and was
widely regarded in England as clever and honourable. One of his ancestors had been Provost of Trinity College, Dublin, and another the
speaker of the Irish House of Commons long before it was abolished
by the Act of Union. His interest in Ireland seemed minimal, however,
and he left the management of his Sligo estate to the old Dublin firm
of Kincaid and Stewart, estate agents. When they suggested that he
pay to remove "surplus population" to New Brunswick and Quebec
City, the sixty-three-year-old Foreign Secretary, newly married and
deeply immersed in diplomacy and politics, gave his assent without, it
would seem, many questions or much thought. At considerable ex-

pense, 2,000 people were transported from his estates in nine different ships, and as Kincaid later admitted, the majority were "those who were poorest."

At first, most of Palmerston's emigrants, who received their passage but apparently nothing else, seemed in reasonable condition, for early in the season there were no complaints except for the case of the *Eliza Liddle*. When she arrived at the northern New Brunswick port of Shippigan, the government agent was shocked at the state of her passengers. "Nothing could exceed the misery and destitution of the emigrants," he reported. "Many had not sufficient clothing to cover them." Seventy-seven of the passengers had come from Palmerston's estate and the rest, including forty-three orphans, had come from the Sligo workhouse, so it was hard to say if Palmerston or his agents were to blame.

There was no question, however, as to where the 428 emigrants came from when the *Aeolus* arrived at Saint John on November 1, the day the Partridge Island quarantine station was closed down for the year. All but half a dozen came from Palmerston's lands and, as Kincaid said, they were from the "poorest class of farmer, very little better than paupers," and so desperate to emigrate they had knelt in supplication on the roads.

The *Aeolus* was commanded by the same conscientious Captain Driscoll who had brought Gore Booth's first contingent in June; deaths at sea had been limited to eight, which was exceptionally low, and from all accounts she was well provisioned. Shortly before the *Aeolus* hove to at Saint John, the vessel's thirteen-man Passenger Committee had written a letter to Kincaid and Stewart in Dublin advising them "the provisions, water and medicines were very good and plentiful, and the captain, his officers, and crew treated us kindly and with every attention to our wants, for which we shall ever feel thankful." The first indication of trouble arose when the master was obliged to pay a heavy fine for late arrival before he was permitted to put his passengers ashore.

Thereafter the case of the *Aeolus* becomes one of controversy. Perley expressed the belief that many of the people from the *Aeolus* would be dead by spring and had they been left at home in Sligo they would have been better off, though given the mortality rate in the west of Ireland in 1847, that seems doubtful. Undoubtedly there were worse ships that year, and the force of the outrage seems to have come in part from the pent-up anger and frustration of a city that had been trying all summer to look after 15,000 destitute people, many of whom were carrying a lethal disease. "Such hordes of human wretchedness, while it will absorb nearly all the revenues of the country is carrying death into the abodes of our citizens," said the Saint John *Chronicle*, whose reporters contributed to the feeling of fear and outrage by describing their "rags, vermin, and loathsome disease … the most miserable wretched that horror can picture."

Dr. William Harding, who had succeeded his ailing brother as health officer, was equally outraged. "There are many superannuated people, and others of broken down constitutions, and subjects of chronic disease, lame, widows with very hopeless families, enfeebled men (through chronic disease, etc.) with large helpless families." Inured as he was to emigrant misery, Harding was moved to a bitter protest. "Who is so tame as would not feel indignant at the outrage," he said in a letter to the mayor. "Ninety-nine of every hundred," he warned, "must be supported by the charity of this community, or otherwise as justice demands."

For the city council, justice took the form of offering free passage to anyone prepared to return to Ireland, but since no one came forward the city resigned itself to supporting the Irish emigrants in the Almshouse, which had been expanded and contained 500 patients and was chronically overcrowded. A gauge of the depth of feeling in the city was the protest the council sent to London, regretting "that one of Her Majesty's Ministers, the Rt. Hon. Lord Palmerston, either by himself or his authorized agent should have exposed such a numerous and distressed portion of his tenantry to the severity and privations of a New Brunswick winter."

Some of the boys and girls on the ship, described as orphans, were said to have been nearly naked when they emerged from the steerage into the November cold. A sailor had to drape one boy in a sack because the boy had no clothes at all. Kincaid later said the emigrants, who he insisted were not evicted but emigrated at their own wish, had experienced hardship when they were obliged to wait at the town of Sligo for a month because the ship had been delayed in Scotland. But he refused to take responsibility for their condition on arrival, and insisted they had all been issued with "blankets, shoes, stockings, petticoats, shawls, shifts, gowns, etc." before they left. He suggested their ragged appearance was due to the "hardships of a rough sea passage." Sir Robert Gore Booth testified at a government hearing that the emigrants were "well clothed by Lord Palmerston's desire before they sailed." He also said that Palmerston's agent had been warned that if he did not take the old clothes away from the people in exchange for their new ones they would put the old ones on when they reached their destination "to make themselves look as miserable as possible on the other side." These were people who had learned that any slight show of affluence usually brought bad luck in the form of increased taxes or tithes.

At the same time the *Aeolus* anchored at Saint John, the *Lord Ashburton* arrived at Quebec City from Liverpool having lost sixty-five of her 481 passengers during the voyage, the greatest shipboard mortality that autumn. The Quebec *Gazette* called the condition of the passengers a "disgrace to the home authorities," and Adam Ferrie of the Emigration Committee was so incensed he dashed off a pamphlet in which he indicted half a dozen landowners for callousness, among them Lord Palmerston. He claimed that "the last cargo of human beings which was received from the Lord Palmerston's estate was by the *Lord Ashburton*," and that of these emigrants "eighty-seven were almost in a state of nudity." According to Kincaid, however, no Palmerston tenants were sent out on the *Lord Ashburton* and he accused Ferrie of faulty research and over-excitability.

And finally the dreadful season came to an end. The last ship of the year was the brig *Richard Watson,* forty-two days out of Sligo, her departure having been delayed several times by arguments with the local emigration officer and then by storms. Most if not all of her passengers were from Palmerston's estate, and although only four had died during the voyage, the condition of the emigrants was said to be deplorable, as Lord Elgin himself stated in a letter to Colonial Secretary Grey dated November 12:

Of the passengers, about one fourth were males and the remainder women and children; and we have been assured by the gentleman who saw them, that a more destitute and helpless set have not come out this year. They were penniless and in rags, without shoes or stockings, and lying upon the bare boards – not even having straw. When the health officer visited them he saw other visible instances of destitution, three poor children – infants we might say from their age – sitting on the bare deck perfectly naked huddled together shivering....

The *Examiner* of Toronto, in an editorial on November 20, protested that the colonies were having to provide clothing, food, medicine and graves for Palmerston's paupers. "Can more inhumanity be shown to them or greater injustice to us? ... Is this province to be turned into one vast lazarhouse – our country swamped, our energies blasted – our prospects ruined in order to relieve the great land gluttons of Europe from the just consequences of their own misdoings and crimes?"

Almost 250,000 Irish crossed the Atlantic that year, of whom about 70,000 came to Quebec City and 17,000 to Saint John. About 20,000 others – mostly English, Germans and Scots – also came to the Canadian provinces. It was estimated that 30,000 of those arriving in British North America needed medical attention.

Precisely how many died was never known, for records were either neglected or lost in the chaos and numbing fatigue of coping with thousands of sick and moribund day after day, week after week. The records that have come down to us are often contradictory. The Emigration Commissioners claimed that more than 6,000 died at sea –

5,293 en route to Grosse Isle and 823 on their way to New Brunswick. An emigration official remarked that if the Atlantic were terra firma, the route from Ireland would be strewn like a graveyard with crosses.

As for Grosse Isle, Dr. Douglas, in his year-end report of December 21, said that 442 ships had been inspected, 8,691 people had been brought ashore to quarantine, and 3,328 had died on Grosse Isle, of whom 908 were children. He later revised this figure upward, and when he erected a monument to his four dead medical colleagues he included a plaque that read: "In this secluded spot lie the mortal remains of 5,425 persons who, flying from pestilence and famine in the year 1847, found in North America but a grave." Four doctors, four priests and two Anglican ministers died of typhus on the island, as did thirty nurses, orderlies and other helpers. Almost miraculously, Douglas himself survived, though the experience left a mark that may have shortened his life. At the age of fifty-five, depressed by recurrent illness, he committed suicide in his home on an island near Grosse Isle.

Figures were imprecise as to those who died in quarantine and emigration hospitals or out on the road in the Canadas, but a Colonial Office note put the toll at 11,543. Montreal suffered the greatest impact, with well over 3,500 deaths. The plaque at the northern approach to Victoria Bridge, mounted on a huge black rock hauled from the bed of the St. Lawrence by the Irish who built the bridge in the 1850s, reads: "To preserve from desecration the remains of 6000 emigrants who died of ship fever A.D. 1847–48." There is no indication whether this was meant to be the total for Montreal or for all Quebec.

At Saint John, Moses Perley's report at the end of the year said 17,074 emigrants had arrived in the New Brunswick in 106 ships and virtually all were Irish. He put the death toll at 2,400: 823 died at sea, 600 on Partridge Island, and the rest at the Emigrant Hospital near Saint John or at Middle Island, Chatham.

Ninety per cent of the emigrants that year were Catholic, a much greater proportion than before, and they consisted of small farmers, artisans, labourers and domestic servants. A large number, a third or more, went on to the United States, like John Ford from Macroom, County Cork, who lost his young wife on Grosse Isle and took his son to Dearborn, Michigan, to farm the 400 acres where his grandson, Henry Ford, the automobile pioneer, was born two decades later.

Of the 38,000 Irish who arrived in Toronto, the greater number were sent on to Hamilton and the Niagara Peninsula by boat, and the rest overland into other parts of the province. Those with friends already settled in the colony invariably fared best. Joseph Carrothers, who had lost his sister Jane to typhus during the migration that year, and had taken ill himself, was able to recuperate for a month at the home of his brother, Nathaniel, who had arrived several years earlier to farm near London. Writing to relatives in Fernaugh, County Fermanagh, Joseph said, "Those that is settled for some years is well off.... I am with a waggon maker learning to make waggons at 20 dollars pr month."

Robert Whyte, taking a stagecoach from Prescott to Bytown, where two hundred had died of fever, encountered a scene reminiscent of those he had seen during the famine years in Ireland. "I saw a poor woman with an infant in her arms and a child pulling at her skirt, and crying as they went along. The driver compassionately took them up and the wayfarer wept her thanks. Her husband had died and she was going to her brother, who came out the previous year; having made some money by lumbering in the woods he remitted her the means of joining him. She told her sad tale most plaintively and the passengers sympathized with her."

Whyte also saw two young men from his ship who had got work on the Lachine Canal. As for the others, "they wandered over the country, carrying nothing with them but disease, and owing to their weak constitutions very few can have lived through the winter." They huddled together for warmth, visited the soup kitchens set up for them and were reduced to begging in the Irishtown, Corktown and Slabtown slums of cities from Saint John to the Niagara Peninsula.

The government empowered thirty communities to establish local boards of health to shelter and feed them, but usually for no longer than a week or two. In Toronto a journalist said seventy Irish people from County Clare, eager to work but finding nothing, squatted in a miserable shed on Front Street "between a dung heap and the stagnant harbour waters." They begged for money so they might go into the country to find farm jobs, though thousands who had previously been sent out were flowing back into the city having been refused farm work.

A.B. Hawke, the Canada West emigration officer based at Kingston, did not help matters by declaring that "more than three fourths of the immigrants this year have been Irish, diseased in body and belonging generally to the lowest class of unskilled labourers. Very few of them are fit for farm servants." He ended this biased generality with the observation that they were lucky, many of them, that they had relatives already settled in Canada as otherwise "the calamity would have been more severely felt."

Even the healthy and able-bodied were shunned by farmers fearing disease, and they roamed the roads like outcasts. A Peterborough woman wrote, "Wherever these wretched emigrants came they brought with them sickness and death. Some of the members of the Board of Health have already fallen under its malignant influence." Thus men like Thomas Brennan from Roscommon were fated to roam the roads all winter seeking work. He had been one of the few to come off the *Virginius* with his health but his wife died on Grosse Isle. He took his motherless children to the Niagara Peninsula in search of work but found nothing, and within a year he was dead.

An estimated 20,000 emigrants died in 1847 and the following winter – en route to Quebec or New Brunswick, in the quarantine stations, the cities and towns, or out in the countryside. At least one in every five or six who left Ireland. To those who died trying to find a new home, the *Dublin Magazine* dedicated a commemorative poem in its issue of April 3, 1849:

Deep in the western forest's shade,
In the green recess of a sunless glade,
Where the wild elk stalks, and where strange flowers bloom,
Is a rough hewn mound – the emigrant's tomb.
To the plains of the western world he sailed
But his eye had dimmed and his cheeks had paled.
He died where the proud ship touched the strand
And they made him a tomb in that foreign land.

16

Counting
the Cost

$\mathcal{T}$HE RIVER that had brought the tide of disaster from Ireland was locked in ice when the Legislative Assembly met in Montreal early in 1848. They were faced with making an immigration policy for the coming season, still not knowing just what to expect. As one member reminded the assembly, they had done so little to deal with the tragic migration of the season past they now were "answerable to the country for the disgraceful conduct they had pursued."

Unlike the Americans, they had not closed their doors to the sick and dying, and while this, one might say, was to their credit, they had failed to anticipate the suffering that ensued to emigrants and Canadians alike. Some wanted to blame others – the Irish landlords for sending the sick and helpless, or the English government for allowing this to happen. A French-Canadian nationalist accused *les anglais* of deliberately dumping diseased Irish on Quebec to complete the conquest begun by General Wolfe ninety years earlier. Another insisted the province had been "invaded by an army more destructive than any other which could be sent against it."

Some were for jacking the immigrant tax so high it would discourage all but the healthy and wealthy. But when the shouting died down the lawmakers of the united Canadas adopted an act similar to the laws passed in the United States the previous spring to exclude the sick and destitute. Though blandly entitled "An Act to make better provision in respect to emigrants," it clearly set out to protect the colony from the very people who most needed help. The landing tax was doubled, heavy fines were to be levied on ships detained in quarantine, and captains were to be held responsible for the condition of their passengers. Similar laws were passed in New Brunswick.

Lord Grey was pressured by the colonies into altering the Passenger Act of 1842. Doctors were to be hired to inspect all emigrants before they boarded. Emigration procedures were to be strengthened to guard against the total loss of control experienced in 1847. Ships were to provide more space for each passenger and a proper galley so they would not have to eat the half-cooked food that had often caused dysentery, and in addition to the one pound of daily breadstuffs required by law, the captain was responsible for distributing rations of rice, flour, tea and sugar.

As a result of these changes, combined with a depression in the timber industry, some of the shipowners withdrew from the trade in timber and emigrants, and others diverted their ships to Boston and New York. Thus while the flood of emigration flowed heavily for the next five years, the Canadian provinces were to play a greatly reduced role. Accounts of the terrible conditions at Grosse Isle and Partridge Island contributed to a decline in migration to Canada, and the letters some of the emigrants were sending home spoke of hardships that sounded little better than conditions in Ireland.

From New Brunswick, Owen and Honora Hennigan warned friends that "miserable Saint John is allmost as bad as Ireland." Keating Hurley from County Clare, describing "destitution and misery at Saint John," concluded "it fails me absolutely to recount the afflications that I felt." Bryan Clancey, who arrived with his sister from Gore Booth's estate in Sligo, "offen wished to be home again. Bad and all as we were, we offen wished we never seen Saint John."

Jobs were scarce everywhere, and Henry Johnson from County Antrim wandered for months from town to town in Canada West looking for work of any kind. "I have at last lighted into a farmer's house near the far-famed Falls of Niagara where I am doing a little work for my board," he wrote to his wife, Jane, who had remained in Antrim with their two children. He was lonely, homesick and often ill while he tried to make enough money to bring his family to Canada. "I think if I stop here much longer I will be a pretty good Canadian farmer, so that I am not altogether losing my time," he said. Given the grim accounts of the previous season, he was in no hurry to risk the lives of his wife and children on the coffin ships.

As the mayor of Toronto said, people in Canada were awaiting the first ships of the new season "with universal alarm." Dr. Douglas himself was dismayed when one of the first vessels he boarded was much like the worst ships of Black '47. She was the brig *Governor*, which left Limerick with 174 passengers, of whom twenty had died at sea and twenty were so ill on arrival they were put straight away in hospital. "These people were huddled on board, almost destitute of clothing and without beds or bedding, the captain having furnished many of the women and children with spare sails to cover them," Douglas reported. "Their sole provision had consisted during the voyage of the ship's allowance of biscuit and a small quantity of tea and sugar. A great number of them have assured the master and surgeon that their sole subsistence for two years previous was green food – turnips, nettle tops, etc. with a chance and precarious supply of Indian corn meal." The surprising thing to Douglas was that these were not refugees from a workhouse but people who claimed to have been tenants of Colonel Wyndham, whose record was better than most.

Wyndham himself was at his home in England when he heard of the matter and he sent Douglas's report to his agent at Ennis, who insisted the emigrants on the *Governor* had not been *bona fide* tenants at all, but people who had settled unbidden on the land of one of Wyndham's legal tenants who had been evicted for failure to pay his rent. When these people demanded they be sent to North America, said the agent, he had thought it proper to send them, and supplied them with extra rice and made sure there was a doctor on board. He accused them of exaggerating their plight; nothing further was done and the people were thrown on the charity of the Emigration Agent.

There were one or two similar cases, but within a few weeks it was clear there would be no repetition of Black '47. Visiting Grosse Isle in June, Lord Elgin assured himself that the quarantine station was well prepared for whatever the new season might bring. He found a new system to segregate the sick from the healthy, and supplies of beef, vegetables and milk, the latter a sideline carried on by Douglas from the little farm he operated at the end of the island despite charges he was making a personal profit thereby. "The establishment for healthy passengers contains accommodation for about 2,000," Elgin reported to London, "but I found very few there at the period of my visit, the ships which had recently arrived having been free of sickness, and consequently permitted to proceed with their freight at once to their destination. The hospital sheds are calculated to admit a greater number, but the patients actually there did not, I was happy to observe, amount to 200 in all."

As the season progressed, it was evident the stampede to the British provinces was over, though the emigrant traffic to the United States was considerably more than it had been in 1847 or any previous year. Only 25,000 people, about a sixth of the total bound for the States, arrived in British North America in 1848. The death rate, instead of being in the thousands, was expressed in hundreds, perhaps 500 or so, reflecting the new legislation and the smaller total of arrivals, about a fourth of the total of the previous year.

THE NEW ARRIVALS brought news of renewed – if illusory – hope among those they left behind. The blight had failed to appear in the previous season and people were back in the fields, trying to plant enough potatoes to see them through another year. "We were all in the greatest spirits at the approach of plenty," wrote the priest at Kenmare, County Kerry, and it was well into July before tragedy struck again. "The blight has made its appearance," he wrote, "the whole country in consequence has been thrown into dismay and confusion."

"Is it not possible," demanded the *Freeman's Journal*, "to contrive some means of saving people from this painful and lingering process of death from starvation? Do we live under a regular or responsible government? Is there justice or humanity in the world that such things could be, in the middle of the 19th century and within twelve hours reach of the opulence, grandeur and power of a court and capital first upon the earth?"

The reply, from a government maintaining a costly army of occupation in Ireland – bigger, it was said, than the combined army and navy of the United States – was that England was suffering a severe financial crisis. Parliament could vote no more aid. Lord John Russell's comments must have sounded devastating to any Irishman who heard them. "I do not think any effort of this house would, in the present unfortunate state of Ireland, be capable of preventing the dreadful scenes of suffering and death that are now occurring." England, it seemed, had done all it meant to do.

The winter of 1848–49 brought horrors reminiscent of 1847, and there was little aid from outside, for even the Quakers had withdrawn their charity. "From all sides," wrote William Bennett, a Quaker relief worker, "came expressions of despair, such as 'Poor Ireland is done' or

'It can never recover.'" Lady Wilde, mother of the poet Oscar and wife of a doctor who was compiling a census for the government, described the rural population as a "helpless crowd of crushed, dispirited peasants, dulled by want, oppression and despair." Thomas Hayes of Roscrea, Tipperary, writing to his uncle Thomas Hopper in the Ottawa Valley, said, "Large quantities of land are untenanted and the tenants sent to the poorhouse of which it is no disgrace to be an inmate. Robberies and murder every day transactions of the most glaring character taking place – landlord shooting – tenant ejecting – auctions of farming stock and implements of husbandry every day taking place for rent and arrears of rent."

Landlords evicted tenants at a faster rate than ever in the western counties of Clare, Leitrim, Tipperary and Limerick. Some 10,000 tenants were evicted that year, and the *Illustrated London News*, which more than any other English journal attempted to report the famine developments, suggested that if evictions and emigration went on, the country would become a wilderness. "The landlords evict their miserable tenants by hundreds and thousands," it said, "the miserable tenants go to the Union or receive outdoor relief at the rate of 7/8's of a penny per day, until the munificent allowance lapses in the grave; while the small farmers still in possession of a portion of the soil struggle with the landlords and the constabulary for the crop."

In the region of Kilrush, a County Clare market town of stone houses and broad streets on the edge of the Shannon, there had been 6,000 evictions and the workhouse had become the sad centre of community life. "Kilrush gives its name to a Poor Law Union that will be celebrated in the history of Pauperism with Clifden, Westport, Skibbereen and other places," said the *Illustrated London News*. Not only the very young and very old were dying, but young men and women in the prime of life. "John O'Dea, twenty-four, died within an hour of admission," said the workhouse record book, and Michael Ryan and Biddy Kelly, both aged thirty, died soon after.

In its list of bankrupt Poor Law Unions the *Illustrated London*

News might have included Kenmare, once a pleasant little export centre for cattle, butter and sheep, where at one time the principal landowners, the Lansdownes, had contributed a hospital, orphanage, model school and other amenities. The current Marquess of Lansdowne, a politician, spent most of his time in London and left the running of his 60,000 acres to an incompetent manager. His land lay on the shores of a long sea loch enclosed by mountains whose slopes afforded little that was arable. The estate was burdened with a population it could not support, no restrictions having been placed on subdivision of land. The children of cottiers had married young, confident that their relatives would split up an already-small patch of land and give them half.

"The estate in fact was swamped by paupers," wrote William Steuart Trench, who arrived to become Lansdowne's new manager three years after losing his own plantations in the potato blight. "The destitution which a sudden failure of the staple food of the people, in a remote valley like this, must necessarily bring along with it, may be imagined. The scenes in Schull and Skibbereen were here enacted over again. Kenmare was completely paralyzed. Begging, as of old, was now out of the question, as all were nearly equally poor. Many of the wretched people succumbed to their fate almost without a struggle.... They died on the roads, and they died in the fields, they died on the mountains, they died on the relief works, they died in their houses; so that villages were left almost without inhabitants; and at last some of them despairing of help in the country, crawled into the town and died at the doors of the residents and outside the Union walls." He believed that at least 5,000 people had died in the Union of Kenmare during the famine.

Trench convinced Lord Lansdowne that sending people to Canada would cost less than supporting them for a year at home. Lansdowne, who had opposed the high poor law rates, which he said were driving landowners into bankruptcy, agreed to pay the fares of all of his tenants who wanted to go in batches of 200 each, with a little extra to help them get started in Canada. "And thus," said Trench, "200 after 200, week after week, departed for Cork, until the Poor House was nearly emptied of paupers chargeable to the Lansdowne estate; and within a year 3,500 paupers had left Kenmare for America as free emigrants, without any ejectments having been brought against them to enforce it." The *Illustrated London News* correspondent reported: "We found ourselves on the road to Kenmare in the midst of a train of from 200 to 300 men and women, boys and girls, of varying age from ten to thirty years. They looked most picturesque in their gay plaid shawls and their straw bonnets and were all on their way to Cork to go on board the emigrant ships. This is better than leaving them to pine and perish from want, as in the too-wretched Union of Kilrush, though it is sad to see so much young blood sent from among us; and that, too, as a gentleman from Kerry told me, when it is found difficult to get hands to do the necessary farm work."

The government, or at least the agency that managed crown lands in Ireland, also found itself caught up in the round of eviction and paid transportation common to other landowners. Having taken possession of an estate at Ballykilcline, it had done nothing to solve the problem of overcrowding and overworked land and had begun to evict fourteen families so as to increase the size of the farms to a more profitable twenty acres. This caused such an uproar that the agent in charge of the estate talked a reluctant government into offering the people the alternative of going to Canada at government expense on the ship *Roscius*. Several elected to go, and it was decided to extend this offer to two other ailing crown estates, at Boughill and Irvilloughter near the village of Ahascragh, on the River Suck in Galway.

At Irvilloughter, the larger and more destitute, a hundred tenants had paid no rent for five years and were dependent on government relief. Henry Dempsey, fifty, his wife and eight children were reported to be "in a horrid state of poverty;" the widowed Biddy Loftus, forty, was in a state that "beggars description;" and Mary Gormley, wife of a

labourer and mother of four, was "almost naked" as she had been obliged to pawn her clothes with the gombeen men, the usurers who lent money. Some of the 243 to emigrate to Canada from the estate had known better days. John "Black" White, fifty, had once farmed six acres, but now was "very poor and half naked."

At Boughill, a tract of 111 acres of arable ground surrounded by a bog, the tenants had once been "happy, contented people, ready to pay rent." Certainly Edward Kelly, the middleman, had found it a profitable place, since in pre-famine years he had received high rents from his seventeen subtenants, plus fifty-six days of free labour each year. With the potatoes gone, no rent had been paid and a third of the population was anxious to leave.

The first group, gathered from the two estates and totalling 250 people, sailed on the *Seabird* in June 1848, and a second contingent departed the next summer on the *Northumberland*, two voyages that demonstrated that when proper care was taken there need be little suffering. They were examined by a doctor before boarding, and though there were no potatoes or vegetables to ward off scurvy, their shipboard diet was otherwise adequate – two pounds of bread or biscuit daily, two pounds of beef and one pound of butter per week, and a pound of tea and nine pounds of sugar per person during the journey. There were only four deaths at sea, and at Quebec City they received money to travel to Upper Canada.

All told, the government sent fewer than a thousand people to Canada in this manner, a small fraction of the tenants sent by landowners. The cost was modest, the emigrants were willing to go, and with their departure came farm consolidation and improvements that permitted the sale of the estates at a net profit. Why did the government not do more of this? Lord Grey at the Colonial Office had toyed for a long time with the idea of transplanting whole villages of people, including their priests, to backwoods Canada and setting them up in new hamlets of their own. This plan, ambitious if ill thought out, would have provided them land and enough money to keep them for

a year and was somewhat like Peter Robinson's experiment. The Canadian government was not enthusiastic, since most accessible sites in Upper Canada had been taken. When the scheme was costed, Grey shelved it in favour of sending people to Australia, where the distance was such that people could not be expected to pay their own passage in large numbers. The government did, however, agree to send 500 young women, all under twenty-five and most of them orphans, to Montreal to work as servants. Otherwise, the government preferred, in Trevelyan's cold phrase, "to leave things to the operation of natural causes" since people would cross the Atlantic in tens of thousands without government aid.

At all events, Canada would have been hard pressed to cope with more than the number that actually did arrive in 1849. The total was 40 per cent more than in the previous year, and during the spring there was yet another cholera epidemic, much like those of the early 1830s. The first weeks of May brought 2,000 to Grosse Isle, half of them tradesmen, labourers and mechanics and the rest small farmers of the sort Lord Clarendon, the new Lord Lieutenant of Ireland, would have preferred to keep at home. "They cut their corn on Sunday, sell it on Monday morning and are off to America in the evening," he complained, "leaving wastelands behind them and the landlords without rent." Some had no clear idea where they were going. "On board the *Duke* from Dublin," reported A.C. Buchanan, "there were large numbers of very poor persons; more than one third of whom I had to assist to enable them to leave the city; the majority of them had no particular destination in view." Some had been sent by Poor Law Unions to ease overcrowding in workhouses afflicted by the new cholera epidemic, which increased the death toll at sea and in quarantine that year to 1,000. In addition scores of emigrants lost their lives in the sinking of the *Hannah* from Newry and the *Maria* from Limerick, which foundered in the ice floes of the North Atlantic.

One of the passengers in the *Riverdale* from Belfast late in May was Jane Johnson of Antrim, with her two children, on her way at last

to join her husband, Henry, whose fortunes had improved enough to send for them. "There is no question, my dearest Jane, as to which of the two countries is best for parties situated as we are here," he wrote. "Every kind of living is four times cheaper and at the same time work of every kind is trebly paid, for a family of children has infinitely better prospects of being provided for and receiving excellent education free. Dearest Jane, anything I can do shall be done to make you happy."

Just before sailing, Jane had written Henry a reply: "I hope it will be a happy meeting with us and I hope that the Almighty will protect and take me safe. PS Dear Henry do not neglect to meet us at Quebec. Your loving wife, Jane Johnson." But Henry did not meet her, and on arrival at Quebec City she learned he had died of cholera on his way to her side, one of the first victims in the epidemic that killed 2,000 people in Canada, at least half of them in the cities of Montreal and Quebec. In normal years such an outbreak would have been a major disaster in itself; now it was but another in the series of fearful illnesses brought by the emigrants.

When the emigration season opened in 1850 an improvement was reported in the health and the appearance of people coming ashore. There were fewer that year, about 24,000, not much more than an eighth of the number now sailing directly to the States. The North American economy had improved and they could look forward to getting jobs, for the colonies were caught up in the railway boom and Irish were needed to lay tracks, as they had earlier been used to dig the canals. They worked fifteen-hour days, six days a week, and given the ordeals they had been through in Ireland, their stamina was surprising. Many settled at Griffintown on the southwest outskirts of Montreal, where they worked for the Grand Trunk Railway and built the Victoria Bridge.

One of the railway builders, twenty-two-year-old Michael Byrne, sent a letter of thanks to the government agent who had sent him to Canada from Boughill, County Galway, where his home had been a

mud hut by the bog. "I am to inform Your Honour that I am employed in the railroad earning five shillings a day in your Irish money. And instead of being chained with poverty in Boughill I am crowned with glory and I am better pleased to come to this country than if you bestowed me five acres of land in Boughill."

"This is a fine country for a man to live in," wrote Nathaniel Carrothers, who had settled near London, Canada West. "There never was a better time for emigration here. Wages of all kinds is good.... They are giving a dollar a day to all the labourers on the Great Western Railroad which is through this part of the country. London has become a large and fine place since we came to this country." Carrothers had come from County Fermanagh nine years earlier to settle near the land pioneered by the Talbots in 1818. He had amassed 187 acres of his own, a span of mares, a yoke of oxen and a fine spread of wheat fields and orchard, and his potatoes, a superior breed of Pinks and Cups, were the best on the local market. "Our eating and drinking are very good in this country," he said, "when compared to that of the farms of Ireland."

"Dear Brother," he wrote to William Carrothers at Besbellaw, County Fermanagh, "if you had only plucked up courage to come to America a few years ago and got a good farm in this part of the country before the land got dear, you would have no cause to rue it and I am sure your children would bless the day they came to Canada; I never was sorry for coming, but ever shall be that I spent so many of my days in Ireland." He advised his brother to disregard the "murmer, after I know not what" of their brother Joseph, "who seemed to be discontent when he came – suffice it for me to say that he never was as well off in Ireland and could save money if he likes." Joseph had been one of the famine refugees in 1847.

The famine years had brought many more emigrants of the labouring class. "The wild western Irishman," Lord Grey told the Governor General, Lord Elgin, "now goes out to Canada, utterly ignorant of every useful kind of labour, and till he gets gradually instructed is

fit for no employment requiring more than brute strength. But he is a singularly teachable animal, and one very easily brought under discipline." This biased view of the Irish working man, so common in England and reflected in the cartoons of the middle-class magazine *Punch* with its drawings of tattered and witless "bog trotters," was inevitably carried into British North America, where the embers of racial and religious prejudice sprang into flames here and there.

Since 1845 the population of Irish-born in Canada West had doubled to a total of 120,000 so that they were now, as in New Brunswick, the largest ethnic group. Two-thirds were Protestant, including the Ulster Presbyterians who had established themselves firmly on the land before the famine years. Indeed, the majority, whether Protestant or Catholic, had settled on the land but it was in the towns that trouble usually flared up.

Resentments, fears and pressures arising from the famine migrations appeared in tragic force in the summer of 1849. In a fight between Orangemen and Catholic Irish in Hamilton's Slabtown slums, four men were killed and six wounded. At Saint John, where 90 per cent of the 32,000 Irish who arrived since 1845 were Catholics, there was a battle on July 12 when the Orange parade, with its provocative slogans and songs, entered the York Point neighbourhood, which Catholics called their own. Chanting "Stay off our ground," the Catholics threw stones at the parade, but turned it back only long enough for the Orangemen, 600 strong, to arm themselves with guns and open fire . Before troops could arrive, a dozen people were killed and many wounded in what became known as the Battle of York Point. People blamed old animosities brought over from Ireland, but whatever the background of feuds between the Orange and the Green, there were also new frustrations and jealousies peculiar to North America, particularly evident in the cities of the eastern United States, where the Know Nothing Party spread prejudice against Irish Catholics. In Saint John, an influential Irish-born journalist and politician, Timothy Warren Anglin, deplored the Protestants' habit of marching with banners and songs that they knew were "insulting to every Irish Catholic." In a letter to the Saint John *Morning News,* Anglin expressed dismay at finding "Orangemen and Catholics fighting each other at a time they were working together in Ireland to help the suffering."

In Ireland, if people did not help each other, it seemed there was no one else to do so. Charles Edward Trevelyan, under the illusion the famine was over, turned a deaf ear to pleas for government help, even those of his own agents. "I want to have it distinctly on record," wrote a Poor Law Commissioner in Dublin, "that from want of food many persons in these Unions are at present dying or wasting away."

Money the government was investing in Ireland went not into food but into security, the maintenance of 50,000 soldiers and police to meet the shadowy threat of firebrands who called themselves Young Ireland. Impatient with Daniel O'Connell's moderate efforts to repeal the Act of Union, the Young Ireland party plotted insurrection but received so little popular support their efforts ended in a useless encounter in which they were routed by police in a cabbage patch near Ballingary, Tipperary, in 1848. Their leader, William Smith O'Brien, a Protestant Limerick landowner – an unusual background for a southern Irish rebel – was arrested and transported to Australia, along with John Mitchel, the writer for the *Nation.* Thomas D'Arcy McGee fled to the United States and turned up in Montreal a dozen years later to devote himself to the welfare of Irish immigrants and a vision of a united Canada.

Though the famine had changed Ireland forever, a slow and painful recovery began as the blight disappeared in 1850. Whole villages, particularly in the west, had been deserted, and much less land was under tillage. "The famine, in the strict acceptance of the term, was then nearly over," wrote William Steuart Trench, "but it left a trail behind it as formidable as its presence." Most of the victims had been the poor living in overpopulated regions where land had become so overworked and divided it could not support them; the famine was above all a tragedy of the Catholic peasants, particularly in the western counties, who depended on the potato, unlike the Presbyterians of eastern Ulster, whose farming was better organized and who depended on grain. Throughout the famine, northeast Ulster was the one region where the Quakers did not consider it necessary to organize soup kitchens.

Between 600,000 and 800,000 people died in the years 1847 through 1849, a fatality total four times above normal in the western counties. In County Cork alone, 95,000 died; the total for the pre-famine years of 1842-44 had been only one fifth that number. Some believe the total was closer to a million, basing this on the census finding that the population had declined by 20 per cent since the early 1840s. Since a million were believed to have emigrated to the United States and Canada, they argued, this left a million people unaccounted for in any way but death.

·Whatever the precise figures, they were lost in the immensity of the tragedy. Whole parishes had been stripped of population, and survivors were like victims of a terrible accident. "Sport and pastime disappeared," recalled an old woman in County Donegal. "Poetry, music and dancing stopped. They lost and forgot them all, and when the times improved in other respects, these things never returned as they had been. The famine killed everything."

17

An Irishman's Canada

BY 1851 the Great Famine was over and food supplies and the general living standard had improved, but the emigration continued, bleeding Ireland as from a wound that would not heal. Ireland had already lost 10 per cent of its population, and during the next twenty years another two million left, most of them bound for the United States, until there were more Irish abroad than at home. Fares to the U.S. now were cheaper than those to Canada, which received hardly more than 175,000 Irish in the 1850s and '60s, and would never again attract the large numbers of earlier years. In 1855, for example, only 4,022 Irish emigrants arrived in Quebec City, 277 in New Brunswick and 46 in Newfoundland. The following year there were half that number.

Both the British and Americans had improved their passenger laws; sail was giving way to steam; Atlantic crossings were faster and easier, and there was less illness, though 1853 saw another cholera outbreak in which an estimated 10 per cent of Irish emigrants died. Large sums were being remitted to bring relatives and friends to join earlier emigrants; the British government, in the form of the Colonial Land and Emigrant Commissioners, had provided funds for 120,000 to emigrate to British colonies, including Australia; and the Irish Poor Law boards sent tens of thousands as well. There was an increase in the number of single women coming out, and, a typical instance, the Nenagh Workhouse in Tipperary sent 387 women in 1852. Most went to Bytown, where they were hired as domestic servants within forty-eight hours after arrival.

At Westminster, aging English politicians, the very men involved in the famine disaster, expressed concern at "this annual wasting away of the strength and very life of a nation." Earl Grey, who had been Colonial Secretary in the 1840s, was moved to tell the House of Lords one evening in March 1866 that the vast Irish migration to the United States was nothing less than a "great calamity." Among those in the audience was John Francis Maguire, editor of the *Cork Examiner* and a member of parliament, who was accompanied by a visitor from overseas, Dr. John Sweeny, the Catholic Bishop of Saint John, New Brunswick. Though Lord Grey's distress was shared by many, there were those in the audience who wished the emigrants good riddance.

"I do not agree with his lordship," one man told Maguire. "On the contrary my deliberate conviction is, unless the Irish go away on their own accord, or are got rid of in some manner or another and are replaced by our people – I mean the English or the Scotch – nothing good can ever be done with that unhappy country."

To Maguire, a Catholic nationalist who had seen the terrible famine in west Cork, the Englishman's words were "an insolent slander ... a sweeping indictment of the Irish race." What made them worse was the way they were spoken. "There was no hostility, no anger, no passion, but a deep-seated belief in the truth of the terrible sentence thus tranquilly pronounced on a whole nation. A similar opinion has been too frequently expressed or insinuated in the public press of England, not perhaps so frequently of late as in former years."

As editor of the *Examiner* and a representative at the parliament in Westminster, which had been open to Irishmen for a generation now since the passing of Daniel O'Connell's Emancipation Act, Maguire had been thinking for some time of going to North America to see how the emigrants were faring. "I desired to ascertain by personal observation what the Irish – thousands of whom were constantly emigrating, as it were, from my very door – were doing in America; and that desire, to see with my own eyes, and judge with my own mind, was stimulated by the conflicting and contradictory accounts which reached home through various channels and sources of information, some friendly, more hostile." Bishop Sweeny, an emigrant himself forty years since, told him: "Come to New Brunswick and I'll show you some Irishmen who are doing extremely well."

Sweeny recalled how as a priest in Saint John he had witnessed the "ruinous tendency" of emigrants "to hang about town," resigned to a life in the ghetto, where they drank too much and depended for existence on uncertain work as common labourers. In 1859 Sweeny had organized the Emigrant Aid Association and persuaded the provincial government to offer 100-acre grants of wilderness land. "I wish all to understand," Sweeny said, "that in going into the woods to make a home for themselves and their children, they will have to labour hard, endure many hardships and privations and practise industry and frugality for a few years, but in so doing they have the hope of securing an independence for themselves and their families – what the majority of them can seldom hope for, depending on day labour in our large cities and towns. We do not encourage tradesmen or artisans who are not used to hard labour to undertake the making of a farm in the forest."

Some 700 families had been settled in four separate regions and Sweeny was particularly proud of the settlement in Carleton County,

200 miles northwest of Saint John and thirty miles from the village of Woodstock. It had been named Johnville in his honour, and from its beginnings in 1860 had grown to a farming community of 600 Irish. They had cleared 1,460 acres, grown potatoes, turnips, wheat, hay, buckwheat and barley, and acquired forty-eight horses, 773 cattle, 247 sheep and 262 hogs. "In an almost incredibly short space of time," said Sweeny, "they won their way to rude comfort and absolute independence."

"It was arranged," said Maguire, "that I should specially visit this latest settlement of our unjustly deprecated countrymen. The appointment, made in London in the month of March, was faithfully kept in New Brunswick in the month of October." Thus it was that early one chill morning Maguire found himself beside Bishop John Sweeny jolting along the trail that led through a forest of pine and spruce to Johnville. Mounting a hill crowned with a small chapel he saw a rough-hewn clearing two miles long and a mile wide, dotted with two-foot stumps and surrounded by crude fences of logs. Though it was unlike any farmland in Ireland or England, Maguire had an impression of backwoods prosperity: "comfortable dwellings, substantial and even spacious barns – horses, cattle, sheep, hogs and poultry of all kinds."

Their first stop was the cabin of Hugh and Mary Jane McCann, where Mrs. McCann served tea and told of how they had been the first to arrive six years earlier, "making light of trials and difficulties that would have daunted many a lord of creation." A childless couple, the McCanns had come to Saint John in the famine years and, taking advantage of the offer of land, had travelled up the St. John River by boat. Borrowing a team of oxen from an Irish family, they had made the six-mile trek to Lot 1, Range 2, carrying provisions and a "few sticks of furniture." "It was as good as any theaytre," Mary Jane McCann laughed, to see Hugh and "herself" tramping after the oxen, with all their possessions "nodding and shaking" on the wagon. They built a dirt-floored shanty with log walls and a pole roof covered with sods, and settled in for the winter, miles away from any neighbour. By the following autumn they had cleared several acres and raised a crop of potatoes, buckwheat and oats.

Other families arrived – Reillys, Sullivans and O'Keefes. Thomas Crehan and his wife and children had come direct from County Galway, where their priest had read of Bishop Sweeny's call for settlers in the local newspaper. The Crehans had run afoul of their landlord, who had raised their rent, impounded their pig when they could not pay, and deprived them of grazing rights on the mountainside. "The Crehans made up their minds to go somewhere – anywhere – 'to the end of the world' – rather than remain in a state of abject vassalage, dependent on the caprice or avarice of the gentleman," wrote Maguire. Now they had thirteen acres under wheat, peas, potatoes and turnips. Crehan could neither read nor write and spoke little English, but Bishop Sweeny said he had become "prosperous, independent, contented and happy, and very soon he will, no doubt, be positively wealthy." Whereas in Ireland it was rare to find a farmer with more than thirty acres, they had in New Brunswick acquired a second 100-acre lot for their eldest son.

Mrs. Crehan, a "dark-haired, sharp-eyed, comely matron," told Maguire of her loneliness, "and not a living soul near us but the childer." Fresh from the open, treeless lands of Galway, she was frightened of losing her way in the woods, where her only guides were blazes on the trees. "And twas the owls – the devils – that would make a body's heart jump into their mouth. Oh, Sir, they screeched and screeched, I declare, like any Christian, till they frightened the childer out of their senses. The little boy – he's a fine fellow – would catch hold of me by the gown and cry out, 'Oh Mammy, Mammy! What a place Daddy has brought us to! We'll all be ate up tonight.' You know, Sir, it's easy to frighten childer, the craychers."

"But, Mrs. Crehan," asked Maguire, "I suppose you don't regret having come here?"

"'Deed then no, Sir, not a bit of it. Thanks to the Lord, and blessed be His holy name, we have plenty to ate and drink, and a good bed to lie on, and no one to take it from us, or to say boo to us. The grief I have is that there's only the 200 acres, for I'd dearly like another 100 for the second boy. And, Sir, if you ever happen to go to Galway and see [the landlord] you may tell him from me that I'm better off than himself, and more independent in my mind; and tell him all the harm I wish him is for him to know that much."

Another settler, Bartholomew Reilly from Macroom in County Cork, had come first to Yarmouth, Nova Scotia, but finding the land rocky had crossed the Bay of Fundy with his son Timothy, leaving his wife and ten other children to travel on later when he had prepared a home. Within two months he had cleared three acres and seeded a crop, and when Maguire met him five years later he had cleared half of his 100 acres, owned a yoke of oxen, six cows and several sheep and hogs, and had built a fine house and barn. Maguire described him as a "man of middle age, grave countenance, handsome features, including a marked aquiline nose, deliberate utterance, and the richest of Munster brogues."

"Well, Reilly, I congratulate you," said the Bishop. "What you have done in the time is most creditable to you."

"Well my Lord, I am getting along pretty well, I thank my Maker for it. We have reason to be grateful and contented your Lordship, with what we've done. There is a good prospect for us and the children. Sure enough, 'twas a great change from the Old Country to this. Glory too, to the Lord, for that same!"

Labour was a thing to be honoured at Johnville, said Maguire, not a badge of inferiority, as in Ireland. "Nor is the poor man here a drug, a social nuisance, something to be legislated against or got rid of, regarded with suspicion because of his probable motive or intentions, or with aversion as to a possible burden on the property. In the old countries, the ordinary lot of man born to poverty is that poverty shall be his doom – that he shall die in the condition in which he was brought into the world."

There were 100,000 Irish in New Brunswick, almost equally divided between Protestants and Catholics and numbering more than a third of the total population. Sixty per cent of the Protestants were farmers and 35 per cent of Catholics, while a somewhat larger number of Catholics than Protestants were labourers and artisans. Half the population of Saint John was Irish, most of them Catholics, though there was a substantial minority of Protestants. "The Irish, Protestants and Catholics, hold a most important position in Saint John," said Maguire, "and may be said to own fully half the property and wealth of that bustling, active city. Of this property and wealth the Catholics, who, with scarce exception, are Irish, possess a considerable share. And what they possess they realized for themselves."

The success achieved by Catholics was evident in the career of Timothy Warren Anglin, who had arrived from Clonakilty, County Cork, in 1849, established the *Freeman* newspaper and become a spokesman for the Irish of New Brunswick. Anglin was elected to the provincial legislative assembly, and though he opposed confederation he later became a member of the federal parliament and Speaker of the House of Commons.

The Catholics, said Maguire, inevitably had a harder road in the British colonies. "Similarity of religion with that of the wealthier portion of the mass of the population was always of great assistance to the Protestant emigrant to America. And yet while labour, rude or skilled, is the lot of the majority of the Irish of Saint John, and throughout the province generally, a considerable proportion are to be found in every department of business, and enjoy, as merchants, traders and manufacturers, the highest position which character and wealth can secure to their possessor."

Travelling the neighbouring province of Nova Scotia, where the Irish were long established and few emigrants had arrived in the famine years, Maguire estimated the Irish at 40 per cent of the population. "In no city of the American continent," he said, "do the Irish occupy a better position, or exercise a more deserved influence than in Halifax."

As early as 1823 Lawrence Kavanagh had become the first Irish Catholic to sit in a legislative assembly, five years before Daniel O'Connell won the right for Irish to sit in parliament at Westminster. As a measure of Irish progress, Maguire was struck by the healthy appearance of school children, so different than those in his native Cork, where "too many of them exhibited the unmistakable evidence of intense poverty, not only in their scanty raiment but in their pale and anxious faces."

In Prince Edward Island, where a fifth of the population was Irish, he spent a day in the settlement of Monaghan, which had attracted settlers from Ulster in the years before the famine. It was autumn, and he found them harvesting the potatoes "of healthy purple hue" which would make the island famous:

The Monaghan settlers had long since passed the log cabin stage, and were occupying substantial and commodious frame houses – those Irishmen who had begun 'without a sixpence in their pockets' – had brought up families with care and responsibility, could drive to church on Sundays in a well-appointed wagon with a good horse, or a pair of good horses, and probably had what they would call 'a little money' laid by in the bank. As a rule, admitting of only a rare exception, I did not for the entire day – during a circuit of sixty miles – see a single habitation that was not decent in appearance or that did not evince an air of neatness and comfort.

In not one proof of progress or evidence of solid and substantial comfort were the Irish settlers behind their Scottish or English or native born neighbours. Their land was in good condition, their cattle were as numerous and valuable, their hay and their potatoes were as good and abundant. There was not even the suspicion of inferiority in any respect whatever.

During his six-month tour of North America, Maguire was intent on viewing the Irish emigrants through exceptionally rosy spectacles. As he had decided that the Irish could only be better off in the New World, his book *The Irish in America* sometimes reads like a tract by an emigration agent. While admitting that "in some places there are evils to deplore" – slums, alcoholism, battles between Catholics and Orangemen – he insisted such things were being remedied. Maguire's visit occurred in the months leading up to Confederation – the union of the Canadas with New Brunswick and Nova Scotia – when hopes were high for the future of the Dominion and the timber and railway booms of the 1850s had brought prosperity. Weary of the misery in his own country, Maguire's picture was over-optimistic but contained a core of truth: "One is enabled almost at a glance, to recognize the marked difference between the Irish race in the old country and the new. In the old country, stagnation, retrogression – in the new, life, movement, progress; in the one, depression, want of confidence, dark apprehension of the future – in the other, energy, self reliance, and a perpetual looking forward to a grander development and more glorious destiny."

Travelling up the St. Lawrence to Quebec City, the world's greatest timber port, Maguire noted that the labour force was largely Irish; and the Quebec Ship Labourers' Benevolent Association, founded in 1851, was the first labour union in the country. The most skilful – the cullers who sorted and measured timber rafted down from the Ottawa River and the Great Lakes – made £300 a year, compared with the £20 they might expect to make in Ireland. Maguire estimated the Irish population at well over 10,000, a thriving community that had built St. Patrick's Church and founded Saint Patrick's Literary Institute. He quickly disposed of the darker side of the Irish emigration. "In Quebec, as in too many places in America, there are instances of drunken, reckless and improvident Irishmen, but happily, these cases are exceptional; for as a rule, the Irish of that city are sober, prudent and thrifty."

There were fewer Irish emigrants passing through Quebec City now, English and Scots having become the major emigrant groups since the mid-1850s. At the same time, the Irish were drifting out of Quebec province in increasing numbers, some to Upper Canada, most to the United States. The main reason for this was economic, the driving force for most emigration: the French had long since taken up the best land along the St. Lawrence, leaving the Irish only the poorer land of the interior, far from centres of commerce. Typical of this trend was the migration from the settlements at St. Malachi and Frampton on the Etchemin River in Dorchester County, where Cornelius Lyons had put down roots, as recounted at the beginning of this book.

When Cornelius Lyons arrived in 1823, having defied his landlord, evaded the magistrates and emigrated from Limerick with his family, there were 200 Irish living in these farming communities sixty miles southeast of Quebec City. The first years were difficult, and Lyons, like his neighbours, likely augmented a scant living with seasonal work in the Quebec City timber coves, while managing to develop a small dairy industry. There were 235 Irish families in the 1850s, but the soil was thin and the region hilly, and by 1866 half had gone to the United States, including the Lyons family, led now by Peter Lyons, who found a new home in Minnesota.

The most heroic trek from the Etchemin River was that of Martin Murphy, a Wexford man, with his sons, daughters and grandchildren, twenty-five people. Travelling in wagons and on foot to Quebec City, they took steamers up the St. Lawrence, across Lake Ontario and Lake Erie to Cleveland and down to Missouri, where they settled for a time. They joined a wagon train of other Irish to cross the plains and mountains to the San Jose Valley south of San Francisco, and there, said Maguire, Murphy became a wealthy stockman, and "died at a grand old age, the founder of a prosperous race." That was in the 1840s, and as the years went by the Frampton priest lamented that the "flower of the youth left, and went to California." The land was occupied by French Canadians, and there are few Irish there today to tend the graves of the Fitzgeralds, Kellys, Doyles, O'Neills and Redmonds.

There were 50,000 Irish in Lower Canada in 1866, of whom most were Catholics, who found the religion, if not the language, compatible and conducive to mixed marriages. They lived in Quebec City, Sherbrooke, Trois Rivières and Montreal – labourers, artisans and merchants who made up 40 per cent of the Irish in the province. Farmers, who accounted for more than half of the Irish population, could be found all the way from the Gaspé in the east, which had been electing Irishmen to the Legislative Assembly since the 1790s, through to Beauharnois in the west near the Ontario border. Between those two points they had settled south and north of the river – in St. Sylvestre or St. Patrice, in the township of New Ireland, at Shannon in Portneuf County north of the St. Lawrence, in the Laurentian valleys and up the eastern fringes of the Ottawa River.

The largest concentration, not only in Quebec but in all British North America, was in Montreal, the most prosperous city. When Maguire arrived, Montreal had weathered the threat posed by the abortive Fenian invasion of June 1866. Named for the legendary *Fianna*, the warriors of ancient Ireland, the Fenians, otherwise the Irish Republican Brotherhood (IRB), had evolved out of the Young Ireland movement during the 1850s. Dedicated to the overthrow of English rule in Ireland, though too far from Ireland to achieve it, the Fenians took it into their heads that an invasion of Canada would somehow help their cause. Kidnap Canada and the English would release Ireland. Montreal was a prime target. "With the reduction of Montreal," said their manifesto, "a demand will be made upon the United States for a formal recognition of Canada, whose name will be changed at once to New Ireland." They had expected to enlist Canadian Irish Catholics but had little success. According to Thomas D'Arcy McGee, who had been a Young Ireland rebel in his native land but was now a loyal Canadian and member of the Legislative Assembly, only 355 Montrealers heeded the Fenian call to arms.

The Fenians, many of them veterans of the American Civil War, had planned three separate invasions. The one aimed at Campobello Island in New Brunswick never materialized; that at Fort Erie and Ridgeway in Upper Canada was driven back after some initial success; and the effort to invade Quebec's Eastern Townships near Frelighsburg was thwarted by Montreal militia, among them Patrick Devlin, president of the St. Patrick's Society, and other Catholics of the sort the Fenians had hoped to recruit.

D'Arcy McGee told his Canadian followers that their first duty must be to Canada; however much they wanted an end to English rule in Ireland, they had no right to bring Irish politics to Canada. "If Ireland were governed in my day as Canada is now, without distinction of class and creed," he said, "I should have been as zealous to uphold authority in Ireland as I am to advocate it in Canada." He was less concerned with the military threat than with the prejudice the Fenians fostered against Canadian Irish among the Anglo-Scottish community.

Maguire believed Irishmen there had little cause to rebel. "In no part of the British provinces of North America," he said, "does the Catholic Irishman feel himself so thoroughly at home, as in the beautiful and flourishing city of Montreal. He is in a Catholic city, where his religion is respected and his church is surrounded by dignity and splendour." Between Catholics and Protestants, the Irish made up a quarter of the city's population; the Catholics alone, who outnumbered Protestant Irish, Scots and English combined, were a fifth, though the Protestants dominated the city's industry and commerce.

A large proportion of Montreal's captains of industry were Calvinist Scots, but there were Protestant Irish as well, living on the privileged slope of Mount Royal known as the Square Mile. Most notable was Francis Hincks, a Protestant from Cork, who got his start in Toronto selling dry goods and liquor. Entering politics and coming to Montreal, he had become a cabinet minister and premier, and served as president of the Grand Trunk Railway. Another was Thomas McCord, the property owner, both of whose sons became judges. The Workman family from Ulster included Thomas, a hardware merchant and banker, and William, who served as mayor and, after Confederation, a member of parliament.

Lewis Thomas Drummond, a Catholic lawyer from Coleraine, County Derry, married a French Canadian, defended the French-Canadian rebels in 1838 and became a judge and a cabinet minister, and profited, like Hincks, in railway speculation. Maguire said both

Hincks and Drummond had infused life and spirit into the Irish of Montreal, giving them a "sense of pride and consciousness of strength which they much required."

Using water power provided by the Lachine Canal, Montreal experienced Canada's first taste of the Industrial Revolution. Foundries, cotton mills, soap works, paper mills and sugar mills grew up along the canal. The Grand Trunk Railway, whose workshops were nearby, built the Victoria Bridge which linked Montreal to markets east and west.

The city had given birth to a community of Irish shopkeepers, artisans, tailors, shoemakers and ship chandlers, having become a port second only to New York. *MacKay's Montreal Directory* for 1866–67 lists forty-four O'Briens in central Montreal, and though there were labourers among them, many are listed as small businessmen, and one was a policeman. Thomas McKenna, sometime president of the St. Patrick's Society, founded in 1834 and the first of the city's national societies (predating the St. Jean Baptiste Society), was a plumber, and his vice president, Denis Downy, a fruiterer.

Thomas Ryan from Kildare, a wholesaler, was one of the new middle-class Irish community leaders, respected among Protestants and Catholics. He had been president of the St. Patrick's Society when it embraced both Catholics and Protestants, before the latter created their own Irish Protestant Benevolent Society in 1856. Another was Richard Holland, who had come to the city at the age of nineteen, started his own business and became a city councillor and park commissioner in a city whose flag included the shamrock as well as the fleur de lys, the rose and the thistle.

The Irish had built two Catholic churches, St. Patrick's and St. Anne's, and the community pride Maguire found so striking was evident when the Bishop of Montreal, Ignace Bourget, took it upon himself to refer to the Irish as "God's unfortunate people." Apparently stung by the bishop's words, the Irish of St. Patrick's parish made it clear they would prefer to forget past misfortunes but their rebuke was mild. "Your Lordship, referring to the sad events of 1847, is pleased to call us an 'unfortunate people'; we admit it, we were 'unfortunate' in 1847 through the inscrutable ways of God, who, however, often chastises in love. In 1866 we are still 'unfortunate' – for your lordship will not allow us to forget our sad destinies."

The majority of Montreal's Irish were labourers, servants, coachmen, blacksmiths, carpenters, living in the ill-built quarter in southwest Montreal called Griffintown, near the factories by the Lachine Canal. It had been developed by Robert Griffin, an Irish soap manufacturer, on land once owned by Thomas McCord. Griffintown was prone to flooding from the nearby St. Lawrence, and suffered a mortality rate twice as high as the rest of the city. Typhoid and diphtheria were common.

The French-Canadian newspaper *L'Opinion* said parts of Griffintown resembled the slums of Boston or New York, and a visitor to Griffintown recalled a "collection of typical Irish cabins built low on the ground and covered with sods. These cabins were inhabited by a party of squatters, men who I understand had worked at building the railway and waterworks and squatted on these plots with their families, cultivating the ground and keeping poultry and cows and paying no rent. They lived there for a number of years before being compelled to move." Conditions, it seemed, were not unlike those that emigrants had fled from in Ireland.

"In Griffintown, poverty and wretchedness, miserably clad children and slatternly women are occasionally to be seen," said Maguire, "but they are comparatively rare; while it is true that the Irish Catholic feels himself more at home in Lower Canada than in other provinces, Upper Canada especially, it must not be supposed he had not had many serious difficulties to contend against."

In Thomas D'Arcy McGee, member of the legislature for St. Anne's ward, southwest Montreal, the people of Griffintown had a powerful champion. "We are fighting in Griffintown the battle for Irish equality," he said. He fought for better education, illiteracy being one of the emigrant's greatest burdens, and campaigned for a united Canada, "a Canadian nationality, not French-Canadian, nor British-Canadian nor Irish-Canadian – patriotism rejects the prefix."

Nineteen years earlier in Ireland, McGee had described England as "that hoary harlot," and his intention was "to rend the British flag – to blast the British name – to wreck the British edifice of power from cornerstone to cornice...." Forced to flee Ireland disguised as a priest for plotting against the English, the young Wexford militant had gone to work as a journalist in Boston. But while his comrades of the Young Ireland movement joined the Fenians, McGee suffered a sea change. "Politically, we were a pack of fools," he said.

In 1859, disillusioned with the lot of the Irish in the United States, he accepted an invitation from the Saint Patrick's Society to launch a newspaper, the *New Era,* in Montreal. The newspaper became his springboard into politics, and in nine years he had become a surprisingly ardent Canadian. "We must vindicate our loyalty to the free-est country left to Irishmen on the face of the earth," he said. Comparing Canada with the United States, he said, "There we are always aliens. Here we are citizens in possession of a large portion of the governing power of the state."

Journalist, author, lawyer, poet and compelling speaker, McGee became the leading Irish-Catholic politician in Canada, a cabinet minister whose duties included immigration, and one of the Fathers of Confederation. His vendetta against Fenians was to cost him dearly, for though Irish Canadians wanted no trouble on Canadian soil, they did support Fenian aims to topple English rule in Ireland, and McGee's passionate attacks on everything the Fenians stood for was resented. His political rallies became so violent he needed police protection. He was dumped from the St. Patrick's Society – and from the cabinet, his ability to bring in votes having been impaired. Then one night in Ottawa in April 1868 he was on his way to his boarding house after a late session of parliament when a man stepped out of the darkness and shot him. A young tailor named Patrick James Whelan, a man with Fenian sympathies, was arrested, convicted and hanged for the murder, despite his insistence of innocence.

In martyrdom McGee regained his popularity. The press lamented his loss to the nation, and the morning after the murder Sir John A. Macdonald paid tribute to him before moving adjournment of the House as a mark of respect. "He who last night, nay this morning, was with us, whose voice is still ringing in our ears, who charmed us with his marvellous eloquence, elevated us by his large statesmanship and instructed us by his wisdom, his patriotism, is no more – is foully murdered. If ever a soldier who fell on the field of battle deserved well of his country, Thomas D'Arcy McGee deserved well of Canada and its people." In Montreal, thousands turned out for his funeral as for a state occasion. Six grey horses pulled his glass-panelled bier, which was draped with a black cloth embellished with the likeness of a silver harp and shamrock. A poet compared his death with that of Abraham Lincoln.

Maguire's book contains no praise for this remarkable Irishman, but Maguire's sympathies were with the Fenians. His prejudice was also evident on his visit to Upper Canada, where he managed to ignore most of the Protestants, who made up two thirds of the Irish in that province. So far as the Presbyterian Scotch-Irish were concerned, Maguire held that they were not true Irishmen at all, and their hyphenated name meant to him that they were "ashamed of their country."

Maguire had curiously little to say about Toronto, though Irish were a quarter of the population of 50,000 and the largest national group in the city. They had settled in shanties along the lakefront or in what became known as Cabbagetown, because of the proliferation of backyard cabbage patches that flourished well in sandy soil and hot summers. There were many Catholics among them, but to Maguire Toronto was a Protestant stronghold, the "Belfast of Canada." With seventeen lodges, it was the centre of Canadian Orangeism, which Maguire called a "dark shadow in this bright picture of prosperity."

There were 150,000 to 200,000 Orangemen in Canada, not all of them Irish, and most of them in Ontario and New Brunswick. In Ontario one of every three Protestants was an Orangeman. Lodges were almost as common as crossroads general stores, functioned as social centres and supported a vision of an English-speaking Canada under the British flag. Since many Protestant Irish suffered difficulties in the New World, if not on the same scale as their Catholic country-men, lodges such as those in Toronto were of considerable help to those in need of aid.

Maguire believed the Irish should stick to the land, where the majority of Catholics as well as Protestants had settled, particularly in Ontario. "As a rule, admitting of rare exceptions, the Irish who settle on the land and devote themselves to its cultivation do well, realize property, accumulate money, surround themselves with solid com-forts, and bring up their families reputably. Hundreds of cases could be mentioned of Irishmen, originally of the very humblest condition, who, when they came out first, worked as farm labourers for others, and now occupy, as owners, the very property on which they toiled for their daily bread."

Whether Catholics fared as well as their Protestant neighbours was often determined by the quality of their land. Of the 580 families in the southern region of Montague Township, where it follows the Rideau River near Smiths Falls, Catholics who had settled there early – workers on the canal – had the best lots and therefore prospered as well as or better than Protestants. On the other hand, both did poorly on the northern lots where soil was inferior and of which John Now-lan, a government agent, wrote: "The people in general is very poor. The most part of them gets their living by working out in the winter and raising a little crop in summer." Protestants were as prone to mis-fortune as Catholics. William Flood, for one, lost his cattle and horse. "Those losses together with the failer in the grain crop, renders him incapable of supporting his family, leaving him a burden on the neigh-bours," said a petition in the township records for December 1860.

When their crops failed them, there was winter work in the lumber camps to make ends meet. "I am assured that Irishmen make better lumberers than the natives of other countries," said a letter in the *Londonderry Standard* from an Irishman in the Ottawa Valley on August 4, 1853. "It appears that the good and abundant food they receive here expands not only the muscular frame but also the intellect; no one who has not seen the contrast between the downcast, ill-fated ragged Irish peasant in his own country, and the same man after even a few months residence in these provinces, could believe in its completeness."

For Maguire, a prime example of a famine emigrant who had done well was Jimmy Cuffe, who came penniless from County Roscommon and now, seventeen years later, had 800 acres on Wolfe Island near Kingston. A man of nimble wits, "low-sized, broad-shouldered, well-knit and vigorous as a 'four year old,'" Cuffe had built a good house, barns, a herd of cattle and a stable for horses. "In a word," said Maguire, "everything that the heart of any rational Irish could desire. He drives his family to church in a spring wagon, drawn by a pair of good horses, 'as grand as the Lord Mayor of London, or any real gentleman in the old country.'"

If Jimmy Cuffe epitomized the pluck and progress of the individual, Peterborough epitomized community progress. "Not a few of those who sailed from Cork in 1825," said Maguire, "have passed away after a life of hard and ceaseless toil, and others now stand, as it were on the brink of the grave; but their sons, and their grandsons, their daughters and their grand-daughters flourish in the midst of prosperity and comfort, of which those who went before them were creators." Tom Hay, writing to his uncle in Dublin, said: "A very large proportion of our population are Irish or descendants of Irish, and a more profitable and law abiding people never existed."

Typical of the Peter Robinson emigrants was the family of Garrett and Mary Galvin of Listowel, Kerry. Like the majority of Irish in Upper Canada, they clung to their land, increasing their original seventy acres in Ennismore Township, north of Peterborough, to more than 200. According to the census of 1851, a year in which Ireland was recovering from the famine, the Galvins owned twelve cattle, including four cows that supplied them with 600 pounds of butter, two horses, seventeen pigs and forty sheep. They had planted thirty-four acres to wheat, peas, potatoes and corn, and cleared sixteen for pasturage. For the winter they put down four barrels of salt beef and cured several barrels of fish. The current head of the family was Patrick, who had been twenty years old when, twenty-five years earlier, he had leaped from the boat that ferried his family across Chemong Lake and said, "Behold, I am the first settler in Ennismore." He had sired fourteen children, having married again when his first wife died. He became the township's first postmaster and tax collector and a member of the Peterborough County Council. One of his great-grandchildren, Douglas Galvin, was to become, a century later, mayor of Peterborough.

A glance at Ennismore Township, which had been named for Lord Ennismore of County Cork, neither the best nor the worst of the seven townships settled by the Robinson people around Peterborough, gives us some idea of how average Catholic settlers had fared. The population was somewhat more than 500, spread over nearly 10,000 acres, of which one third was used for pasture and for crops of wheat (by far the largest), barley, oats, peas, potatoes, turnips, corn, hops and a few other things. They owned 231 cows, 199 calves, 707 pigs, 861 sheep and 105 horses. They produced 2,000 pounds of maple sugar every year and 2,000 pounds of wool, as well as flannel cloth. They had built a school for 180 pupils and it was well attended.

They had not spared much time for their housing. The only substantial place in the township was the two-storey stone house put up by Jeremiah McCarthy, the other seventy-two being log houses and shanties of one storey. Presumably men such as Daniel Costello, who had eighty acres under cultivation and owned seven cows, could have afforded better housing, but it did not seem to be a priority, or it may have been a holdover from those days in Ireland when ostentation was sure to bring the grasping hand of the landlord and the tax collector.

By 1867, the year Francis Maguire published *The Irish in America*, 850,000 people had left Ireland for British North America during the past fifty years. Many had moved on to the United States; many more had stayed. "As a rule," Maguire concluded, "they have enormously benefitted their condition by leaving the old country for the new. In every walk and department of life they are making their mark...."

IN THE 1870S, the proportion of Irish to other Canadian ethnic groups was at its peak. A quarter of all Canadians spoke with an Irish accent, and when a French Canadian in Montreal referred to "les anglos" he meant, as often as not, the Irish, who outnumbered the English and Scots combined. By the end of the decade there were close to a million people of Irish extraction in the British provinces, 60 per cent of them Protestants – Anglicans, Presbyterians, Methodists. About half the Irish lived in Ontario, where Protestants outnumbered Catholics two to one; the proportion of Catholics was larger in Quebec and New Brunswick. Prince Edward Island had joined Confederation, as had Manitoba and British Columbia, but there were as yet few Irish in the latter two provinces. One of the reasons Newfoundland, described by one visitor as a "transatlantic Ireland," had declined to join Confederation was the fear that Confederation would mean domination by the Protestant Irish of Ontario.

For Nicholas Flood Davin, however, an Irishman was an Irishman, regardless of creed, and in praising their achievements in his book *The Irishman in Canada*, published in 1877, he lumped them all together with little reference to religion. A journalist and lawyer, Davin had come from Kilfinnane, County Limerick, a few years earlier and settled in Toronto, a member of the new generation putting down roots in a country headed by an Irish Governor General in the person of the affable Lord Dufferin.

Though Davin believed the Irish fared better than in the United States, he was distressed by the prejudice he found in Canada against Irish Catholics. Police records suggest there was no more trouble among poor Irish than the poor of other groups, but their infractions got more space in the newspapers. There is no doubt that Irish Catholics suffered from a bad press, though in Toronto the *True Witness*, for one, insisted that the few Irish "criminals" who appeared in the courts were guilty of nothing but poverty, being simply hungry and homeless and in need of help. In Halifax, where Irish Catholics were 33 per cent of the population, court records suggest their transgressions – drunkenness, vagrancy and assault – were actually slightly less than those of other ethnic groups. With the confidence of a young newcomer, Davin aimed "to sweep aside misconceptions and explode cherished falsities, to point out the truth and raise the self-respect of every person of Irish blood in Canada."

The Irish had come to Canada as early as English or Scots, Davin said, had tamed the wilderness and fought off invaders. "The Irishman has played so large a part in Canada," said Davin, "that his history could not be written without, to some extent, writing the history of Canada." D'Arcy McGee had been only one of the Irish Fathers of Confederation; others included Jonathan McCully in Nova Scotia and Edward Whelan in Prince Edward Island. Robert Baldwin of the County Cork family, who with Lafontaine had headed the first Liberal government of United Canada in the 1840s, had been a pioneer of responsible government; Edward Blake, whose family had come from Galway, was premier of Ontario and leader of the federal Liberal party; Paul Kane, from Mallow, County Cork, had become a celebrated Canadian artist.

Nor did Davin forget the less exalted, like Mrs. Foley, née Sullivan, from Killarney, who had married young and had four children.

One day she said to her husband: "We shall never do anything here. They say Canada is a fine country, let us go out there, in the name of God, and try our luck." But the husband would not hear of it. She then said, "Well, I must go myself;" and the brave little dark-eyed woman saved enough money to bring her to Toronto. In Toronto she took in washing, and saved enough money to send for her husband. She then said to her husband: "If we are to do anything for our children, we must push out into the woods." She heard there was land to be had in Victoria [a newly-opened county west of Peterborough] and thither she went with her family, and worked like a brave woman. She has now 200 acres of land well cultivated, and each of her four sons has 100 acres. All four are married and are raising happy families.

Davin enlivens his book – which with Maguire's constitutes the only exhaustive survey of Irish in Canada published until recent years – with anecdote and history, and above all with names – hundreds of them – of doctors, lawyers, clergy, businessmen, contractors, politicians, artists. It was a Who's Who of upwardly mobile Irish of the time.

His method was largely that of making thumbnail sketches of men such as Daniel O'Meara from Tipperary, who founded the lumber town of Pembroke on the Ottawa, brought immigrants up from Quebec City at his own expense and built not one but two Catholic churches with his own money. But to tell the history of all the Irish in the Ottawa Valley would take a whole book, he said, and thus he could not tell of all the little communities such as Mount Saint Patrick or Lucan or Killaloe and similar places that preserved their ethnic identity and sent dozens of priests and nuns to the Church. Or of the Foley brothers, Timothy and Michael from Ramsay Township who became two of the greatest railway contractors in the United States and Canada.

He wrote of Arthur McQuade, who had come to Emily township with his widowed mother in 1837. A Protestant from County Cavan, McQuade laboured for two years for a farmer, saved enough to make a down payment on 100 acres, became a major property owner, a school trustee, tax collector, member of parliament, and one of the wealthiest men in the province. William Cluxton from Dundalk, County Louth, who had come out as an orphan at the age of twelve was president of two railways – the Midland and the Lake Huron and

Quebec City – and president of the Marmora Mining Company east of Peterborough. He told of Dr. William Hingston, mayor of Montreal, and Owen Murphy, mayor of Quebec, and of many forgotten now but influential in their time, such as R.H. Oats of Toronto, who founded the United Canadian Association. The most impressive thing in Davin's book is this seemingly endless list of Irish who had made good and left such an imprint on 19th-century Canada. By the weight of their numbers Davin gave the lie, as he intended, to the caricatures of bog Irish that had for so long disfigured the pages of such London journals as *Punch* and followed the emigrants across the Atlantic.

By Davin's time the tide of Irish migration, though running strong, flowed mainly to the United States, where fares were cheaper and the Catholics, who were now the majority of emigrants, would be free of English power. In the decade of the 1880s, barely 5 per cent of the million who left Ireland came to Canada, where once the Irish had been three quarters of all newcomers.

In two generations, however, the Irish, of all the immigrant groups, had made their mark, not so much through assimilation but because they were in at the beginning, builders of a new society where, as D'Arcy McGee had said, "The British flag does fly here, but it casts no shadow." Their mark has been stamped on Ontario, not only because of the large number of Irish Protestants who settled there, but also in less widely known ways, such as the school curriculum introduced by Egerton Ryerson in the 1840s, much of which was derived from Ireland's National School System, and its school books of the 1830s. Another Irish contribution to Canadian life was the paramilitary organization of the Royal Canadian Mounted Police, modelled in the 1870s on the Royal Ulster Constabulary. The Irish have made their mark on cities such as Saint John, St. John's, Halifax and Montreal. There is an undeniable Irish influence in the popular culture of Quebec, whether in its fiddle music, as perfected by Jean Carignan, or the poetry of Emile Nelligan, whom the Québécois claim as a national poet but whose paternal family came from Buttevant in the Black-water region of County Cork.

The majority had put down roots before the Great Famine, which may account in part for the differences between Irish Americans and Irish Canadians. Unlike their urban cousins of the eastern United States, the majority of Canadian Irish, Catholic as well as Protestant, used the skills they had learned in Ireland and kept to farming. Perhaps because they were so scattered, out on their farms, that they did not – the Orangemen excepted – build the pressure groups so common in the States. In the age of the anti-immigration "Know Nothing" movement in the United States, Davin believed the Irish were better received in Canada, despite an obvious residue of prejudice, and had less need to look back over their shoulders at the old country to affirm their identity.

"The Canadian immigrant will, with time, lose many of the peculiarities of his race," wrote the Irish-Huguenot William Canniff in *The Settlement of Upper Canada* in 1869, "and in the end sensibly approximate to the character and appearance of the people among whom he has settled. The children of the emigrant, no matter what pains the parents may take to preserve in their children what belongs to their native country, will grow up quite unlike their parents."

For whatever reasons, memories of the "old country" seemed milder in Canada, more in tune with the Canadian way. Their sympathy for Ireland ran deep, however, as shown by Edward Blake – whom Sir Wilfrid Laurier called one of Canada's greatest political figures. Born in Canada shortly after his Anglo-Irish parents immigrated, he left Canadian politics in 1892 and went to Westminster as an Irish Nationalist MP representing County Longford to defend Irish interests.

One difference between the Irish experience in Canada and the United States lay in the trauma of Partridge Island and Grosse Isle, which the Americans, by turning back the sick and starving in 1847, had largely escaped. The famine migration, the worst episode of human misery in Canadian history, was fading into painful memory when, in the summer of 1897, representatives of the Ancient Order of Hibernians visited Grosse Isle on the fiftieth anniversary of Black '47. They found the graves neglected and overgrown. "The desolate and neglected aspect of the particular portion of the island allotted for the resting place of so many of our blood and our faith seemed to strike us with reproach," wrote Jeremiah Gallagher, president of the Quebec chapter of the order. The Hibernians, as defenders of Irish culture, resolved to erect a monument.

On August 5, 1909, hundreds of pilgrims gathered on Grosse Isle for a commemorative service and the unveiling of a forty-six-foot granite shaft topped with the Celtic cross. The inscriptions, in Gaelic, English and French, read: "Sacred to the memory of thousands of Irish emigrants, who, to preserve the faith, suffered hunger and exile in 1847, and stricken with fever ended here their sorrowful pilgrimage."

Select Bibliography

Adams, W.F., *Ireland and Irish Emigrants, from 1815 to the Famine*, New Haven, 1932.

Akenson, D.H., *The Irish in Ontario, a Study in Rural History*, Kingston-Montreal, 1984.

Bhaldraite, Tomás de (trans), *The Diary of Humphrey O'Sullivan*, Dublin, 1979.

Banks, M., *Edward Blake, Irish Nationalist, A Canadian Statesman in Irish Politics*, Toronto, 1957.

Beames, Michael, *Peasants and Power, The Whiteboy Movement*, Brighton, 1983.

Bennett, Carol, *Peter Robinson's Settlers, 1823–1825*, Renfrew, Ont., 1987.

Bennett, William, *Six Weeks in Ireland*, London, 1848.

Bilson, Geoffrey, *A Darkened House*, Toronto, 1980.

Burritt, Elihu, *A Journal of a Visit of Three Days to Skibbereen*, London, 1847.

Carrothers, Joseph, *Irish Emigrant Letters from Canada 1939–70*, Belfast, 1951.

Cowan, Helen I., *British Emigration to British North America 1783–1837*, Toronto, 1928.

Crawford, E. Margaret (ed), *Famine, The Irish Experience 900-1900*, Edinburgh, 1989.

Cross, Michael S., "The Shiners Wars: Social Violence in the Ottawa Valley in the 1830s," *Canadian Historical Review*, Vol. 54, March 1973, p. 1–26.

Cushing, J. Elizabeth, and Teresa Casey and Monica Robertson (eds), *A Chronicle of Irish Emigration to Saint John, New Brunswick, 1847*, Saint John, 1979.

Daly, Mary E., *The Famine in Ireland*, Dublin, 1986.

Davin, N.F., *The Irishman in Canada*, London, 1878 (Irish U. Press, reprint 1969).

Donnell, James S., *The Land and the People of 19th Century Cork*, London, 1975.

Edwards, R. Dudley and T. Desmond Williams (eds), *The Great Famine, Studies in Irish History 1845–1852*, Dublin, 1956.

Elliott, Bruce S., *Irish Migrants in the Canadas, A New Approach*, Kingston-Montreal, 1988.

Ellis, Eilish, *Emigrants from Ireland, 1847–1852: State-aided Emigration Schemes from Crown Estates in Ireland*, Baltimore, 1977.

Finan, P,. *Journal of a Voyage to Quebec in 1825*, London, 1828.

Fitzpatrick, Rory, *The Scots-Irish Epic*, London, 1989.

Galvin, C.F,. *The Holy Land: A History of Ennismore Township*, Peterborough, 1978.

Gesner, A., *New Brunswick, Notes for Emigrants*, London, 1847.

Gibbon, J.M., "Ireland and Canada," in *Canadian Mosaic*, Toronto, 1938.

Gourlay, Robert, *A Statistical Account of Upper Canada, complete with a view to a grand system of emigration*, London, 1828.

Guillet, E.C., *The Great Migration, Atlantic Crossing by Sailing Ship 1770–1860*, Toronto, 1937;
— *Documents Relative to the Peter Robinson Emigration of 1825*, Peterborough, 1956;
— *The Valley of the Trent*, Toronto, 1957.

Hall, Basil, *Travels in North America*, (3v), Edinburgh, 1830;

Haydon, Andrew, *Pioneer Sketches in the District of Bathurst*, Toronto, 1925.

Horton, R.J. Wilmot, *Ireland and Canada*, London, 1839.

Inglis, H.D., *Through Ireland in 1834*, London, 1835.

Kee, Robert, *Ireland, A Natural History*, London, 1982.

Kelly, E.T., *The Coming of the Newfoundland Irish*, Newfoundland Quarterly, 65: 18–20, 1967.

Kilfoil, W.P., *Johnville, The Story of an Irish Settlement,* Fredericton, 1962.

Kirouac, J.A., *Histoire de la Paroisse de St. Malachi,* Quebec, 1909.

King, J.A., *The Irish Lumberman–Farmer: Fitzgeralds, Harringtons & Others,* LaFayette, Calif., 1982.

Kingston, W.J., *The Story of West Carbery,* Waterford, 1985.

Lucas, Sir Charles (ed), *Lord Durham's Report,* London, 1912.

MacCraith, Rev. Michael (ed-trans), *Humphrey O'Sullivan's Diary,* Irish Text Society, 1937.

MacDonagh, Oliver, *A Pattern of Government Growth: Passenger Acts and their Enforcement 1800–1860,* London, 1961.

Maguire, John Francis, *The Irish in America,* London, 1868.

Mannion, J.J., *Irish Settlements in Eastern Canada,* Toronto, 1974.

McCarthy, Michael J., *The History of Newfoundland 1623–1800,* St. John's, 1982.

Miller, Kerby A., *Emigrants and Exiles, Ireland and the Irish Exodus to North America,* Oxford, 1985.

Moodie, Susanna, *Roughing It in the Bush,* London, 1838 (reprint Ottawa, 1988).

Nelligan, J.M., *Life of a Lumberman,* 1929.

Nicholls, G., *A History of the Irish Poor Law,* London, 1856.

O'Driscoll, Robert & Lorna Reynolds (eds), *The Untold Story: The Irish in Canada,* (2v), Toronto, 1988.

O'Gallagher, Marianna, *Grosse Isle, Gateway to Canada, 1832–1937,* Ste. Foy, Que., 1984.

Parr, G.J., *The Welcome and the Wake, Attitudes in Canada West toward the Irish Famine Migration,* Ontario History, v. 66 pp–101–113, 1974.

Pool, T.W., *The Early Settlement of Peterborough County,* Peterborough, 1867.

Power, Bill, *Mitchelstown through Seven Centuries,* Fermoy, Co. Cork, 1987.

Punch, Terrance M., *Some Sons of Erin in Nova Scotia,* Halifax, 1980.

Radcliff, Rev. Thomas (ed), *Authentic Letters from Upper Canada*, Dublin, 1833.

Redmond, P.M., *Irish Life in Rural Quebec, A History of Frampton*, Chicago, 1977.

Robinson, C.W., *The Life of Sir John Beverley Robinson*, Toronto, 1904.

Salaman, R.N., *The History and Social Influence of the Potato*, Cambridge, 1949.

Schier, A., *Ireland and the American Emigration*, New York, 1970.

Senior, Hereward, *Orangeism, The Canadian Phase*, Toronto, 1972.

Stewart, Frances, *Our Forest Home*, Montreal, 1902.

Stewart, H.I., *The Irish in Nova Scotia*, Kentville, 1949.

Strickland, Samuel, *Twenty-Seven Years in Canada West*, (2v), London, 1853.

Talbot, E.A., *Five Years Residence in the Canadas*, London, 1824.

Traill, Catharine Parr, *The Backwoods of Canada*, London, 1836.

Trench, W. Steuart, *Realities of Irish Life*, London, 1868.

Trevelyan, Sir Charles, *The Irish Crisis*, London, 1850.

Whalen, James, *"Allmost as Bad as Ireland,"* Saint John, 1847, Archivaria, 10:85:97.

Whelan, Kevin (ed), *Wexford, History and Society*, Dublin, 1987.

Whyte, Robert, *The Ocean Plague, or a voyage to Quebec in an Irish Emigrant vessel by "A Cabin Passenger,"* London, 1848.

Wilson, David A., *The Irish in Canada*, Canadian Historical Society, Ottawa, 1989.

Woodham-Smith, Cecil, *The Great Hunger, Ireland 1845–49*, London, 1964.

Young, Arthur, *A Tour of Ireland*, (2v), London 1780.

Source Notes

<small>PRIMARY SOURCES</small>

Irish University Press (IPU) Shannon, 1968, British Parliamentary Papers (BPP):

- Emigration, v.1, 2, 1st, 2nd, 3rd Reports on, 1826-27;.v.4., 5. Select Committees (SC) House of Lords Colonization from Ireland 1847; v.6. SC on Passenger's Act, 1851; SC 1st and 2nd Reports on Emigrant Ships. v.19, 20; SC 1825 [200] Minutes, Evidence before the House of Lord's Select Committee appointed to inquire into the disturbances in Ireland, 1825; SC Report from Select Committee on the State of Ireland 1831-32.
- Reports, Returns and Correspondence Relating to Emigration 1828-38.
- Famine, v.1-8, including Distress Papers, State of Union Workhouses and Board of Works reports.
- Colonies – Canada; v.1-17, includes weekly reports of the Emigration Agent, Quebec City, v.8 and v.17.
- Correspondence Explanatory of Measures Adopted by Her Majesty's Govt. for the Relief of Distress HC 1846; 1847.
- Papers Relative to Emigration to the British Provinces in North America HC 1847-48.

CAC: County Archives, Cork

CO: Colonial Office Records, 384-5 series [Emigration]. RG 9, A 1 v.31-32 New Brunswick [NAC] and RG 7G 14 l84l-51 v.55, Governor General's Office.

JLA: Journals of Legislative Assembly of Province of Canada, 1847 App.L, including reports of Superintendent, Grosse Isle.

NLI: National Library of Ireland, Dublin.

PRO NI: Public Records Office Northern Ireland.

SPO: State Papers Office, Dublin

<small>INTRODUCTION AND CHAPTER 1</small>

Page 9. "evening and the end of the day," *Five 17th Century Political Poems,* Dublin, 1952.

11. "Do not make a union," Boswell, *Life of Samuel Johnson,* v.III, p.66.

18. "Newfoundland is a fine plantation," Two Irish Poets in the Wild Plantations, Essays in Canadian Writing, Toronto, No. 31.

19. "The number of people who go," Young, v.I, p.406.

20. "Whereas a great number," quoted in McCarthy, p.33.
    "For the better preserving," Maguire, p.163.
21. "The simplest method," in J.D. Rogers, *Historical Geography of Newfound-land*, Oxford, 1911.
22. "The common dialect," W.S. McNutt, *The Atlantic Provinces*, Toronto, 1965, p.157.
23. "a very industrious," Chas. Morris, Provincial Surveyor's Report, 1764.
    "The first five families," Uniacke, SC March 22, 1826.
25. "By what I hear," Thomas Moore, *The Life and Death of Edward Fitzgerald*, London, 1831.
26. "The Irish are not fond," MG 23 H II 7 NAC.
27. "We had seven weeks," *Diary of Humphrey O'Sullivan*, 8/28/1830.
28. "Oh what scenes of misery," *Lachrymae Hibernicae*, By A Resident Native, Dublin, 1822.
    "What could I do?" Miller, *Emigrants and Exiles*, p.163.
    "For Halifax and Prince Edward Island," H.I Stewart, *The Irish in Nova Scotia*, Kentville, 1949, p.140.
    "For tradesmen and others," ibid.
    "One of the peculiarities," *Evening Post*, Dublin, 3/18/1815.
30. "Thousands of unfortunate sons," Talbot, *Five Years Residence in the Canadas*.
31. "cheerful, healthy, and the hope," ibid.
35. "It is a melancholy thing," Adams, p.104.
    "Nothing can be more," Edward Chappell, *Voyage of HMS Rosalind*, p.218.
    "all our population," Uniacke, SC March 22, 1826-36.
    "In the fifth year of peace," *Lachrymae Hibernicae*.
    'The end of 1820 was distinguished," 1851 Census V, p.238-.
37. "It would be impossible," *History of Sligo*, Dublin, 1822, p.66.
    "Were it not for the aid," Miller, p.38.
    "The poor people are lying," Report of the London Committee for Irish relief, July 1822.
    State-aided emigration: In 1815, 699 persons; 1818, 600; 1820-21, 3,200; 1823-25, 2,591.

CHAPTER 2
40 "With honey and with milk," St. Donaties, 9th century.
    "Out of every corner," Thos. C. Croker, *Research in the South of Ireland*, p.74.
46. "to enlighten the minds," Power, p.44.
    "The cottages," Young, p.47.
48. "lights upon the hills," Blacker, SC 1825 (200), p.23.

"The insurgents it appears," *Report on Present State of the District in S. Ireland,* Dublin, 1822, p.55.

49. "Their perseverance," ibid.
"to quit this place," *Kilkenny Moderator,* 6/11/1832.

50. "among them some very bad characters," SC 1825 (521), p.434.
"Not every young man," IFD MS 1234, p.321. O'Donovan Diary, in Bath Ref. Library, England.
"We are oppressed," State Papers, Dublin, 1821, 2299/12/SPO

51. "very intelligent, smart fellow," Annual Register, Cork, 1822.
"Here I am ... Captain Rock," Beames, *Peasants and Power,* p.67.
"Notice to Mr. Hill," Cork Hist. & Archaeological Soc., 1893 v.3, p.159.

52. The gentlemen of Ireland," Young, v.2, p.56.
"One of the great misfortunes," Kingston to Bathurst, 6/20/1822, CO 42.

54. "One of the remedies for Irish misery," Peel to Goulbourn, Peel Papers British Museum, MSS 40329.

55. Cornelius Lyons: J. Kirouac, *Histoire de la Paroisse de St. Malachi,* Quebec, 1909, p.71.

CHAPTERS 3 THROUGH 6

Peter Robinson's two emigrant groups, in 1823 and 1825, are among the best documented in history. For Robinson's activities, comments, and letters, as well as those of his emigrants, the author has relied on the vast amount of material in the National Archives, Ottawa, and the Ontario Provincial Archives, Toronto. NAC RG 1 L3 v.435 (Settlement of Irish emigrants in Bathurst District) 1823-25. Emigrant letters CO 384 vols. 10, 12; The Robinson Papers, MG 24 B 74 at NAC, and RG 14, A 3 Jnl of House of Assembly, UC 1826-27; Also RG 1 L3 v.435, etc.

58. "The general appearance," Reid, *Travels in Ireland,* London, 1823, p.299.
"Crossing the Ballyhourie," Croker, p.102.

59. "a poor town," ibid, p.86.

72. "If accounts," Horton, 1824, CO 324/95.
"In the years 1822 and 1823," Horton, *On Emigration from the United Kingdom,* p.323.

76. "burned at the stake," B. Robinson to Bathurst, 7/12/24 CO 384/12.
"for wanton and outrageous," *Pioneer Sketches in the District of Bathurst,* p.158.

77. "be stopped at once," Dalhousie to Bathurst, 5/18/1824 CO 42/200.
"little disturbance among the Irish," CO 42/377 Maitland to Bathurst 3/31/1826.

78. "The existing state," SC evidence 4/27/1826.

80. "A rumour reached us," S.R. Bellingham Memoires, MG 24 B 25 NAC.

88. "My charges," Reade Report, 3/13/27 CO 384/17.

93 "My first," Bellingham.

94. Kingston death toll, CO 42/380 J.B. Robinson to Horton 1/22/1827.

95. "The white tents," Guillet, *The Great Migration*, p.174.

96 "superior to any place," Traill, *The Backwoods of Canada*, p.70.

99. "Behold I am the first," Early History of Ennismore, *Peterborough Examiner*, nd.

100. "Upon the industry," Dalhousie to Horton, CO 42/204 16/12/1825.
"no less than thirty," *Colonial Advocate*, 12/6/1825 also 12/8.
"I am here in the midst," Stewart to Crowley, Douro, 1/20/1826, Appendix 4, SC Emigration, 1826.

101. "On Saturday last," F. Stewart, *Our Forest Home*, p.173.

104. "The man who had," 1824 RG 5 A 1 UC Sundries v.69 Reel C-4613 pp 36570-1.

105. "we had a good," Jean McGill, *A Pioneer History of the County of Lanark*, 1968, p.99.

109 "I would not employ any Irish," MacTaggart, *Three Years in Canada*, v.2, p.243.

110. "it generally came on," ibid v.2, p.17.
"Ague is the disease," *The Canadian Settlers Guide*, p.205.

112. "We shrank," Moodie, *Roughing It in the Bush*, p.210.
"reeking with smoke," Traill, p.112.

113. "When the weather," Traill, p.74.
"Former indolent habits," Hall, *Travels in North America*, v.1, p.321.

114. "Were it not for the ague," Hall, *Travels*, v.1, p.286 passim.
"Would you like," ibid, p.152.
"We have been taken from misery and want," Hall, *Travels*, v.1, p.150.

115. "Grew up as if by magic," Ireland and Canada, p.41.
"thereby injuring," Hall, v.1, p.335. The cost had been reckoned at 12 pounds per head or an average of 60 pounds per family at a time unassisted emigrants were arriving at a cost of three or four pounds sterling for the passage.

116. "Small farmer with a large family," Buchanan, BPP 1826-7, No.550, p.435.
"The labouring population," Strickland, p.191.

CHAPTER 7

117. "The moment the very name," quoted in Thomas Gallagher, *Paddy's Lament*, 1982, NY, p.68., also *The Edinburgh Review*, v.XI, 1807.

118. "The landlord of an Irish estate," Young, v.2, p.53.
"It was an injustice," A. MacDougal, *Treatise on Irish Fisheries*, Belfast, 1819.

"So far from being," SC on Employment of the Poor, 1823. 128.

"The proctor has a double objective," Dr. John R. Elmore, Cork, SC 1825 (20), p.415.

129. "One clergyman within thirty miles," P. Somerville-Large, *The Irish Grand Tour,* p.46, London, l982.

CHAPTER 8

134. "Symptoms giddiness, sick stomach," *Quebec Mercury,* 1/14/1832.

136. "only then did the truth," in Bilson, p.23.

137. "Imagine our feelings," Mary McLean [Walsh] MS ll.428, NLI.

138. "It has pleased the Lord," Anderson, at Quebec City, in letter to his home in Coleraine, 7/1/1832, NAC MG 40 R v.2-42.

139. "We none of us," Alexander Hart quoted in Bilson, p.25.

"From south to north," *Kingston Chronicle,* 4/7/1832.

140. "emitting deadly," Belson, p.55.

"The excitement caused," *The Life and Times of the Rev. Anson Green,* Toronto, 1877, p.159.

142. "August 12. We reached Grosse Isle," Traill, p.18.

"A crowd of many hundred," Moodie, p.20.

144. "When I see my country in mourning," in G.N. Tucker, *The Canadian Commercial Revolution,* Toronto, 1936, p.275.

"There are many tradesmen," Brady, 9/17/1832 PRONI T. 3028.

145. "We left Belfast," Peterborough, 10/28/1832 PRONI Acc.1.

147. "The despondency we suffered," Dec. 1832, *Authentic Letters,* p.88.

"The cholera raged," *Letters from Settlers in Upper Canada,* London, 1834, p.12.

CHAPTER 9

152. "In the awful light," *History of the North Part of New Brunswick,* Halifax, 1832.

"The most miserable," to Simonds, 9/5/27, CO 188/35.

153. "No one more," CO 188/35 to Goderich, 2/14/1832.

157. "Took a great deal of time," J.A. King, *The Lumberman-Farmer,* Lafayette, Calif. p.60.

...onds *Colonial Magazine,* v.1, 1844, p.462.

...JC Sundries, v.174-75, Jan.-March 1837

...ıble," J.B. Robinson, p.170.

...)range Lodge 7, April, 1927, UC Sundries

172 "We are ready at all times," ibid.

173. "The manner in which they met," Ireland and Canada, p.22.

174. "A set of ragamuffins," CO 42/233.

177. "The committee acting," Records of the Col. Wyndham assisted emigration, Reel A-1642 NAC.

178. "Getting rid of the surplus," Brydone, SC 6/18/1847.

179. "On the 22nd of May," Wyndham Records.

181. "We are all," ibid.

CHAPTER 11

184. "I went to a hamlet," *Rural Rides*, v.3, 10/17/1834.
"It was the most appalling sight," Kee, p.85.

186. "There exists the most," *Peasants and Power*, p.111.

187. "With one hand," de Beaumont, *The Great Famine*, p.209.

189. "Shovelling out the paupers," in Woodham-Smith, p227.

190. "To throwing starving," Sydenham to Russell, 12/26/1840.

192. "I don't delay," Garry, March 8/48 in 3rd Report on Colonization from Ireland, 1848, appendix.
"On board one vessel," Douglas BPP, 1844, No. 181, p.25.
"It is out," Correspondence, Pat. Nowlan, Weymouth, N.S. MG 24 I. NAC.

193. "The weavers in Bandon," 7/29/1827, CAC.

CHAPTER 12

200. "A pauper emigrant," *Durham Report*, p.127.

201. "Of all the seaports," Redburn, *His First Voyage*, N.Y., 1847.

203. "The Irish emigrant," SC 22/3/26, p.46.
"nothing in the annals," 4/1/1828 CO 384/20.
"that beggared all description," Hansard, 1828 XVIII, p.1212.
"scanty nourishment," *The Royal [N.S.] Gazette* of Sept. 27 said all 60 died.

204. "partly from the hardships," CO 384/70.
"It is notorious," Cowan pp 207-8.

206. "worse than can be imagined," SC Passenger Act, 1851, HV v.19.
"noisesome dungeon," *The Times*, 12/27/1853.

207. "The passengers were thus," *Niles Weekly Register*, Baltimore, 9/27/1834.

208. "On Sunday the 25th,"Guillet, *The Great Migration*, p.127.

209. "My ill luck," ibid, pp 125-6.

210. "Awakened by cries," Letters, McConnell family, Toronto Central Library.
"The wind howling dreadfully," Finan, *Journal of a Voyage to Quebec*, p.19
"to die of fear," Miller, p.256.

211. "all could not induce," Schrier, p.91.
"The desire for gain".

212. "The hold was full," York, Aug. 1832, Authentic Letters, pp 98-103.
213. "We had as good a captain," PRO NI Acc.6298.
    "a pleasant man," *Journal of a Passage from Belfast to New York,* 1849.

CHAPTER 13
217. "Mark the Irishman's," Young, p.45.
218. "It was scarcely," Census 1851, Pt.V, p.241.
222. "Good God, are you to sit," in Norman Gash, *Sir Robert Peel,* p.106.
226. "Tipperary is in insurrection," *The Nation,* 4/18/46.
230. "On August 1st," W. Steuart Trench, *Realities of Irish Life,* p.50.
231. "this doomed plant," Mathew, in Census of Ireland, 1851, p.270.
232. "I cannot make my own mind up," Russell papers l/23/47 PRO 30/22/
    1846.
233. "From the poor," SC 1847, p.188.
234. "Every man of rank," Distress Papers, Co. Clare 11/6/46. "Unless actually
    seen," Daly, p.72.
236. "They were employed," Transactions of Central Relief Committee Society
    of Friends, 1846-47, Dublin, 1852, App.III.
    "to want of sufficient," Board of Works. W. Cork, I pp 219-220; Police
    report 11/2/1846. 237.
    "One had been dead," Cummins, *The Times,* 12/24/1846.
239. "The tears of agony," Kee, p.90.
241. "For God's Sake, take us," SC 3rd Report, p.13.
242. "I am persauded," in *The Great Famine,* p.371.

CHAPTER 14
43. "The people sink," Bishop to Trevelyan, 1/29/47. Relief Commission Corr.
    II, p.302.
244. "It is scarcely possible," Census 1851.
    "We deeply sympathize," Woodham Smith, p.177.
    "two cartloads," Distress Papers, 2/14/1847.
245. "Fever, dysentery and starvation," *The Times,* 3/11/47.
247. "I did not see," Trench, Appendix.
    "A ha'penny," Burritt, p.37.
252. "He must sell," *Irish Journals of Elizabeth Smith,* p.131.
252. 'Prices were so high," Society of Friends, p.159.
253. "Under such a calamity," *The Economist,* 1/30/1847.
    "They wait on the outskirts," 4/24/1847.
254. "women returning home from Ennis," Relief of Distress Papers, Jones to
    Trevelyan, 1/19/1847.
255. "Something more," *Lancet,* April 1847.

256. "horrible silence," *The Nation,* 6/19/1847.
   "my hand trembles," Bennett, p.26.
257. "passing and repassing," Kee, p.94.
258 "In the city of Cork," SC 6/25/47.
259. "It is my opinion," Kee, p.96.
   "There is much reason," ibid, p.95.
   "The people," MG 24 I 121-7 NAC.

CHAPTER 15

262. There is disorder," SC Colon, 1847 Appx. pp.122-32.
   "classed among," ibid.
   "The difficulties," Colebrook to Grey, 10/17/1847 enc. 7.
   "All the sick," JLA weekly report, 5/15.
263. "The population," JLA 5/29/47.
   "I did not have a bed," JLA 5/21/1847.
265. "Out of the 4, 000," JLA 5/21/1847 App.R.
266. "The fearful state," SC 1847-48; CO 384/79535 Canada.
267. "In almost every," Devere SC H. of Lds 1847, p.45.
   "The number of sick," O'Gallagher, p.147.
269. "Corpses were allowed," SC to Inquire into management of the Quarantine Station at Grosse Isle, JLA 1847, v.6. App.RRR.
270. "The sick remain," ibid.
   "I was eight days," ibid.
271. "This was affected," SC 1848 v.47 Douglas 12/8/47.
. "Vast charnel house," Ga*zette,* 9/5/1847.
274. "The passengers were dressed," Whyte, *The Ocean Plague.*
281. "On mustering the passengers," BPP Colonies, Canada, v.17, p.385.
282. "By all appearances," SC 1848 App.X., p.126.
283. "I have no doubt," App.X.
285. "When I left Ireland," ibid.
288. "There are many," Harding CO 188/102 11/25/1847.
   "that one of Her Majesty's Ministers," ibid.
289. "the last cargo of human beings," *Montreal Pilot,* 12/11/47.
290. "Of the passengers," Elgin Grey Papers (A. Doughty, ed), 1846-52, Ottawa 1937.
   "I saw," Whyte, *Ocean Plague.*
293 "more than three fourths," Accounts and Papers, 1847-58 XLVII, Canada.

CHAPTER 16.

295. "answerable to the country," JLA 1848.
297. "miserable Saint John," SC 1848 App X 3/17/48.
   "I have at last," O'Connell Papers, Toronto Central Library.

"These people were huddled," BPP Papers Relative to Emigration, 1848, v.47 (Douglas's annual report).

301. "The estate in fact," Trench, pp.113, 134.

305. "There is no question," McConnell family papers, Toronto Central Library.

306. "I am to inform Your Honour," 9/13/48, Ellis.

"This is a fine country," Carrothers, 12/5/1853.

309. "Sport and pastime," Hugh Dorian, *Donegal 60 years ago,* IFD, p.16.

CHAPTER 17

311. "a great calamity," Maguire, *The Irish in America.*

312. "I wish all to understand," Kilfoil, p.13.

321. "If Ireland were," MG 27 111 B. 8 v.35. no. 14420. [Murphy Papers] NAC.

322. "God's unfortunate people," The Case of St. Patrick's Congregation, Montreal, 1866, p.19.

323. "Collection of typical," D.C. Lynn, *Irish in Province of Canada,* MA, McGill, p.76.

324. "A Canadian nationality," McGee Speeches and Addresses, Toronto, 1937.

324. "We must vindicate," *Gazette,* 4/9/1854.

"The people in general," Reel C-11732 NAC.

333. "The Canadian immigrant," *The Settlement of Upper Canada,* Toronto, 1869, p.637.

"desolate and neglected," O'Gallagher, p.84.

334. Monuments to the Irish famine victims were erected in Kingston in August 1899 and at Partridge Island in October 1927.

Index